"The world is my oyster..."

Falstaff, The Merry Wives of Windsor

Shakespeare

This is a companion book to "A Treasure Hunt",
but, it is not a sequel, nor a prequel --
it is an Equal

To my mother's nursery rhymes,
her gift of an *itchy foot* and a cat.

Contents

Prologue,

Not all those who wander are lost.

J.R.R. Tolkein

That's true, but I think it might actually start out that way, being lost I mean. Traveling, wandering begins with fat, untried baby legs starting to stand, shakily moving each tiny foot out in front of the other.

This walking thing is scary and exciting but--wait! *Running--oh, running is incredible!*

Head up, arms outflung, mouth wide open, eyes squeezed shut in the ecstatic feel of the whooshing air against the cheeks. *Oh, yes, running is the greatest until*

DEAD STOP EYES WIDE OPEN

Where am I? I don't know this place, these strange people, where's my Lil Bear, where's my house -- Where's MOMMY? Oh, there she is, half way down the block, so far away, calling me, arms reaching! I run as fast as I can into those arms -- safe!

WOW -- I'm never going to do THAT again!

Well, maybe just a little bit, maybe tomorrow?

So it begins, the brave journey into life, the simple physical joy of moving, running, dancing, feeling the body take up space, reaching out, smelling, tasting, experiencing what has not been before. Then the desire to see what's next, what's down that block: the hesitation, that little zing of fear, the racing for home to curl in safety for a while before the feet begin to itch again. That little zing of fear, of suddenly feeling *lost* is actually a moment of awareness. We know in the instant that we are in a strange, a new, accidental place. Early on we turn and run for *knowing*, but soon we want to stay awhile, look around, touch, see and learn what it's all about.

Wandering is how we do it; meaning and purpose come later, but in the beginning we just move to move and in that seemingly aimless wandering we discover ourselves.

Many years ago when I was still a typical suburban wife and mother, totally involved with all that that life entailed, always busy with some task or another, I happened to have an open moment. No one was around--amazing--and I was just sitting on the porch, daydreaming, woolgathering--*mind wandering* in all the wonderful places I would love to visit someday. Looking across the street, I noticed a cat strolling along the sidewalk who suddenly, easily and gracefully, lay down in a patch of sunlight on that sidewalk and immediately fall asleep. I felt a thrill go through me. I was suddenly aware of the enormity of what that cat had just done and what was possible for me as well. I knew then that that was how I wanted to be, to feel so comfortable anywhere in the world that I might, like that cat, lie down and sleep--*totally at home!*

Being *at home* doesn't preclude sometimes feeling lost or afraid or confused or delighted or excited or any of the myriad emotions traveling brings. It does mean "I am here on my own two feet, capable, able to choose, free to move in any direction, face whatever and find a solution." Traveling out of the comfort zone we all like to live in is a challenge and takes courage. The rewards of going are so great, however that after many such forays into the unknown being lost itself becomes a lure to go again.

So, fellow travelers, wander with me now through my many *goings*, my journeys and adventures. No need to feel afraid or lost. I promise we will always be *at home.*"

At home in Europe...

This adventure originally appeared in *A Treasure Hunt*. If you have already read it please take a cat nap and move on.

"Innocents Abroad"

The Statue of Liberty is beginning to soften around the edges, grow less distinct, start to melt into that fantastic panorama of the New York City skyline. There is a catch in my throat, a few stomach flutters and deep inside I feel those awesome, booming whistles as the ship moves slowly out into the ocean. *La Flandre* is an old World War II destroyer, sold to the French and remade into a modest tourist-fueled ocean going liner; to me, however, it is a flying carpet to carry me over the world to England, Wales, Ireland, Scotland, Holland, Germany, Italy, Switzerland and France for a mystical, magical, most wonderful nine weeks of my life. Tucked into the pocketbook at my side is a brand new red leather Travel Journal, given to me by my mother, "I will let you go BUT only if you promise to write in this every day!" Her eyes shine with excitement for me, knowing that she cannot experience all the coming adventures herself but that she will live them vicariously through me. Also at my side...

Although it is August 19, 1953 the planning for this wonderful trip actually began in the fourth grade. "Class, class settle down now. We have a new student with us. She has transferred in from another school. Let's welcome her. Her name is Marilyn McBride." Skinny, cute, acting bashful, making silly embarrassed faces, getting everyone's attention.

"Mmm, I'm not sure I like this--another Marilyn to boot. " I'm the leader here, who is she?"

And thus I began a sneaky, whispering campaign against this unwelcome intruder into MY territory! What I said thankfully I can no longer remember but it worked--at least, halfway. The girls all stop talking to her, the boys do not! Two days, three days--*I'm feeling a little sick, how could I have been so mean, so nasty--now I'm a little afraid as well!* Four days, Saturday...

I give the operator her number in a shaky voice.

Her phone rings, "Hello, hello--"

"I'm sorry, I'm really sorry."

I don't even say, but she knows it's me. There is a long and for me, anxious pause, "Okay, want to come over my house for lunch?" I'm floored.

That long, long walk down to the corner, right on Ridge Road, through Third Ward Park, past Hughes Lake to her house (a trip I would travel a thousand times or more in the next few years), heart beating, talking to myself, trying out various apologies, feeling frantic--*oh, dear, there she is on the porch, actually smiling!*

We have grilled cheese sandwiches on paper plates, orange paper napkins, and non-stop talking! We are both entirely impressed with each other, I can hardly believe she could be so forgiving. She later confesses that she had never in her life apologized to anyone and thought it was awesome that I had actually said, "I'm sorry".

What a great beginning for a friendship and, oh, we had some wonderful times being "best friends." There's really nothing better to have when you are young and new to life. Egging each other on, doubling the 'dares', doing things you'd not try on your own! Can you see us running barefoot through downtown Paterson, playing hooky to go to New York to the Paramount Theater to see Frank Sinatra, sitting through three shows, leaping over the seats to get closer to heaven each show? Or braving cold winter days to stand in line outside the Metropolitan Opera House to hear "*Madama Butterfly*" or watch "*Swan Lake*", sipping coffee some gallant 'other standee' had run across 39th street to buy? As we got older our sights widened, our adventures, bolder. We graduate, go to college, get jobs and in the summer of 1951 we sail to Bermuda for a week's vacation. Enamored of ships and the sea we decide to take a trip to Nantucket the next year and love that as well. In August of 1952, Marilyn and I take my mother to an outside concert in Lewisohn Stadium in New York. It is a lovely, warm summer evening, music from the ballet *Giselle* playing. During intermission we regale my mother with stories about our trips to Bermuda and Nantucket. She grins and coyly asks, "What island will you go to next year?" Amazingly, without hesitation, both of us reply in tandem, "The British Isles!!" We might have talked about it at some time, not seriously, but this is an instant, irrevocable decision. Planning begins.

A year of scrimping, saving, smoking each cigarette three times, eating liverwurst sandwiches on a hard roll, only 25 cents, every day and here I am leaning against the ship's rail, watching New York disappear into the mist, with my, often-times other self, Marilyn, at my side. I am shaking with excitement, awe, and can feel with an almost physical reality all the bonds that tie me to family, home, work and country dropping away. I am uncaught, freewheeling, sailing into a new, unfamiliar world knowing with certainty that when I return in nine weeks I will be different.

We turn, facing forward, outward, with that sharp, slanting, salty ocean breeze making prickles along our cheeks and look farther than we have ever looked before, out over the edge of the world, five days away to England!

There are four of us in a tiny, compact cabin; an American girl going to France to teach English in the American School; Micheline

Freibourg, a Parisienne returning gratefully home, Marilyn and me. There is also a very tiny porthole which gives an eye level look at the great rolling waves that are beginning to make the ship sway sideways and back, sideways and--*whoops, not a great idea to watch that too long.* Additionally, the only way to see out this very small round opening to the world is to sit, hoisted up, cramped on the equally small sink with a faucet poking into one's back. A much more comfortable view is up on deck, sitting in a deck chair, wrapped in a warm plaid blanket drinking hot bullion each morning. There are six of us at table and we quickly make friends with this varied and interesting group, one of whom is Lucy, who is making her tenth trip. She is filled with helpful information and we make her our model. There are two bottles of red wine at each meal and by the end of the voyage we quickly polish off both of them.

Two days in I wake in the middle of the night. *What's happening? What's different?* Oh, silence--the deep thrum of the engines that lay below each moment of the day and night is suddenly stilled! For one hour we drift, "a painted ship upon a painted ocean." I hear some noises out in the passageway, a muffled word here and there but no excitement or confusion so as the engines purr back into life I drift back to sleep. The talk at breakfast is of some minor repairs occurring during the night, so glad I didn't panic!

That day we run into some rough seas, so rough that no one besides Marilyn and I show up for a meal. The table is ringed with a two inch raised edge which keeps the dishes from sliding off. Mal de

Mer has everyone else locked, groaning in their staterooms while Marilyn and I roam the decks with impunity. Oh, we also finish off one of the bottles of wine!

The weather improves, people recover, Marilyn begins a bit of a shipboard romance with a young, delightful French cadet, Henri Dal, we turn our clocks forward each day and Gala Night happens. Music, dancing, paper hats, champagne, my first Pernod, to bed at 5:00 a.m! Shipboard magic, no hangover. Wonderful conversations, lounging on deck with Lucie, a Belgian lawyer proud of his very fractured English and a Hemingway look-alike Freudian psychiatrist making funny pronouncements on women. Marilyn and I speaking our own much fractured French, amusing everyone.

We see five small fishing boats off the bow and a low, dark smudge against the horizon--five days gone and we are here! There are gulls circling, a salty tang that smells of harbors, the sea touching land sweeps in and we must say goodbye, au revoir to *La Flandre* and our shipboard friends.

"Here we are, Mother, just as we impulsively said, 'The British Isles." I have this absurd feeling that we are actually standing on the ragged southern edge of a map of England looking left through rocky Wales to a small green island, Ireland and up toward the highlands of Scotland, where my secret heart lies. Breathing begins to settle down, pulse beating normally again but my legs can't seem to find the rhythm of walking on land. Hand in hand Marilyn and I weave our way across Plymouth Hoe to our first European hotel, the Duke of Cornwall. We are giddy with excitement and proceed to make fools of ourselves in the ultra-staid atmosphere of the formal dining room--a pair of giggling noisy Americans in this oh-so-quiet English environment.

We survive our first night in England, or should I say, England survives us. We take the train to Swansea, Wales. The lovely, green, hedge-rowed English landscape gives way in time to a more rugged scene and eventually to the scabrous piles of slag from the colliers that dot the southern Welsh hills. We book into the Civic Hotel with some difficulty because no one here speaks English, well, not the American kind! All goes well, however, and after a night on the softest bed so far we spend a day wandering the steep streets. We have a tour of the Guild Hall and eat cockles in Mumbles castle, wrapped in local newsprint--the cockles, not the castle. Our boat train to Dublin leaves in the evening and two men, Mr. Tanner and Mr. Jones who were staying at the hotel insist upon taking us to the station, presenting us with a big clump of leeks, the official vegetable of Wales. So exhausted, we sleep through the ferry ride and subsequent 6:30 am train to Dublin. Barely making it through lunch we retire to our room and promptly sleep through to the next morning.

On to Belfast to be met by Desmond McGivern. Marilyn had befriended Desmond's brother when he visited her church at home in Passaic, New Jersey. He had insisted upon us visiting his family and arranged everything with them beforehand. They are truly delightful and welcoming people, even taking us out into the countryside to find Marilyn's family, the 'Sooty McBrides'. There are so many people bearing the same last name that whole families take on nicknames. Why hers would be "Sooty" no one is sure, but there is probably a great story behind it. Driving the countryside which is much as America had been 50 years ago we take turns trying to invent the funniest one.

Checking family records in small local churches is a good way to start. We have hardly begun when, lo and behold, we find a priest who takes us to see an old woman in his parish. She had immigrated to America long before but had recently returned to her homeland. Welcoming us into her home she tells us that she had spent most of her years in America in Paterson, New Jersey and had actually known Marilyn's grandfather, a well-known Paterson doctor!

For two more days we are dined and entertained by these truly friendly and lovely people. Although everyone seems to have such trouble with my so English surname, Holdsworth, as soon as I mention that my grandmother was Celia Feeney they all chime in with, "The Feeneys are just over the hill!"

Scotland is calling so we have to give the Feeneys a pass. The boat train leaves from Belfast, arriving in Glasgow station where we catch the train to Mallaig. In our compartment there is an older couple, pleasant and quiet. I don't really even see them, I am so beside myself with excitement. All my life I have heard stories of my Scottish Clan, MacLeod, read funny, old fashioned books written by long ago family vicars, all named Norman. Here I am actually on my way to the 'home place', Castle Dunvegan on the Isle of Skye! I literally cannot sit still, running from one side of the compartment to the other, singing "My hearts in the highlands, my heart is not here." Marilyn keeps apologizing to the couple, explaining that I have wanted all my life to come to Scotland. We are passing Rannoch Moor on our way to those highlands. If ever there was a place that looked like the desolate surface of the moon, this is it but I keep saying, 'so wonderful, so wonderful.' We move swiftly on through mountains and valleys, passing rushing waterfalls indescribably beautiful and wild lochs. The soft haze of purple heather is everywhere.

Arriving at Mallaig we discover that the small ferry to the Isle of Skye is not sailing. Apparently, the driver of the bus that meets the ferry and drives people to the town of Dunvegan and elsewhere has broken his arm and can't drive the bus. In tears I frantically explain to the Harbor Master who I am and that I must get to the island. After listening with monumental patience to my seemingly endless explanations of how my great, great something, Alexander MacLeod, came to American in 1792, and imploring him to do something, he grabs the phone, calls a number and equally as patiently explains to the party on the other end," I have a MacLeod here whose ancestor went to America in the stone age! I'm afraid if we can't make some arrangement she will dive in and swim the channel." After a while he hangs up, turns to me and says, "Too late tonight but first thing in the morning the ferry will sail and a substitute bus driver will meet you and take you to Dunvegan. You can stop crying now--and talking." For the first time I notice he's actually smiling, patting my arm kindly and wishing me well.

"Over the Sea to Skye"--at last!

As the heavy doors of Dunvegan Castle open, I say, "Good morning, may we tour the castle? I am a MacLeod!" Boldly.

"That's nice" comes the quick reply, "One shilling, please."

Later, checking in to our guest house, Skeabost Inn, I am welcomed by the owner Angus MacLeod as a "clanswoman." My hurt pride is somewhat restored. There is a great "do" at the castle that evening and many of the guests, staying here at the hotel, appear in full Highland regalia on their way to the festivities. *I guess they forgot to send my invitation.* One of the 'invited' is having some difficulty setting out, it's Angus MacLeod himself, splendid in kilt, sporran, blue velvet coat, immaculate white ruffled ascot, knee socks with a skgian dubh (that's a stag horn knife) and definitely 'three sheets to the wind'. He is being encouraged by two English visitors, "Oh, Angus, gives us a song before you go. You can't leave yet, come on."

"I like MacKay and MacKay likes me."

Angus, weaving unsteadily across the room, performs. He is finally whisked away to stumble through the gala evening and we, to bed. About two miles into our six mile walk the next day we suddenly find ourselves surrounded by a ragged group of highland cattle, long, shaggy reddish hair, big wide horns and large liquid brown eyes on an exact level of our own. We stand still trying to appear unconcerned as, with one disinterested look, they swish their tails at us and lumber on.

Leaving Skye, Edinburgh is next, another castle, another shilling, the Royal Mile, Princess Street, the Castle, shopping, bagpipers playing on street corners for pennies. A whirlwind visit just for a day, we catch the 10:20 night train to London. Sitting up for eight hours--we are learning to sleep upright.

A stop at British Tourist Information gets us a nice room in the Warwick House (15 shillings a night--that's $21.00) which is right around the corner from the British Museum. There are so many sights to see and experience in London and in our four days here we pretty much visit them all; Tower of London, changing of the guards at Buckingham Palace, Trafalgar Square, Covent Gardens. A visit to Oxford and Stratford-upon-Avon to thrill at Shakespeare's birthplace and weep a few tears at his tomb is wonderful and precious.

"Are you Marilyn Holdsworth?" A gorgeous, tall, blond young man in a tuxedo is speaking to me. I feel like Cinderella. I had booked a tour "A Night in London" at home before we left and was expecting the usual tourist bus to lumber into Piccadilly Circus where we are waiting as per instructions, instead here comes a luxurious limousine replete with "Prince Charming." Eric is our guide and escort for the evening which includes stops at Hemicky's Wine Bar, Collins Music Hall where we see old-timey vaudeville and a nude tableaux, Nag's Head Pub in the theatrical district and a visit to the Stork Room Club, where Eric shares conversation and stories of his early life in Finland. He dances in turn with Marilyn and me and walks us back to our hotel at 3:00 am. These English certainly know how to give a tour!

After checking out of our hotel on our last day in London we confirm our tickets on the boat train leaving Liverpool Station that night for Holland. Somewhat at loose ends, we decide to just wander, and putter around this fantastic city. As we walk through quiet streets I am beginning to realize that the wonder we have been feeling has been shadowed by the sight, eight years after the end of World War II, of so many bombed out buildings, churches, homes, businesses--indiscriminate ruins amid the splendors and everyday new growth of this metropolis. Now I remember listening to Eric Severaid and Ed Murrow on the radio reporting from war torn London during the Blitz, hearing in the background the actual sounds of bombs falling. I shiver suddenly in this warm summer afternoon, seeing the city multi-layered, filled with real people with a living history beyond the tourist attractions. Still filled with that wonder but somewhat subdued now I feel that I actually, really have been to London.

"Oh, I can't read any of the sign–I don't understand a word that people are saying to me! Where am I, is this Oz, was that the Yellow Brick Road I traveled?"

Calm down, self--it's Amsterdam, Holland and these are Dutch people speaking Nederlander not Munchkins!"

For the first time in my life I am truly in another world, 'a stranger in a strange land.' Fortunately many people speak and understand a bit of English, and along with sign language, we are at least able to order breakfast. Roode Leuw is our hotel and after a somewhat garbled checking in we take a boat tour of the canals. Amsterdam is truly lovely. Tall, slender medieval and renaissance buildings frame the canals, people are friendly and with a lot of laughter seem to enjoy our amateurish attempts to communicate. We later try to pay our way on a bus but this arouses a lively, animated discussion by a noisy group of travelers who won't let the driver take our money.

I have always loved the paintings of Vincent Van Gogh and the museums here of his work are so rich with his colors and images. I am in heaven for a little while. Back in the everyday world I touch paradise again, briefly, each time I bite into a wonderful piece of Dutch pastry. Who would have thought Holland to be a treasure house of baked goods? So much for Paris. (We'll see.) I am not sure if those scrumptious tastes are what prompts us to stay here for another day or if it is the Rembrandts, Hals and Vermeers that seem to fill the city with light. Even then, it is hard to leave. We love Amsterdam!

Back in America, the group of young Catholic men who were visiting churches in our home town included not only the Irish fellow whose family so ingratiatingly took care of us in Belfast, but also a young man from Krefeld, Germany where we are now headed. He also had insisted to Marilyn that we visit his family. We have only an address. Unlike Holland, people here do not speak English, even a bit, and getting directions is proving very difficult! We show the written address to several people who try earnestly to make us understand German, talking louder and louder, one woman keeps pumping Marilyn's arm up and down in frustration. We repeat over and over "Ich verstehe nicht." "I don't understand" and soon dissolve into helpless giggles at this comic scene. Using hand motions, drawing pictures in the air, endless pointing finally gets us to our destination. We ring the bell and the door opens. We are greeted by a short, very rotund woman who tries desperately to wrap us both in her outstretched arms, crying, "Kommen sie fum Wolfgang!!" She signs that her daughter, Ruth, speaks English and will be home soon. Meanwhile, we sit with her having a grand conversation, she in her language and we in ours. It is actually amazing how much is communicated. Facial expressions, hand gestures, overall body language are really excellent ways of making meaning clear. Herr Storkman arrives and soon thereafter, Ruth--who does speak English fairly well--a relief as our hands and arms are getting tired. Ruth takes us for a tour of the town. It must have been lovely once but 80% of it was bombed during the war and reconstruction is slow. She explains that the family's home was in that 80% and that is why they are living in the small apartment. This is said quietly, without rancor or conscious blame to her American guests. After a wonderful supper we are shown to our room and sleep like the proverbial babies upon a fantastically warm and light feather bed. The night, however, is not completely without incident. I wake to find that I must leave the apartment to use a bathroom down the hall which is shared by other families. It has a water closet arrangement and I proceed to break the chain! I am mortified to explain this in the morning but Herr Storkman simply gets his tool box and smiling forgivingly takes care of the problem. After being amply fed with a tasty breakfast we are taken to the train station, given gifts of chocolates and perfume and put on the train.

I am, once again, filled with unfamiliar emotions. Thoughts and feelings so strongly held during the war years, fueled by movies of horrors and the viciousness of the German enemy, are turned upside down. Not only are we being treated like any stranger, helped and welcomed, but we have been sharing laughter and family stories with pleasant, ordinary people very much like us. This awareness is further stretched by what happens as we change trains in Cologne. It is so crowded that we must sit on our suitcases, jammed in between the aisles. There are two young German men standing near us and when some seats become available further up the car they take our arms and lead us to them. When we try to say thanks it becomes obvious they do not understand English. With a smile and a wave they disappear only to show up when it becomes necessary to change trains again. They look at our tickets and schedule, shake their heads and indicate that there is a better train to take. They gesture and point and off we go to the other track. When they see that we are making the wrong choice they actually jump over the rails, grab our suitcases, with us in tow, and put us on the right coach! Incredible, with obviously no agenda, no self-advantage, they have gone out of their way to see two perfect strangers find theirs. We never see them again but I will remember their message; *"Forget preconceived notions, see each moment as it really is, be aware and open to what life has to offer without prejudice and fear"* I am humbled by what I am seeing and experiencing on this wonderful journey!

On our way to Heidelberg we pass through several towns and villages. I am shaken once more by the sight of so many bombed out buildings. My heart hurts as I notice that there is absolutely no difference between British ruins and these that we are seeing here. I used to be so sure I knew who and where the enemy was, but no longer. I know now that the true evil is war itself and the devastation it causes to everyone. I hope I never forget this.

In Heidelberg we descend upon our friend, Pat Healey, her husband, Chris, and their 6 week old baby, Candice. Chris is an American civilian working with the army. It is a good thing that they are a really laid back couple because I can see how much work there is to taking care of the baby. In between visits to surrounding sights, castles and pubs we try to give them a break by feeding and taking care of little Candy. We are thoroughly enjoying this visit and there is much laughter and drinking of the local Rhine wine. It is with some sadness that we say "Love you both and thanks for just everything, it was great!"

There are no seats on the train to Munich so we sit in the dining car for the next five hours, drinking endless cups of strong, bitter coffee--I may never sleep again! Although it is still September it appears that the wonderful, noisy, wild festival called Oktoberfest has already started. In one of the many beer halls we find seats at a long table filled with happy revelers and many, many mugs of sudsy amber liquid. Of course there is an oompah brass band and rugged men dressed in lederhosen on the stage stamping in time to the music. It is impossible not to enjoy the hectic hilarity and we willingly enter in, singing and drinking with the best of them. 10:40, which is our departure time arrives too soon and we are traveling once more. This time however we are in 2nd class, and each of our seats pushes down flat to become double so we curl up in the fetal position for a night's sleep in our crowded compartment. A night's sleep did I say? At each border the compartment door opens and a loud authoritative voice says "Passports!" in first a German accent then in an Austrian accent, then another Austrian accent, and finally an Italian accent. We had been warned many time about never letting our passports out of our sights. The war has caused so many refugees and homeless people eager to travel to the states that there was a real possibility of theft. At the first border we watch our documents very attentively but by the end of the long night we just hand them groggily to whoever opens the door. There really must be guardian angels for weary American travelers because we arrive in Rome at 4:15 next afternoon with all our papers intact.

We do not have any place to stay, and in this enormous station filled with people rushing in all directions we are feeling a bit lost. Marilyn approaches a priest and tries to ask for his help. As he shakes his head uncomprehendingly, we are surprised to hear, "Now then, can I be of help?" in a strong Irish brogue. Turning, we are confronted by a short, ruddy faced priest with a big smile and outstretched arms. He tells us that there is a convent here that takes in young women travelers and if we don't think that $2.00 a day for room, board and three meals is too much they can probably take us in. We assure him that we can afford the fee.

Our room is on the fourth floor and we have a balcony that overlooks the "'Circus Maximus." The best hotel in Rome could not be more welcoming nor provide such a view. I think the mattresses might be stuffed with straw but, no matter, we walk so much in the next five days that sleep comes instantly and cuddles us in comfort all night long. After breakfast we take a bus out along the Via Apia Antica to see the Tomb of Cecelia Matella, which is closed. Walking back along this ancient road is thrilling, there are many patches where the original large stones are the actual current surface of the roadway. They are smooth and shiny, having been polished for more than 2000 years by carts, horses, marching feet, and eventually cars. Lunch is, of course, spaghetti at a roadside trattoria where a cat begs for and receives long strands of pasta from us. It is hot and we sometimes stop at water fountains on street corners for a refreshing drink. Unfortunately, many of the places we had hoped to visit--Catacombs, the small "Quo Vadis" church (we peek through the keyhole) and Basilica of San Sebastian are closed. We are finding out, too late, that everything closes between 12:00 and 4:00! However we pass under the Arch of Drusus in the Roman Wall and are able to wander through the Baths of Caraculla and eventually the Coliseum.

In the next two days we visit the Scala Santa, Holy Stairs, and the Church of St. Peter in Chains with Michelangelo's statue of Moses, the Roman Forum, several basilicas and the Temple of Venus. Our next adventure takes us on a bus ride to Castle Gandolfo to see the Pope in his summer home. Marilyn's priest had made arrangements back in the states for this visit and, knowing little of what the encounter would be like, we are quite nervous. We have been told that we should have our arms and our heads covered despite the heat of the day. Clutching several rosaries in our sweating hands, ready for blessing, we enter the gates and are confronted by a mass of humanity crowded into the small courtyard. So much for a private audience! He appears on a balcony and speaks briefly. Whenever a town is mentioned portions of the crowd erupt into cheers, just like a football rally. We are herded back on the bus, having been assured that we have been blessed.

The Vatican is next, on our last full day. Although Michelangelo's frescos on the ceiling of the Sistine Chapel are darkened by time the glory shines through. My heart beats faster as we stand in front of his "Pieta", so close we can almost touch that glowing, milky, marble surface.

Heads filled with the magic and mystery of all that we have seen and experienced, we say goodbye to Rome and entrain for Firenze, Florence. Staying in convents seems to be a great idea so we head for the Sister, Redemptrists. The nuns here are cloistered, necessitating ringing a little bell and waiting for the door to slowly open to let us in. In contrast to the hominess of our place in Rome, the surroundings here are reminiscent of a very nice hotel.

Florence has many treasures and finding that the Uffizi Gallery is closed we visit the Baptistry with its beautiful carved doors, the Gates of Paradise, the Duomo, and the Ponte Vecchio. Everything we see is wonderful and moving but, for me, the most thrilling sight of all lies in a building just off the main square. We enter a long, rather dark hallway lined with paintings which leads to a small rotunda whose ceiling is open to the sky. There, bathed in light, is Michelangelo's magnificent statue of David! Nothing I have seen can touch the beauty and power of this creation--nothing. Walking slowly, approaching him I feel the way I did when I was a little girl first seeing the shimmering Christmas tree. If I ever have a son his name will be David.

Coming back down to earth, we shop in a small store, specializing in leather goods. The wallets are just lovely, embossed with dainty designs and figures. I am trying to decide which one to choose, when I notice a large, officious woman loudly demanding, "I'll take ten of these and fifteen of those and…" I shudder inwardly as I realize she is speaking with an American accent. The European economy is growing very slowly in these post-war years and many countries and populations are struggling, eking out minimal livings. To have an obnoxious, unfeeling person showing off her wealth is what has been giving the world the definition of an "ugly American." I remember that since we sent home our dressy clothes when in London and now wear plaid skirts, sweaters and penny loafers and almost no makeup people keep telling us that they do not think we are Americans. They say, "That is a compliment."

This short stay in Florence has resulted in extremes of thoughts and feelings. In fact, the visit to Italy has stretched my awareness, my understanding and appreciation to such a degree that I feel that I have been turned on my head, upside down. The slow, beautiful train through the Alps to Lucerne, Switzerland slows down the hectic pace allowing the world, and me, to right ourselves. This is a delightful, absolutely undemanding pause. The window in our lovely Des Alpe hotel looks out on a quaint wooden bridge across the inlet to the lake with impressive snow-capped mountains on the horizon. It is the only sight on our agenda. What a glorious relief. Delicious meals, awesome scenery, a date with a charming, old English gentleman who takes us to a quaint beer hall, church bells ringing for a feast day, even getting our shoes resoled replenishes our bodies and our souls. A big deep breath, a cleansing sigh and we are ready and eager to be filled up again with the excitements of Paris.

Bermuda shorts and knee socks had seemed like a good idea for comfort on our overnight train to Paris which arrives at the Gare de L'est at 8:00 am. We count on being able to get a hotel and change into more *Parisienne* attire before becoming laughable sights on the stylish boulevards. About six miles and hours and hours later we are still traipsing all over the city, no longer caring what we look like, exhausted and so frustrated, unable to find rooms even at convents! Apparently there is an international automobile convention happening and it seems that all hotels are booked. In desperation, we have cris-crossed Paris at least three times. We go to the Allied Armed Forces Center where PX cards that Chris Whipple had gotten us from his army connections in Heidelberg get us a room in the Hotel Montcalm. What a room, large, comfortable, with a private bathroom and, ergo, expensive. We gratefully take luxurious baths, sleep wonderfully, order breakfast in bed and quickly downgrade to a small, much cheaper room *sans 'en suite'.*

Despite this somewhat inauspicious beginning our six day sojourn in this magical city fulfills all its promises. Because we have, at last, enough time to visit every sight leisurely, without the hectic pace of having to cram each sight into small, tight bits of time, we are able to enjoy just strolling along the Seine, going to mass at Notre Dame, or eating lunch al fresco in the Luxemburg Gardens. Les Invalides, Rodin Musee, a three dollar omelet in a fancy restaurant on the Champs Elysees, a visit to Montmartre, Place Pigalle all fill our days. We stop at the Louvre to wonder at

"Winged Victory" and Venus de Milo and be disappointed by the small, dark, unimpressive (to me, anyway) Mona Lisa.

In our travels we find that a few of the "toilettes" are 'standing room only' and the paper available in the Hotel Moderne rest room is newsprint, today's date, I'm assuming. We try several restaurants but tend to eat most dinners in a small cafe around the corner from our hotel. The food is basic but good, the people friendly and the cats that often walk across the tables and need to be shooed to the floor with brooms give the place a true 'expatriate' flavor. We really have tried to find Hemingway's "Deux Magots" but must make do with this unassuming substitution.

Our last day--we climb Paris's tallest hill to visit the dazzling white church of Sacre Coeur to view all Paris in one sweeping look. Now, in a small, outside café I am drinking a glass of vin blanc and listening to Edith Piaf singing "La Vie en Rose". Oh, how can I bear to have this incredible journey end?

"STOP, TIME, let me sit a while longer, one small moment among so many, before we rush into the encroaching future!"

Customs on the train to Le Havre the next morning are a breeze. I am sad at leaving but so excited about seeing my friends and family. Emotions are circling willy-nilly inside my brain and I hardly notice that we have arrived at the dock where the *Liberte* is waiting to take us home. Oh dear! We walk off the soil of Europe at 11:30 am. I stand at the rail crying a little, waving goodbye to the most fantastic, rewarding nine weeks of my life.

The *Liberte* is a much larger ship than *La Flandre* and has three classes whereas *Flandre* had just First and Tourist sections. On the trip out, everyone from first class snuck down to Tourist where all the fun was happening but now we feel a bit like 'steerage' passengers. The atmosphere on this trip is actually very different. The majority of the people appear to be immigrants or Europeans who now live in America and have been visiting their former homes and families. There are few young people on board and no one to dance with in the lounge in the evenings. We watch a number of French movies and go to bed early. Oh, yes, we have to turn our clocks *back* each night, making every day longer by an hour. I find that sitting in my deckchair, cozily wrapped in a warm blanket, watching the changing moods of the ocean letting thoughts, memories, snippets of conversation or quicksilver images flow through me is just what I want right now.

... I am standing looking back down the cobbled slope at Marilyn who is gazing at me with a look of awe, "I am looking at you in Edinburgh Castle!"

... a spaghetti eating cat.

... a little boy being lifted lifeless from a canal

... a convent balcony draped with freshly washed underwear which later appears in our room modestly draped over the furniture......

... having to pay 75 cents to take a bath in Lucerne

... Edith Piaf singing

That deep, booming whistle sounds over and over, the Statue of Liberty is still here, welcoming us among the 'huddled masses.' Suddenly we are home, hugging everyone, spilling over with stories, pleased, excited, sad and happy all at once. A time, a trip I will never, ever forget.

It's interesting; I knew I would be different when I returned, how could it be otherwise? To have experienced and learned so much must surely change me but I am not aware of being a new person yet. As I slowly unpack my battered suitcase, I see quite clearly another case that I have been carrying with me all along. What it contains are all those tiny shifts in thought, those moments of change, of growth, of new understandings, of always being ready to drop old ideas, making room for the new. Packed abundantly and overflowing into its corners and pockets, it will be a delight to unfold and try on everything! These are the new clothes that I will dress myself in now and hopefully for the rest of my life.

At home in Greece…

L'audace, l'audace, toujours l'audace

The bus is careening down the switch back roads of a mountain in Greece. I am scrunched down in my seat as far as I can go so I don't have to see how close we are to the totally unprotected cliff edge. The guide is explaining that the small flower shrines we pass are remembrances of past accidents where a vehicle didn't quite make the turn.

Heart racing, breathless, afraid--suddenly I am totally alive!

The slight scratchiness of the arm rest, the scary sound of the bus wheels bumping over the rough road, sporadic talk from fellow passengers, sunlight pushing against the dark blue cover of the seat in front of me, all are real and immediate and I AM HERE!

Funny, that an irrational fear of heights would wake me to a real world.

Making plans, flying on British Airways to Athens, the funny Greek hotel, seeing the sights; yes I have experienced them all but slightly removed, a bit off kilter, not quite there.

It is August of 1980 and I've been a widow for the last seven months. Coping, learning, grieving, growing have absorbed me, leaving living everyday a sort of misty walk-through. Memories are sporadic and skewed and frequently of small, insignificant events because, in some way, my feet have not been on solid ground. Here on this shifting, speeding, noisy bus almost flying two feet above the roadway I have, at last, come down to earth.

It has been 27 years filled with marriage, three wonderful children and a career since my trip to Europe with Marilyn McBride and the first adventure all on my own. One of my husband, Ray's favorite quotes (there were many) "L, audace, l'audace, toujours l'audace" was by Danton, a French revolutionary, and translates as, "Audacity, audacity, always audacity!" This was the telegram I sent home to my son David when I landed, followed by "The odyssey has begun." I have had much use for courage in the last year. Ray would be proud.

Straightening up a bit, leaning back, I am still afraid of heights but beginning to relax and settle in to actually being awake and aware again. My first three days in Athens were remarkable. The bright, warm sunshine, actually visiting the memorable places, walking the Acropolis, losing almost right away the lens cover on my new camera (I told you small unimportant events slid into my consciousness), touching the ancient rough stones of a pillar in the Parthenon, seeing those magnificent statues in the museum all take their places in my memory. I am recalling and owning each experience.

What fun it was to be in a café in the Plaka, the oldest part of Athens, watching the dancers in their flashy costumes, sipping an ouzo, playing at being a true Athenian, admiring the great legs of the male dancers in their short pleated white skirts. Reminds me of Ray, he had such good looking legs. The remembering is good. It is a part of acceptance. For a long while I ran away from memories but slowly the ordinariness of recall is part of daily life again. What a journey and this trip to Greece is an important part of it.

When lives are changed radically by events the tendency is to try to correct, realign, bring back to *the way things were* but that is impossible. In a strange way my choice to make this trip to Greece was a recognition of that fact. A lover of ancient history, of stories of brave Spartan boys, Socrates and Pythagoras I still had never particularly thought of traveling here. This visit is perhaps a statement of a new way of living and being--a bit of *l'audace, a* break in the habitual before stepping bravely onto new and different paths.

As the bus screeches to a stop at our hotel I look up at the mountain and its spiraling road and whisper a quiet *thanks,* to Athena perhaps, for her gift of reality and acceptance.

I wake the next morning more eager than I have been in a long time for the new day. I am rewarded for this anticipation by four days filled with the almost unimaginable sights of ancient Greece. I stroll through Mycenae's awesome five thousand year old Lion Gate, hearing just below the edge of sound the voices, trampling feet, cries of market vendors, children laughing from that so distant past. Epidaurus, Corinth, Patra, magnificent ruins, breathtaking mountainous landscapes, overwhelming--HOT. Temperatures on the second and third days have reached above 100 degrees and, as a treat, we are taken one afternoon to swim in the Ionian Sea!

Back on schedule, arriving in Olympia our guide gathers us under every sparse little tree she can find to provide a wisp of shade while she regales us with stories of those magnificent oiled bronze bodies throwing discuses, javelins, jumping incredible distances and running like young gods in the very first Olympics. A man in the back of the group, mopping his face, somewhat unimpressed, calls out, "No wonder they ran naked."

There is an unusually hot wind, the Sirocco, that blows here from Africa sporadically and we have had the bad luck to experience it. However, the next morning it seems to have blown itself out and the day is sunny but comfortable. The bus is still wobbling up the mountains and careening down the other sides but I have become so immersed in all that we are seeing and experiencing that I am almost enjoying the ride. Sitting in the aisle seat also helps.

As we come over the top of a mountain our intrepid driver actually slows and almost stops in the face of one of the most beautiful views I have ever seen--Delphi, nestling in a ring of soft blue mountains. The ancient Greeks called it *the navel of the world* and I almost believe it. The ruins are extensive and it is still possible to look into the depths of a temple where the Oracle sat, dispensing her prophecies to the dignitaries of that ancient world who came pleading for a glimpse of their futures. We wander about, voices somewhat subdued. I pick a couple of tiny wild flowers growing between the stones and tuck them into my wallet. No one is in a rush or minds picking our way among the tumbled paths.

This lovely mood continues into the evening and early night. My small narrow room in the hotel is almost monk-like. There is a bed, a night stand with a simple vase of tiny flowers, a chest of drawers and a very large window framing a view of the mountain. I fall asleep with the moonlight shining silver on my face.

The view is quite different the next morning as we trundle down the last mountain to the ancient port of Piraeus. A bustling modern harbor but in 490 CE, it is the home of the truly impressive Athenian Empire's fleet that had just sent Persia's ships scuttling for home. The sails and bristling masts of the old ships seem to fade and reappear among the modern traffic. Visiting a place that is so filled with actual physical evidence of ancient life makes staying grounded in the present a dizzying experience.

A sleek top of the line ship, the Stella Solaris, shining white in the hot sun is our next destination. We are welcomed, "Xenos" a word that means both "stranger" and "guest," a synonym we are told proudly that does not exist in any other language. I had booked a double stateroom and go looking for my unknown roommate. As we begin to sail out of the harbor that evening she has not yet appeared. This lovely large room will be all mine for the next week.

There is a welcoming party with luscious drinks and delicious tidbits and as I wander through the crowd I begin to meet some of my traveling companions. The connections here are made more easily and quickly than on the bus tour. There is a quality of openness that happens on a ship, a relaxation. The stress of making

26

decisions, choosing this or that slips away, there is no place to go, everything already planned, moving, not static but ordained. There is nothing to do but let go, live moment to moment and enjoy all that is on offer. I intend to do just that.

The next morning I awake to find we have already sailed through the Bosporus Strait and are heading to Turkey. Our first stop, Istanbul. Once Byzantium, Istanbul is historic, beautiful, exotic, raucous, sometimes serene, sometimes a very noisy hodge-podge. It is the only city in the world to straddle two continents, Europe and Asia. No wonder it looks and feels like no place I have ever been. We tour the Blue Mosque, Santa Sophia, holy places of Islam, beautiful, exotic, strange. There are fantastic geometric designed mosaics on the ceiling and walls and as we walk barefoot on the soft Persian rugs covering the floors we hear the quiet hum of prayers. I am awed by a culture not my own.

27

Musing, subdued, the tumultuous cacophony of the streets hits us like a wave. I love it. This yo-yo of emotions just sweeps through me and leaves me clean and clear and ready for whatever comes. I love it. Laughing aloud I stop to buy a rough wooden flute from a dirty, grinning boy, making his day with my 50c purchase. The Market is next.

The Grand Bazaar built in the 1400s following the Islamic victory over Christian Byzantium now is comprised of 61 covered streets and 4000 shops, every one of which, it seems, is trying to sell me something! The tiny storefronts are filled to the brim with merchandise, ablaze with color, flamboyant wall hangings, rugs, bright shimmering scarves hanging over doorways, there are copper pots, vases, musical chimes. It is like walking in a kaleidoscope. And gold, gold everywhere, warm gentle 18 carat gold fashioned into the most intricate, original designs. I stop to admire a bracelet on display and I am almost kidnapped into the store, the owner showering me with one lovely item after another. I thank him and protest that I am not buying. He immediately begins mentioning prices which fall drastically at each shake of my head. Realizing that I cannot make him understand I push past his foreign haranguing and out the door. He follows me halfway down the street and I have the absurd feeling he would possibly pay me to take the bracelet if I would but turn and respond. I chuckle the whole way back to the ship and serenity.

What a wonderful experience--I've touched another world religion, heard lilting (and shouting) syllables of different languages, shopped in an ancient mall, seen colors and hues I had no idea existed. I have been in Asia.

I enjoy the interesting Greek dishes at dinner but eating alone in the large dining room filled with people talking and laughing makes me sad. I'm beginning to feel a bit lonely; however when I stop in the lounge later I am asked to join two of the couples I had met at the welcoming party. Recounting our adventures, sipping a delicious wine and being asked to dance once or twice completes my evening and I slip away to settle into my sumptuous cabin and, still laughing, no longer lonely, fall asleep.

At each new stop we disembark for an afternoon of sightseeing. It is so nice that my new friends vie for the pleasure of asking me to join them. It's like being invited to the prom and I am very grateful for the company.

Ephesus, bordering the Aegean Sea is next on our itinerary and was home to one of the Seven Wonders of the Ancient World, The Temple of Artemis. The Goddess, later named Diana by the Roman, was worshipped by most ancient peoples. As we explore this historic site, important to pagans and Christians alike and even though next to nothing remains of her center I feel a warm touch and a soft kiss on my forehead from this early celebratory Protector of womankind. *I'm with you, girl.*

Yes, I may be getting a bit fanciful but I am enjoying the freedom travel brings, not only outside of my country and comfort zone but outside all the rules and *shoulds* of my society. The world is very large and varied and I am learning that, in truth, there is no rigid "right way."

Following lunch next day we are grouped near the exit from the lower deck ready for our Rhodes adventure. We've been waiting much longer than usual when an announcement is made over the loud speaker, "We are very sorry that we will be unable to land at Rhodes today. There is social unrest and we have been advised that landing on the island might prove dangerous." A rustle of movement and disappointed comments are interrupted after a brief pause. "The island of Kos will be our host this afternoon. We shall be arriving shortly. Sorry for the delay and change in plans but please enjoy."

What a lovely place, green, almost like a garden, Kos was the birthplace of Hippocrates, the father of medicine. For a while we stroll about the ruins of his early hospital site, The Asklepion. Feeling a bit healthier we board a bus that drives us through the verdant landscape to Faros and a welcoming beach. Refreshed by a swim in the cool water we wander through the remains of a Roman villa, admiring the lovely mosaics and visit ruins of an early Christian Basilica on our way back to the ship.

The Mediterranean is so blue this morning. From my vantage spot at the rail I watch the underside of the small waves of the wake flash a brilliant green for a brief moment, then white, then blue again. Looking ahead I see the outline of Crete, our next stop. I am swept by a long ago childish memory as we approach.

I devoured the wonderful stories from *The Journeys Through Bookland* series I read voraciously when I was young. One of its tales, "Theseus and The Minotaur" told of a young prince born of a Greek princess and a bull for a father. He had the body of a man but the head of a bull. Ashamed of him, the King imprisoned him in the maze of cellars beneath the Palace of Knossos. Enraged, helpless to escape or be treated as a human, labeled a monster, he supposedly ate the king's yearly offering of a Greek youth. Brave Theseus, son of Aegis, ruler of a neighboring kingdom offered himself one year as the sacrifice but vowed that he would kill the demon and save future offerings! He did, finding his way out of the labyrinth by means of a string given him by a beautiful princess, and returned home victorious. I hated the story because I was totally on the side of the poor Minotaur. I felt sorry for it/him and hoped each time I read the tale that he would devour the self-important bragging Theseus, escape the maze and the people who kept him captive. Alas, it never changed, but then, neither did I. When we visit the Palace of Knossos this afternoon I intend to search for the maze and liberate the Minotaur if he is still there!

Crete, the largest of the Greek Islands, is the home of this tale as well as others; remember King Midas whose touch turned everything to gold or Daedalus and Icarus flying too close to the sun on their homemade wings? It is that kind of a place.

Parts of the sprawling Palace were meticulously restored by early archaeologists. The vivid paint, renovated columns, hallway and roofs turn ruins into an actual building. No need for imagination or placards detailing *what was*. Current thinking deplores the practice of restoration of ancient sites and I understand the importance of not thrusting modern ideas which may be erroneous onto pristine remains but as a tourist I appreciate being able to experience the past almost first hand. Mosaic murals line the walls, many showing nubile young men and women vaulting over bulls in a dangerous ritual game. I wonder about a connection to the Minotaur story.

The myths, the tantalizing but obscure rituals and games depicted in the mosaics have their origins in this oldest advanced civilization of the Minoan, 3000 BCE to approximately 1400 BCE, when they were invaded by Mycenae from mainland Greece.

We explore for most of the afternoon this large awesome postcard from the past. Little is left of the fabled labyrinth, and sadly I must leave the Minotaur in his dungeon for another thousand years!

Legends continue as our next port of call will be fabled *Atlantis*. Halfway out of my childhood memory I am plunged back in with a yearning to visit this magical civilization, ancient but far in advance of its world, now buried beneath the sea. Modern people believing that there might be some truth in this myth searched diligently for evidence and found it in the island of Santorini. A circular volcano erupted in 1459 BCE in the most horrific explosion ever known in the Mediterranean world sending the entire middle of the island down under the sea. Despite the fact that no material remains have been found under the now crescent shaped harbor the myth persists.

Steep cliffs lining the harbor lead up to the town. Almost all the buildings are painted white and they dazzle in the brilliant Greek sun. The climb is difficult and almost everyone chooses to ride on the for-hire donkeys. The animals look so worn and shaggy and unkempt and many of us are reluctant to take advantage of the poor beasts. The locals, eager, for the drachmas, promise that the donkeys are really souls working off their time in purgatory! I ride to the top apologizing profusely if silently to my donkey and promise I will use my own two legs to get back down. I wander the narrow crooked streets enjoying the bright colorful flowers that almost leap out from every nook and cranny in the small box-like shining white houses. It seems we have left the past behind, everything is today, now, real people smiling, happy to show off their lofty home.

A slow walk down, relaxed, back to the ship, a gala dinner and dance that evening bring us to tomorrow, our last day on this wonderful cruise.

Mykonos is a very different island from Santorini. Instead of soaring cliffs it spreads itself flat and unremarkable on the sea. There is a welcoming harbor and the same bright whitewashed houses glowing against the blue sky. However, we are amazed at the profusion of windmills that dot the landscape. Of course, the land being so flat the winds sweep endlessly over it and provide a great source of power, beauty as well.

We have truly left the past. Mykonos is a very cosmopolitan place, maintaining a brisk social life, offering upscale restaurants and cafes, showing off its local arts and crafts and handwoven fabrics. It is fun to shop without being kidnapped and harangued by the local merchants, all very civilized.

In the lounge that evening we share our thoughts and feelings about the amazing things we have seen and experienced on this wonderful cruise. Aware that we may not have time for proper goodbyes in the rush of going ashore tomorrow we share addresses and hugs and promises to keep in touch before a last goodnight.

On the flight home I am swamped by memories. Half dozing they come without rhyme nor reason, deliciously random:

... laughing aloud running from that haranguing merchant, skinny arms outstretched covered with golden bracelets chasing me through the Grand Bazaar.

... three ancient pillars at the end of a promontory highlighted by a glorious sunset over the Aegean Sea where I whispered, "Oh, mother, see through my eyes, now, revel with me in this wonderful place where you could never go but, now, share with me!"

... touching every now and then the secrets of ancient people that once seemed so foreign but now are revealed as *much like me*.

... The honeyed sweetness of baklava rolling on my tongue.

... *Delphi*, where in a moment of lost confidence and fear, I turned to the Oracle, a question half formed. She smiled, put a finger to her lips and with an imperceptible shake of her head turned me around and gently but very firmly pushed me into the future!

Stumbling through customs, dragging my suitcase, my carry-on bag and over my shoulder an actual Persian rug, three by four feet, carelessly tied in a round bundle, heavy, awkward, ridiculous. I am arguing mightily with this totally unimpressed and uninterested customs official, explaining that I had been told when I purchased it in Ephesus that if I carried it home rather than sending it by mail I would not have to pay duty on it. Okay, that sounds really stupid even to me now--obviously they saw me coming. Embarrassed by my gullibility I hand over the considerable amount of duty. Turning

I see my children welcoming me and I am so happy, pleased to be home and to let someone else carry my *magic carpet.*

The, *my*, Odyssey complete, I have filled some empty places, learned what I can do all on my own and experienced again the anticipation of every day. How's that for souvenirs?

At home in Oregon…

"Welcome Home, Beloveds"

Half asleep, exhausted from a six hour flight from New Jersey broken by a stop in the dreaded O'Hare airport in Chicago, a mad dash to catch the connecting flight to Portland Oregon and I am stumbling onto an ancient school bus, old enough to have molded plastic seats, for hours of grinding shaking, bumping over mountainous roads in the pitch black. A slow numbing of the spine, bus grinding to a stop, a creaking opening of the bus door, a soft, happy voice--

"Welcome home, Beloveds!"

I am suddenly no longer so tired or numb. Awake, I am ready to sing, to dance, to search my heart, to love my guru Bhagwan and celebrate. I am in Oregon's high desert in an Ashram, new-built by loving hands, Rajneeshpuram--Home!

Not abroad this time, but farther in some ways than I have been before. A journey into the soul, into the mystery, into Me beyond what I can see or touch or feel. Sounds so pretentious but I don't mean it to be because it is really simple, clean, short, now, but words demand their price, each one an ego that loves itself and wants you to love it too! Probably why Master Bhagwan says, "Don't listen to my words, hear the silences between."

Having a Master, a Guru, is also simple. I don't 'follow' him, I don't worship him, I don't venerate him, I learn from him as from a teacher and I love Him, like I love my children. He's wise and funny, a sharer of what he has learned just as my children are bright, witty, clever, and enterprising but that is not why I love them or him. I love them for the sweet, precious connection I feel beyond those prideful words or justifications.

Becoming a sannyasin--Indian name for a spiritual disciple--taking a new name, wearing a string of 112 wooden beads around my neck, a mala, does not mean abrogation of self or a promise to do what a master tells you to do it; is a simple declaration that puts one on a path of discovery leading toward self-fulfillment and enlightenment.

Does this make sense to you? Do you understand? Think of people in your life from whom you learned how to live, what to cherish, how to grow up and enrich yourselves and others. Parents, friends, sometimes just brief encounters along the way, but from whom you learned. Don't you love them all for the gifts they gave without words or demands for payment? Of course you do, and so do I. Special, of course, but also just the latest in a long line of masters I have had starting with my gentle, loving father, Bhagwan has touched my inner being, bringing meaning, bright new ideas, laughter and joy into my life.

I'm happy to be here at the Ranch in 1982, again in 83, 84, 85, watching this little bit of Oregon's dusty, dry, high desert bloom into a very orderly, attractive, self-sufficient village in the wilderness. When I first came here, building had just begun. We slept in tents, slogging through the mud when the occasional summer storms lit up the night sky pouring sudden sharp spurts of rain upon us. Buddha Hall, a roofed but open sided, marble-floored meeting place is big enough for the thousands of sannyasins who come to meditate, dance, sing and celebrate our master and ourselves.

Every morning, leaving our shoes along the shelves provided outside the hall we race inside to drop cross-legged on that oh-so-hard marble floor, wiggling to get the little comfort we can, ready to listen to Bhagwan's words recorded in the past because he has opted to be silent for a while. Once we're settled he walks onto the slight stage, and sits in a chair, crossing his legs, dangling and dropping a sandal from his left foot, serene, smiling, looking happy to see us all. We in turn, grinning, laughing out loud, trying to be sedate and respectful, but failing. Love and joy are so hard to contain, but we quiet down and listen. Wisdom comes in so many different guises; Jesus, Buddha, Pythagoras, ancient Hindu gods, Krishna, modern heroes, silly jokes, Moses. He talks each day about them all. If we complain that when we finally get a clear message from one of them, the next talk will contradict so that we don't know what to believe! "Good, that's what I want," the lilting voice says, "Drop all that you hear and THINK FOR YOURSELVES. Listen, learn, but go inside, forget borrowed truth and find your own. Live as emperors not beggars, don't follow blindly paths carved out by others, lift your foot, step out and make your own!"

Do you wonder why I love this man, who encourages and nudges us on to find a sure and shining place within our own hearts?

It's funny how so many, many people who have never been to Rajneeshpuram, read or listened to Bhagwan have such definite *all-seeing* ideas and comments about this place and this man. They are so sure that what they see through the narrow slit of their pre-conceived ideas and prejudices is the correct, the only truth! I have read and listened and experienced this small commune planned and built entirely by ourselves. It is amazingly clean, hard work in this dusty desert environment. There are acres and acres of fields covered by tasty vegetables. I know because I have picked peas and beans in the broiling 100 degree heat of the summer plateau and eaten them gratefully each night. The people I met are from all over the world. Surveys show the majority are well educated, many are college graduates with professional careers like me.

Others, finding that the materialistic society we currently live in does not bring happiness or fulfillment or peace in their lives and are searching for more meaningful ways to live have found alternate ways to be. This is our way and we thrive.

Because I work in public school settings in special education, planning programs for children which answer their individual needs, I have the summers off. This allows me to visit the ranch for three, four weeks at a time.

I pick vegetables, help to scrub floors in the workshop halls, do wildly active meditations in the early mornings and calming, soft reflective ones at the end of the day. I have my astral chart planned on a computer and discover I'm NOT the Gemini I always thought I was. Born on the cusp, June 21, "You are 12 hours into Cancer!"

"No wonder I could never *find myself.*"

"Naturally," I am told. "The moon is your controlling planet and it changes each day!"

We are off and running. Appropriately, Cancer is a water sign, and my rising sign, Sagittarius, is fire which is where my energy and love of the turbulent ocean comes. Gotcha!

There are new and exciting workshops and I do one each summer. Entering the large room I see red-clad sannyasins randomly sitting on cushions on the floor with a smaller empty cushion in front of each one. I find a place and, instructed to do so, introduce myself to my *"four year old Bhadrena"* who sits, restless and bouncy on the empty cushion in front of me. The instructor explains that when we are four we are small, powerless, and often frightened or confused by things and events we cannot understand. Sometimes we are shaped by these influences, unfavorably, throughout our later lives. For the next few days we will be *taking care* of our little selves, explaining from our now stronger, smarter adult perspective what those scary, happenings and feelings were really all about. We will chase the *boogie man* back into oblivion with patience and love and knowledge hoping to clear away unwanted and misunderstood ways of coping.

Later walking in the garden, feeling tiny fingers curled in my outstretched palm, I am telling little Bhadrena about why her mother seems so distant. I help her to understand for the first time that mommy loves her dearly but isn't always able to show it. Hard for a four year old to grasp *grown up* meanings I keep my words as simple as I can. I actually sense a slight squeezing of that small hand. A simple rush, a sigh, and for a lovely moment I feel an old unhappiness lift and float away.

Watching others walking around the Ranch or sitting on a bench beside a small stream, bent slightly forward, looking down to a four year old height, talking quietly, whispering, concerned or perhaps just grinning with relief is a great picture of this fascinating place. There is such a freedom and acceptance here. No one is pointing or making jokes or denigrating what others are doing. Curiosity, questioning, laughing *with* but not *at* quickly changes society's endless confining *shoulds* into willingness to drop old ideas and search for better more open, broadening ones!

Yes, I was motivated to begin this journey by a desire for a spiritual basis for my life. Something, perhaps sparked by my father's childhood talks, was always there beneath the everyday, a yearning to be *more* or *less* than what I could see or taste or smell. Experimenting, trying this way or that, I found what I needed with Bhagwan. But, I have to confess that one of the things that made becoming a sannyasin so rewarding was and is that sannyasins love to dance, to sing made up songs, to be noisy, free, and hug and greet each other, "Beloved." A softer, looser way, more open to "who knows" and "what ifs."

These are the 80's. There is still a lot of interest in consciousness raising, new and different lifestyles, searching for self, and communes that grew out of the turbulent 60's. I think it is now called "New Age." Whatever it is, I am so glad to be a part of it. The workshops reflect the interest in becoming, in self-realization, "Intuition and Awareness", "Dance and Psychodrama," "Zencounter." The *biggie* is called "Primal Encounter" and I am ready for a two-week long sojourn into the exploration of an entire life cycle: mine.

Wrapped tightly in a sheet holding me in a crouched fetal position beneath the body of a women on all fours also sheet enfolded--mother and child. We will switch roles later but now I am the baby. It's dark, hot and confining and in a short while my only thought is to get out, however I'm held tight. As time passes my *mother* whispers encouragement and love and slowly I relax somewhat. It's the strangest thing, I feel and almost see my body growing, blood vessels and nerves spreading throughout just like all those graphic scenes on public television. Little stubby legs and arms, my sex, a face, even tiny fingernails are all growing to make me, and after a very long while I suddenly feel hands pushing me toward a small bright opening ahead.

Someone is calling, "Push, push!" and in a rush I find myself crawling through a channel of arms and legs out into the world. *Mommy* holds her bent index finger to my face and without thought or question I begin to suck. Not so long this time, less struggling but with an awareness not possible the first time I have experienced a bit of what birth must surely have been! I now meet my 'mother', who finds it actually difficult to stop cradling me, her baby. She is a young German woman and whenever we meet in the daily life of the Ranch I run to her calling, "Mommy, mommy!" In the workshop we change places so that she also runs toward me, calling, "Mutti, mutti." We hug and laugh together.

In the next two weeks we are pledged to silence except in the actual workshop. We wear big pins, IN SILENCE, and each of us has a stuffed animal for physical comfort that we carry with us everywhere. Mine is a little plush, white flying horse and I tuck him into my mala, snug over my heart. We are also encouraged to stop drinking coffee or other stimulants to keep us vulnerable to the intensity of our experience. [

A confession; out in the ordinary realm of the Ranch a good friend hands me his coffee cup on the sly and hides my grateful sipping from inquiring glances. We also whisper with tightly closed lips when no one else is looking, giggling like naughty children. Mea culpa.

We work hard together in the following days learning, doing exercises that give insight to many self-mysteries, large and small. We can't clear up and dismiss every complicated twist and turn that built our egos but some are gone and others made endurable. It is as though each day I stretch and grow and spread myself into all the lovely space around me, freer than I was before. What a gift.

Every day at around 2:00 Bhagwan drives around the ranch, proud of his newly learned ability to pilot a gorgeous Rolls Royce. All work stops for a minute or two so everyone can wave back. Our last day of the workshop we have bought flowers to lay on the hood of his car as he drives by saying "Goodbye, Bhagwan," because we are dying this afternoon.

Lying comfortably on a small mattress covered lightly with a sheet, relaxed, empty, at peace we are preparing to die. The room is dim and quiet, soft music and a softer voice is easing the path to oblivion. It's lovely and I can feel many ties that hold me to life today, slipping free, letting go--but not all. I have a brief feeling of guilt because I can't really drop everything but then I realize the dross, the dreck I've swept away in the last two weeks is what has gone. I am grateful and proud of my somewhat new, cleaner self. Today was--Goodbye/Hello Bhagwan--and I am renewed, ready and able to drink coffee, talk and flirt in public again.

I come to the Ranch for Enlightenment Day in March 1983. There is construction at Buddha Hall so we are all jammed into a smaller inside building. Sitting cross-legged, each time I bow forward over my hands clasped in Namaste my thumbs go up into my nostrils. Trying to laugh and sing and celebrate without being able to really breathe is quite an enlightening experience.

The largest birthday cake I have ever seen is displayed in Buddha Hall on Bhagwan's birthday on December 11, 1984. *Happy birthday is* sung in a myriad of languages at the top of everyone's lungs, shaking the ceiling and sending back funny distorted but joyful echoes.

1985 brings changes, disruption of paradise by ambitious, mean spirited really dangerous people who begin to destroy the Ranch from within and without. Following an aborted attempt by someone to poison his doctor Bhagwan himself calls the authorities to report the evil actions but some in the outside world are eager to discredit him and take advantage of the situation to imprison him, dragging him from place to place until he decides to go home to Pune, India.

…where I will be with him again in 1988.

The Jewel in the Crown

"Want to go to India, see Bhagwan?"

Oh dear, what a wonderful, perfect, possible idea. "Yes, yes, yes!"

It is 1987 and I am in Seattle Washington. Somewhat lonely, lost, certainly at loose ends when a telephone call drops me right back into a fast moving, on-target life!

My audacious trip to Greece seven years ago was an adventure. It was also a boost, a hurrah for a new way of viewing and experiencing life. Begun as a new widow in a fumbling only half aware state it ended in "I can do it--I can accept loss, a destruction of a lifestyle, an ability to change, to trust myself, to pick a direction and move ahead with courage and grace. In the last seven years I have done a lot of that!

For a while after my husband's death much remained the same; job, my house, a diminished but still active neighborhood social life. I am so proud of my intrepid children David, Pamela, and Daniel bravely dealing with their loss and grief, forming their own routines and plans.

I find a beautiful, crazy, somewhat notorious Indian guru, Bhagwan Shree Rajneesh. His talks, for that is really what they are, not lectures or instructions; are on just about every subject; spiritual, worldly, down to earth, mystical, jokes, silence. The few weeks I spend each summer from 1982 to 1985 at The Ranch on the dusty, hot high desert of Oregon wearing red, meditating with thousands of other spiritual seekers, sannyasins, doing workshops, consciousness raising, exploring spiritual paths. Wonderful!

The ordered past is slowly being chipped away. In 1984 I sell my house and move to a one bedroom garden apartment, actually excited about this new experience.

1986--here we go again! Another, earlier phone call tilting, turning my routine sideways. "A voice from your past, Marilyn Holdsworth." George Bramson, my first love, here in Wayne from California, having arranged a business trip to allow him to attend our 40th high school reunion. Discovering that I was now a widow, eager for reminiscing, he is calling. A great conversation becomes an invitation to get together for drinks the following evening at his motel. Forgetting to tell him I am now a wrinkled, blonde old lady I am pleased to discover that he is a wrinkled slightly bald, white haired old man. Amazing, the old spark was still there and after dinner, a goodbye hug in the parking lot and--"Will you stay?""Yes."

This lovely, unexpected meeting, remembered love and I am on my way to California!

Divesting, putting New Jersey on hold, dropping what was, and I am now a California Girl, a Sacramento sweetie with--"What are we? Partners, girlfriend/boyfriend (a little silly at 59), significant others?" Lovers, of course fits the bill but makes us blush! We just smile, hold hands, surprising everyone with our romantic tale.

Begins now a year of Sunday morning breakfasts of eggs and chorizo wrapped like an ice cream cone in a paper thin taco. I learn to make crème fraise, teach two special education classes in two different schools each day as well as testing and planning programs for homeless children. We go panning for gold in the High Sierra, explore national parks, travel to Los Angeles and eat in fantastic San Francisco restaurants while laughing and learning about the newness of each other.

Strange how it plays out at the end of that year when feelings and caring are still so strong. Not strong enough however, to totally sever old lives, habits obligations. Lifestyles are different and for me, having dropped all of mine back in New Jersey, not so easy to accept.

Still trying, talking, both of us crying, I pack my VW convertible with all my belongings, including a small TV and a Yucca plant that does not allow for the closing of the top. Hoping it does not rain I am off to Seattle, Washington. Staying in a $10.00 a night hostel in Ashland, Oregon where I am lucky to see a performance of Shakespeare's Twelfth Night and a Motel 6 just over the border in Washington and I have arrived at a sprawling 1950s house called Duck Heaven.

Seattle is awash in sannyasins, many who have come here to this lovely, young, open city from the Ranch. I had contacted some friends when I realized it had become time to move on, and I am welcomed to this home on the shore of a little lake, filled, obviously, with ducks. A mattress covered in a wild Indian coverlet placed on the floor next to a large picture window overlooking the lake, my yucca plant, which survived the trip intact, in the corner and I am *at home* again. New roommates, Sangit, Suzanne and David, make shaking off sadness a bit easier. We laugh much, meditate, dance, and they help me explore this exciting city.

Home has become fluid, flexible, a verb instead of a noun! Letting go, it seems, has become a way of life and I slip much more easily from one scenario to another. Another phone call, an invitation, a suggestion, "Want to go to India?"

The call is from my east-coast sannyasin friend Richard. Racing to get my passport, airline tickets and I am on my way. It would be quicker to fly across the Pacific but Richard and I decide we would meet at Heathrow in London and so I fly east. There he is, the sweet looking, bearded man who liked to wear hats that I had met and meditated with when I worked in Pequannock, New Jersey. We had kept in touch, sharing cassettes of Bhagwan's recorded lectures the whole time I was in California. Catch up time on the plane gets us to Bombay at night. We have been told that night landings are safest because of the tendency of flocks of buzzards to get caught in the engines in the daytime.

A wild ride in an ancient creaking taxi driven by a bouncing, chattering driver who keeps turning off the lights. *"Saving rupees, no danger, me good driver, giggle, no worry!"* Even the darkness cannot hide the cardboard hovels all over the sides of the road. A man in rags stretches out on small scraps of grass at roadside trying perhaps to get some relief from the hot humid air, two dirty children, bedtime long overdue, sit listless on the curb. I go a little cold inside.

We arrive at the train station in one piece, which was not always the expectation careening through the streets sans lights in the middle of the night. The waiting room or lobby of this relatively new railroad station is brightly lit, showing in detail all the people crowded together, sleeping on the floor, even two families with children. Unlike what we have seen outside most of the sleepers are clean, simply dressed--the men have briefcases as pillows under their heads or clamped tight across their chests. These are poor but working men and women who are unable to find or perhaps pay for a decent place to live. Here they can be clean, showering in public facilities, and safe. I'm beginning to feel the foundations of what I have always assumed to be the basic needs of living that MUST be met shake and begin to fall apart around me. A man, awake, looks up from his book and smiles tentatively at us, a mother turns to cuddle a restless child.

How can this be *home*, a sustaining place that each day renews in the way that I know? But it is and I must change my definition and preconceived ideas. Apparently, the structure is ephemeral and ultimately unnecessary. Home is people with the ability to accept what is and love and laugh, reaching without rancor for a better place. Oh my, my arrogant, all-knowing Western self is humbled. I have forgotten my sleeping cat and my desire to live in the moment, eager to learn from differences without judgement.

I ache for the poverty and pain around me but I am also grateful to see, again, how wide and sustaining the world is, how strong and brave we all are in our particular journeys through life. We find an empty corner, lie down, curling around our luggage, and actually, I think, sleep for a little while.

Morning is just beginning to happen as we catch our train to Poona. The crowded car is filled with smiling coach mates offering to share breakfast bits they've carried with them. I, smiling also, answer, pointing, gesturing (I really don't know what they are saying) hoping I am making some sense. Actually, it doesn't seem to matter. Come to think of it, why is always making sense so important anyway?

When will I learn?

Giving in, letting go I giggle and clap my hands when everyone else does, absurdly happy to be just where and when I am, free from all the *shoulds, the must bes,* constraints we live with every day, thinking there is no other way. Up yours, society--catch me if you can!

The scenery rushing by matches my mood. Free of the city's squalor it is lush and green, beautiful. We rattle over a deep valley on a high, skinny bridge looking down at a small stream tumbling far below. I had no idea that India is so rural and lovely. I see fields here and there between the trees where tiny figures with sticks are driving what looks like oxen, small ponds, and faint in the distance the hushed gray rise of mountains.

The soft, rhythmic clickety clack of the wheels against the rails and the soothing scenery work their magic. The whole compartment quiets down, loud laughter fades to smiles and a few gentle snores dislodge breakfast crumbs on the belly of the slumping figure in the corner. Leaning back against the seat I think I am actually dozing off.

Whoosh, screech, a shudder of brakes and we have arrived in Poona. The doors of the train station open to a blast of hot, very humid air into the incredibly noisy, rushing-about, crowded town center. I don't believe it but right there in the intersection of two main roads are a couple of enormous brown cows gazing languidly at the crowds milling about around them. Instead of yelling at or goading this snuffling, shuffling cause of a massive traffic jam people are cajoling, tempting, coaxing the beasts in lilting Hindi to "Please move, c'mon, let's go, please."

Besieged by what seems like hundreds of taxi drivers cajoling, coaxing us to ride with them we settle, for the nearest, noisiest one who whisks us away before we can see what happens next. The street is packed side to side with taxis, bicycles, filled to over-flowing buses painted all over with garishly colored designs, and the ubiquitous three wheeled motorized rickshaws all swooping, cutting each other off, calling out, waving. Despite the hurly-burly and the madness no one seems angry. The drivers are smiling, heads bobbing enjoying the melee. I decide very quickly to close my eyes.

"You can look now, we're here." Hotel Srimaan is a small, rather woebegone building, not terribly inviting but it is cheap and near Bhagwan's Ashram. Surprisingly the room is quite comfortable and the bathroom is all marble. I am learning quickly that India is a land of contrasts and the lessons have just begun.

We walk three blocks to Osho Rajneesh, the Ashram. It is evening and the Ashram is closed for the lecture but I am so excited about being here that I crouch down to peek under the gates. Someone touches my shoulder and a gentle, chiding voice says, "Please, Ma, I know you want to see and hear him but be respectful and behave yourself. Come back tomorrow." Chagrined, subdued we walk back to the hotel, properly unpack, shower in our marble bathroom and sleep.

Next morning battling a massive jet lag of a full twelve hours, out of sync we are back at the Ashram. A wall encloses the lovely park-like setting of low attractive buildings. Fountains and benches are placed in quiet secluded corners. Reminiscent of the Ranch's Buddha Hall, but smaller, there is a roofed, open sided meeting space. It is also floored in marble and my legs begin to tingle a bit in anticipation of hours of cross-legged meditations. It is very peaceful, an oasis in the midst of the hurly-burly life of the city just outside the gates.

The energy here is different from the Ranch in Oregon. It's softer, more accepting, spread out, somehow. There was a sharpness to the moments and days at Rajneeshpuram, a speed and excitement that has mellowed here in the East. The edges have blurred, easier, more comfortable to lean against. The next three weeks seem to flow past.

We use the fact that we are staying at an outside hotel to avoid the wildly active 6:00 am Dynamic meditation, but participate in others throughout the day. I love Nataraj, three quarters of an hour just dancing free to lovely music, a fifteen minute relaxing on the marble floor which now feels soft and yielding. Kundalini, done at 4:30 each afternoon, is a gentle shaking of every part of the body, loosening the tensions and cares of the day. Loud screeches from the peacocks that wander in the gardens showing off their magnificent almost luminescent tails accompany us. Bhagwan devised these active meditations because he said Westerners find it difficult to suddenly sit down immobile to contemplate as most Easterners do. The pace

of the different lifestyle needs a moment of active letting go before the quiet introspection can begin. Each evening we sit cross legged on that marble floor wrapped in the love of my guru and all the sannyasins we share him with.

Here in India Bhagwan is more frequently called Osho which quickly rolls off the tongue just as easily. "A rose by any other name..." Each evening there is a lecture, a wisdom sharing that we love.

Leaving the Ashram, walking back to the hotel each evening is almost a carnival scene. There are hucksters selling just about everything, gold jewelry, garishly painted figurines of Hindu gods, beautiful saris, scarves, of course, beggars and one very small, dirty, barefoot boy offering a bedraggled bouquet of wilting flowers, grinning from ear to ear. Each night I promise that I will have a gift for him before I leave. I'm quite sure he doesn't understand me but he never loses his sweet smile even when I walk away.

Being with Richard is also lovely. Our lives are much different since we worked together on a Child Study Team in Pequannock, reading Bhagwan, spending many lunchtime meditations in a nearby park, doing the Tarot, laughing, questioning and loving the journey. We, apparently, are still travelers together on the pathless path. Perhaps, whether we see each other in the future or not, we will always be. I hope so.

Richard, leaving a week earlier than I do has a horrendous trip home. Cancelled flight connections, abrupt change in plans and airlines, two days all but stranded, nervous and wary in Rhiad, Syria and eventually safe and home. He sends me a warning to be careful of thieving taxi drivers in Bombay.

Walking, wandering, about the ashram, meditating, feeling at last like that ubiquitous cat, at home, my last few days are sweet. I revel in the quiet, undemanding moments, gathering this new, lovely experience around me. Hours pass browsing in the bookstore, listening to the soft buzz of far flung accents, watching the passing parade. Bhagwan, wanting us to realize that we are not the clothes, the accoutrements we wear asked us to dress in shades of red and it amazes me again how clear, strong and *right now* everyone's faces are when the clothes just seem to fade and melt into that amorphous sea of red. I love it! I love seeing all the vivid expressions as we talk with each other and I see an answering enjoyment, like a mirror of my own face. I know that people say the ashram like other spiritual places is apart from and not the *real world* but I beg to differ. The outside world of daily living changes all the time, societies built on so called eternal truths are temporary at best, rising and falling. Through all the myriad changes that have marked mankind's progress there seems to have always been a spiritual yearning for a deeper, more honest and meaningful way to live. Searching has taken many forms but the basic human desire to explore and experience what I may call enlightenment appears to flower when the arbitrary demands of society have been removed. Ashrams of whatever persuasion offer a place where learning to absorb and live fully in both worlds is happily possible.

Everything slows down, opens up, on my last evening. I am aware of how very lucky I am to be in this lovely space, to know Osho and these funny, loving people I am with. I don't forget on my walk back to the hotel to look for and find that raggedy boy with his wilting bouquet. He almost falls over with excitement and delight as I give him the promised 100 rupee note. I treat the stumpy flowers with care as he jumps and bows, grinning from ear to ear!

My trip home begins with a memorable taxi ride to the airport! The real world comes crashing in, "Here's change madam," as he gives me cash for a 10 rupee note instead of the 100 note I handed him.

"I gave you 100 rupees."

"No, no, see," holding up a 10 rupee note.

"NO! 100 rupees!" I start to roll down my window, leaning out, shouting, "Police, police!"

"Oh, so sorry, missus....here change for 100"

Laughing, proud of my quick thinking, my spirituality unbesmirched, grateful to Richard for his heads up about cheating taxi drivers, I settle down for the long return.

A long return it is involving delays, cancelations, computer breakdowns, and unexpected layovers. It takes me 40 hours to land, way overdue, in Seattle. Exhausted, 2:00 in the morning; plodding through a seemingly endless customs queue I see a very familiar face in the waiting crowd. George had thought to surprise me by flying up from San Francisco to meet my incoming flight. Surprised himself by the long wait for the delayed arrival he still smiles and welcomes me with open arms. We spend the next few days catching up and exploring options. We really do care for each other and wonder why we can't seem to make *every day* work. A tentative idea begins to surface. What if we spend two maybe three weeks together each year exploring, traveling my east and his west coast? Finding new places, discovering old and new history, learning our country and its past has been of interest to us both and was a good part of our being together this last year. Loving, enjoying each other without the strain of *having to make it work* may be the best of both worlds.

Sad at knowing that our first experiment failed but pleased we've found a doable option we hug, few tears, goodbye and I must start to ship myself and furniture back to New Jersey.

A different New Jersey this time--south of the Raritan River, below the 88 mile marker on the Garden State Parkway it is a whole new world. Quieter, friendlier, slower, where it is okay to chat for a bit with the supermarket checker about her mother's rheumatism, the entire waiting line sometimes entering in to the conversation. Outside in the parking lot it is not unusual to see pedestrian and car in a dance routine insisting the *other* go first. South Jersey!

My South Jersey lies along those beautiful, white beaches on that lovely strip of barrier islands that protect the gentle southward curve of the state. Ever since 1958 when Ray and I discovered this land almost unknown to Northern vacationers and began those wonderful holiday years, the resort town, Stone Harbor on seven-mile island, has been a very important part of our family's lives.

Just three miles inland from the Harbor on the mainland is the town of Cape May Court House, home, of course, to the county courthouse and approximately 5,000 people. Although it is the county seat, it is just a small town that becomes MY small town and home. I am now a Guide at the Mid-Atlantic Center for the Arts in Cape May, sharing all the Victoriana of this lovely old town with the thousands of tourists who come to revel in the frou-frou of the late 1800s.

***

"Baba, Baba!" There he is, taller now, a year later but just as raggedy. No flowers this time but arms outstretched in welcome. It appears that the one hundred rupees, six dollars, I gave him last year have bought me an Indian grandson. Bending down to hug him I am touched that he remembered me.

Of course, I am in Poona, India again, 1988, staying, this year in the Hotel Kapila (means cow), more at ease this time with the poverty, the crowds and the horrendous traffic. Laughing again at the sweet crazy way the Indian people just smile and wag their heads at all the chaos and confusion of Poona's streets. No road rage, threats or nasty looks--just a karmic acceptance of *that's how it is—-next time will be better!*

Settling in to Ashram life is smoother the second time round and quickly we, yes, Richard is here again, pretty much pick up from where we were last year. A cozy café tucked beneath some sheltering trees becomes a favorite place for a leafy lunch. The food at the eating places here in the Ashram is delicious and varied but all vegetarian. The water that food is cooked in as well as all the drinking water is double boiled to eliminate those stomach-aching bugs that westerner's digestions just are not familiar with. For a change in routine we opt to have a meal or two at our hotel, but continue to buy bottled water or lime juice. I am not fond of most vegetables and chicken tandoori is so tasty.

A week into our stay and my stomach has apparently become home to some of those nasty foreign bugs! A visit to the Ashram doctor frightened that I may have contracted dysentery and a sample sent off to the local hospital show no serious bug invasion. I reveal, when asked by the doctor, that I was here last year. "Oh, you just have reentry diarrhea, no need to worry, be gone in a day or two."

She's right, the bugs have departed, we eat only in the ashram and all is well.

It is interesting this time that *meditations* have become *meditating,* more of a flow with less division between crossed legs, the marble floor and a stroll about the ashram, conversation with friends and just being. I'm so glad I came again.

Enriched, still chuckling over some of Osho's really bad jokes, but loving his profound and sweet words, we get ready to bring back what we can from this adventure to our everyday lives. These trips to India involve many real difficulties, expense, an upside down time change, culture shock and physical discomfort but there is a Zen story which says:

Enlightenment is an accident, there is nothing you can do to achieve it, but if you do not work as hard as you can for it satori will never happen.

So, we strive to become *accident-prone!*

Once a sannyasin asked Bhagwan what we would do when he died. Smiling he announced that when he left his body *we would all be Bhagwan with the gift of satori inside of us, just waiting to be discovered and set free!* In January 1989 we get the chance to experience this as truth when he leaves his body.

Sad to lose his physical presence but carrying this gentle promise I get on with my changing South Jersey life. A bit tired of hand-holding tourists as a guide at the Mid-Atlantic Arts Center and missing the school environment, particularly the children, I now work on a Child Study Team as a Learning Disabilities Teacher Consultant (what a mouthful) in Margaret Mace School in North Wildwood. Good to be back observing and talking with students, caring for special children, planning programs for their individual learning styles, helping teachers and parents to understand the different ways learning happens and that growth comes individually in its own time.

I buy a wooded lot in town, build a house surrounded by trees and good neighbors. I acquire Joshu, a lost dirty stray dog of inde-terminate provenance and in quiet moments, sitting on my deck, cradling a cup of coffee I think about India.

India was Queen Victoria's *jewel in the crown* of empire, for me, a journey halfway across the world to a style of living so different from my own. On a scale of 1 to 10 I rate India as 0 to 11! Heart-wrenching poverty in the cities, crowds jostling, horrendous traffic, gold encrusted dancing, flying Hindu gods, shrines on every corner, the rat that ran over my foot one dark walk back to the hotel, the amazing acceptance of the Indian people who believing in karma, smile and find *home* on the crowded train station floor. In contrast, the green beauty of the countryside and the mystic, majestic rise of the Himalayas far off on the horizon. The flashing, vivid colors of the women's graceful saris, and, again for me, the very real, enticing possibility of a way of living spiritually as well as worldly.

My coffee cools as I feel gratitude to India for its lessons and begin to wonder where else in this big kaleidoscope world there is joy and excitement and lessons to be learned. I will have to find....

At home in Italy…

La Famiglia

"What are you are singing?"

"Opera singing, *La Boheme, Aida*, opera!" "You no know?"

I am 14 years old, at my first job as a stock girl in a narrow little ladies dress shop in Passaic New Jersey in 1942. I feel so grown up caring for the dresses, taking them from the fitting rooms, placing them neatly on the hangers, doing up buttons, tying belts and putting them back in the sale merchandise. Slow times I spend on the crowded second floor which I share with Maria, the young Italian seamstress who does alterations. Opening boxes of new dresses I iron and get them ready for sale downstairs. Maria is very quiet but she often sings to herself while sewing and today I ask her about the songs.

Suddenly excited, almost out of her chair "Opera singing, *La Boheme, Aida! Opera!*" "You no know?" Appalled at my lack of knowledge, laughing at my bewildered look she begins in her broken English to educate this poor ignorant American girl. Each opera is a story of people and places, events that are as familiar and real to her as her family and neighbors. At her home in Italy she grew up with opera as part of her everyday life. Like a missionary in the wilds of Borneo preaching to the natives, she regales me with those passionate stories, interspersed with bits of the arias, thrilling and lovely. Her halting English becomes clear to me and I soak up each story with delight. We laugh at how silly some of those characters are and weep with the tragic heroines dying in their lovers' arms. What an education, what a delight. I love opera from that day and all the storied, singing days thereafter. I want very much to go to Italy.

In 1953 it happens on that wonderful nine week European trip with Marilyn McBride. A bit more than half way into that journey, having sat up all night on a train from Germany we arrive, at last, in Roma, Italy. Weary from the trip, feeling somewhat lost in the large train station without any idea of where to stay we meet a ruddy faced Irish priest who gifts us with an introduction to a convent where we could stay. Room and three meals would cost $2.00 a day which we assure him would be "just fine."

The convent overlooks the Circus Maximus, one of the must-see sites in Rome. The coveted view from our little balcony, straw stuffed mattresses, instant coffee (a treat because we are American) and the lovely sisters make this a perfect base for our treasured days in Rome. We stroll the ancient, foot-worn, stones of the Appian Way, climb the Scala Santa and even make a memorable visit to the Pope, with a thousand or so others, at his summer palace, Castle Gandolfo.

Having enjoyed the Roman ruins, the Sistine Chapel at the Vatican and all the magnificent churches we headed off to Florence and the rest of that memorable trip.

I wonder now if Maria could have made an opera out of the exciting, even dramatic everyday moments of that journey. Singing in her soft Italian voice could she have woven all the disparate happenings into an opera? Delighted and excited could she have done it all over again with what is to follow?

Perhaps not, so what follows is not an opera, it is a story, just a story but a really good one and very particular to me.

Once upon a time, long, long ago a little baby was left on the steps of a convent in a small town in northern Italy. The village was called Villaromagnano but the tiny boy did not have a name. The nuns took him in and named him Raimondo--Raimondo Restione. Raimondo is a fine Italian name but *Restione* had never been heard of before. It was made up, brand new, an original gift from those kindly sisters who raised him.

He grew up to be a serious, quiet young man helping in the church and working for local farmers. In the winters he went to Genoa to work in the steel mills, returning to his preferred life in Villaromagnano in the summers. Strong and healthy, he worked long hours, saving to buy his own land. He purchased three plots in the surrounding farmland, met and married Angela Rolandi from a neighboring village, built a large fine house in his town, and had six children.

His oldest son, Giuseppe immigrated to America in the early teens of the 20th century. Tucked inside his small suitcase was a set of long woolen underwear, a special gift from his family worried about the winters in America. His new landlady in New York, not understanding Italian but wanting to help her shy young boarder, proceeded to boil the set. A neighbor's six year old son became the recipient of a new pair of long johns! Although Giuseppe had planned to just stay for a few years, he met Tersilla Carbone, fell in love, married and following the birth of three more Restiones, settled in northern New Jersey. He named his son Raymond after his own father.

You have probably guessed by now that this Raymond was *my* Raymond.

We meet, marry, make three Restiones ourselves, and in 1997 my daughter, Pamela and I have come to Italy to search for more.

And here they are, standing on the side of the road waiting for us.

"Stop, stop the car, there they are!"

I would have known them anywhere. Carletto and his two sons Guido and Massimo. They look just like my husband. Whatever the unknown background of that little baby on the convent steps was it is very strong. The Restione Look is alive and well and oh so dominant. Each time we meet another member of the family my daughter says through her tears, "You remind me so of my father," or, "You look just like my grandpapa!"

Ray died in 1980, seventeen years ago and my father in law, Giuseppe, in 1983. "Grandpapa," as a three year old Pamela named him was a very private man. He attended school in Italy only until the third grade. They were a farming family and needed all hands. Arriving in the United States at sixteen he began his lifelong pursuit of learning, becoming a very knowledgeable man. He was quiet and spoke little of his family in Villaromagnano, only occasionally mentioning stories of his childhood on the family farm. Ray and I, in our turn so busy with our three children, David, Pamela and Daniel, and with all the minutiae of our daily lives, asked very few questions.

Perhaps it was the times that motivated Giuseppe and Tersilla to forgo diversity to become the best, the strongest Americans they could. They moved to a small suburban New Jersey town where there were few, if any, other Italian families and much to my regret never taught their children to speak their native language.

We, therefore, knew little about the only other Restiones in the world. What a surprise it was then when in 1986 my son David traveled to Milan, Italy on business and on a whim opened a local telephone book. There they were, listed right there in Torino and Milano.

"Gli Americani, uno momento, Elio!" An excited voice on the other end of that first telephone call! Elio comes to the phone and asks "Quanti anni hai?" How old are you? *Are you my first cousin or his son?* David stumbling through the few Italian words he had picked up, surprised at the heavily accented but understandable

English these first and second cousins of his were greeting him with assures Elio that he is Giuseppe's thirty year old grandson. An invitation is extended and a rich, rewarding family connection begins.

They knew more about us than we did of them. Apparently grandpapa wrote to them occasionally. They even had a letter telling about the marriage of his son Raymond and, proudly, the birth of a new grandson, David. How exciting! How sad that it has taken so long for this vital, broadening connection to happen, too late for Ray and grandpapa but gifting the rest of us with a whole new vibrant famiglia.

Buon giorno, come stai, io il tuo cugino, David begins to learn Italian, driving that awful Washington DC commute from his home in Maryland with the lilting syllables of his new language shaping his American tongue into more musical patterns. He becomes expert. He and his wife Camille, juggling their work assignments, make a few trips to the Restiones, and now include visiting with Camille's Italian famiglia, the D'Adamos as well.

Meanwhile my itchy feet have calmed down and, as much as I like travel I am busy now enjoying my new house, my work and my scruffy dog. Joining a Gourmet Club that accepts me despite my really poor cooking skills, gives my family cause for much laughter and joking at my expense. Life is good, relatively quiet and calm.

I should have guessed.

It is now April, 1997. "You have to go, it's only $259.00 to fly round trip to Milan!" My daughter-in-law Camille's voice is shaking with excitement. "David, my mom and I are going a week earlier. You can meet up with my sister Karen in Washington DC and fly together meeting us in Milan."

"Okay, okay, that's incredible. I can only take five days from work BUT I am on my way, dear." A quick turn around and I make a call to my daughter, "Pam, guess what? I have your 40th birthday present, I'm taking you to Italy and we are going to search for Restiones."

Find them we do!

Even Laurina, grandpapa's baby sister, now 92 years old, greets us with a sweet smile from the end of a family table lush with delicious dishes cooked to welcome the Americani. This is just the first of many festive tables surrounded by first and second cousins all named Restione that we will be asked to share. Such a welcoming famiglia. What we had always thought would be simple rural farmers have become doctors, Fiat executives, teachers, export-import business men and CPAs. Grandpapa would be so proud of his illustrious family. The younger generation all speak English having learned it in grade school. We are made to feel so welcomed and special.

The Milanese part of the family claims us for the first two days, designating Guido, my children's second cousin, as our guide. Rightfully proud of the beautiful gothic cathedral in Milan's center, Guido brings us here first. The graceful slender pillars surrounding and covering the façade seem to lift this magnificent building up to the sky. The Gothic style was born in northern Europe but has reached a pinnacle here.

The nearby Galleria Vittorio Emanuelli II is our next stop. Milan has come to be known as the fashion capital of the world (move over Paris) and this beautiful enclosed mall attests to that claim. There are unique, artistic displays of the very latest styles in the shop windows, boutiques and specialty stores. Fashionable restaurants, coffee bars and cafes have displaced gloomy office build-ings as meeting places for the business community. As such it is popularly known as 'Milan's living room.'

In the center, under an awesome curved glass ceiling is a striking mosaic of a large bull. It is bright, realistic and the colors are sharp except in one almost worn-out section. Guido rather reluctantly explains that if you place the heel of your foot on the depicted testicles of the bull and turn round and round you will have good luck. Somewhat embarrassed but laughing aloud the women of our group proceed to do just that. I notice that David and Guido have disappeared around the corner.

We tour the Scorza Castle, once home of the Milanese rulers and the Poldi Pezzoli Museum where we view ancient manuscripts and priceless works of art including statuary by Michelangelo, and paintings by Picasso. Just walking about the city is a treat for us. There are very old Romanesque churches, and, of course, the warm vibrant busy streets of today. It is Spring and lush sidewalk displays of colorful flowers are everywhere.

We had gotten tickets to view DaVinci's famous painting *The Last Supper* displayed on a wall in the Monastery of Santa Maria delle Grazie However, purchasing them in advance did not guarantee early admission and here we are the next afternoon in line with many, many others. There are busloads of foreign group tours waiting as well. In casual conversation I mention to Pam that I thought the people from northern Italy did look a bit different from those from the southern regions. Carefully studying the large amount of camera toting Japanese tourists she states mischievously, "I think you are right. It's surprising how many here look Asian!"

We have been warned that due to a current restoration of the famous fresco-like painting we may not be able to see all of it. Entering at the far end of the room we spot scaffolding in place cutting off some sections from our view but I am overjoyed to glimpse the essential beauty of DaVinci's masterpiece. The colors, soft-rubbed by time, still warm with grace, shine through here and there past all the poor attempts to save the crumbling fresco. In 1652, believing that the masterpiece was past restoring a door was cut into the bottom middle of it! Further work stopped the deterioration for a while and the door was closed and painted over. While there is so much lost what is still visible is the love, the adoration and power of DaVinci's original offering.

Another lovely meal that evening, still catching up on family stories from both sides of the Atlantic. Next morning we are off to

Turin to visit with the other part of la famiglia. Carletto's brother, Elio and his wife Fernanda welcome us and we meet their son, Fabrizio who becomes our guide eager to share his proud city with us. A beautiful city it is, with lush green parks and botanical gardens stretching along the banks of the Po River. We spend the next day and a half with him, his wife, Lorella and daughters, Gulia and Claudia exploring. We make a visit to Turin's beautiful cathedral and see what Fabrizio translates as *The Jesus Towel*, The Holy Shroud, said to carry marks of Jesus's face where it covered his head in the tomb.

As a truly fitting end to this exciting visit we travel to the original Restione house in Villaromangno, now a summer home for the family. Fernanda states in serious tones, pointing to the ancestral bed, "This is where it all began!" Now where all 26 members of the Restione Clan meet together. Warm hugs, loud, laughing conversations in both languages accompanied by much pointing, hand wavings and halting translations by the younger generation--oh my, it truly is a family. I have come full circle, enriched, rewarded, accepted by this remarkable famiglia.

***

Siamo novamente in viaggio! Five wonderful days four years ago were great but I have known all along it was not enough. It is now May 2001 and I am again in Milan being greeted by Giovanna Restione who points to the blocky concrete façade of the train station where Mussolini used to harangue the public and laughing, mockingly says, "Fascitsti, fascisti!" How pleased they are to be free of that awful time.

A quick reprise of that visit in 1997, meeting briefly with the Milanese famiglia (I'll be back in a week or so) and I am off to meet David and Camille in Roma. Of course we visit all the fantastic sites we touched and loved in past trips and add a few new ones.

David and I climb what feels to me like a hundred steep steps to see Michelangelo's brooding statue of St. Peter in Chains, only to find the small church is closed for repairs. Trying hard to catch my breath and weather my disappointment seems to arouse the sympathy of a nearby ragged vender of souvenirs and he offers in broken Italian to help us sneak in. We manage a slanting peak of one side of Peter behind a slightly pushed back door. Not quite what we had hoped for but a nice try by our new friend in need. He offers me a small statue of the saint in compensation and surprising him wide-eyed I hug him gratefully.

A visit to the Sistine Chapel is such a surprise and delight. Having glimpsed the staggering beauty of the ceiling back in 1953 when it was dark and covered in years of dust and dirt I am overwhelmed now by the cleaning and renovation done in 1994. To see bright, sharp colors and the clean-limbed forms painted by genius all those centuries ago. I wish I could lie down on the floor and revel in this gift. Unfortunately that is not allowed so we wander back and forth, necks craned, heads tipped upward as far as possible absorbing the magnificent scene.

Venice is our next stop. It is lovely to experience this floating city of canals, fascinating shops where I buy small glittering Mardi Gras masks, outdoor restaurants and small cafes fronting what seems like endless waterways filled with graceful gondolas and singing boatmen. We sit at a tiny table outside our hotel in the afternoon to drink wine home-made by Teodoro, Camille's somewhat ancient D'Damo relative whom David and Camille had visited last week in Celole. David pours the wine from the orange soda bottle it is in and toasting this gift we drink. Without comment we stash the still almost full bottle under our table and laughing sheepishly we move on.

A boat ride to the island of Murano to see the truly beautiful glass made there rounds out our time in this almost fairy-tale city and we are off to Verona. There is a charming patio in the middle of the town that houses a small balcony high above the street where Juliet leaned forward to hear her bedazzled Romeo. Yes, I do know that Shakespeare's story of true and tragic love is not based in reality but what delight to pretend it really did happen.

There is one more sweet visit with all the famiglia in Villaromagnana. It is a little bit harder this time to say goodbye but promises of visits on both sides of the Atlantic make going easier.

Looking back at this saga of the Restione Famiglia I have changed my mind. Young Giuseppe's courageous voyage to America lacking the new language, making ends meet by selling chestnuts on the streets of New York, meeting a lovely young woman recently arrived from a neighboring Italian village and falling in love. Making a family that became a true American family separated through the passage of time from the home place but reunited by a grandson who traveling in reverse found an interesting, loving group of cousins and a 92–year-old aunt. Sorrow at the passing of Giuseppe himself, his son Raymond and cousin Elio is woven into the joy and excitement of our visits. Journeys back and forth over the Atlantic Ocean by three generations of the family have enriched us all, broadened our horizons and taught us how wide is connection and love. So much more than just a story.

No wonder I have changed my mind. This saga is truly splendid opera. Maria should have been able to sing it into being, all those years ago, sweeping my 14-year-old self into an unknown but wonderful future!

At home in Belgium and France…

Ils Ne Passeront Pas

1914-1918

"This is… " My son, David is showing pictures from his recent trip to Belgium and France. On the screen is a shot of a flat empty landscape boringly identical to the five or six that have gone before, though each one has an impressive battle name. I stifle a yawn and someone whispers, "It's just another field." There is a pause, the screen goes blank and David laughs a bit shamefacedly.

"True." he says, "but let me tell you what lies beneath those empty places!" and he begins.

It's an evening in the spring of 2001. We've been sitting for quite a while now, scrunched together on the couch watching David show pictures on the TV screen of his trip to the World War I Western front in France. His voice deepens taking on an emotional undertone as he shares the incredible story of men digging in the dirt of those fields, burrowing, scrambling to make trenches under an almost constant rain of shells as big as the men themselves. "The Artillery never seemed to stop. It was ripping soldiers apart, leaving them torn, screaming in the empty spaces between the enemy trenches and themselves."

"I know that sounds overblown, too dramatic, but it was quite simply the way it was for four unbelievable years." David continues and puts up one more picture on the screen. This one is of himself standing next to a shell propped up on the side of one of those fields. He explains that almost one hundred years after the battles people still find unexploded shells under the soil. They gingerly place them on the side of the road for teams that come through regularly to pick up the armament and safely carry it away.

The stories continue.

It grows late but no one makes a move. David has great enthusiasm and a gift to transmit his excitement and interests to others--in this case, me. I am appalled, stricken but totally caught in the desire to really know about this important part of history that I surely never learned about in school. My father was in the navy in World War I and he would occasionally tell a story but I never truly understood this "War to end all wars." It is time!

I begin reading, searching online. A map of the actual *Western Front, 1914-1918* is the best way to begin to understand.

In 1914 war was declared and Germany invaded Belgium on the way to capturing France. The first battles were fought in the northwest corner of Belgium. Ypres became the focal point of the area. Germany was stopped on the way to Paris and never made it, thanks in large part to an army of Parisian taxi cabs that carried soldiers to the front!

Rebuffed but still committed to invasion, German troops began to move westward along a line that ran from Ypres all the way south east to Switzerland. They were met by French and British soldiers who blocked their advance, resulting in stalemate and the beginning of the horrors of trench warfare. Each side threw battalion after battalion at the enemy trenches, gaining, if anything, sometimes only yards before losing them again at the next skirmish. No one was able to devise a way to break out of this decimating, static situation for the next seemingly endless four years. Casualties mounted incredibly and each side was being bled white. The entrance of America into the fray in 1917 brought thousands of fresh energized troops to strengthen the weary British and French armies, helping to bring victory to the Allies.

In July I receive a brochure from the Tour Group, Elderhostel, listing the tours scheduled for the following year. It has been a few years since I traveled abroad, and then usually with family or a close friend. I am retired, working on call as a Learning Disabilities Consultant taking assignments in county schools only when I choose. This leaves me with a great deal of time and I had begun to think of traveling with a formal group tour organization, choosing Elderhostel.

My life is filled with *aha!* moments and here is the latest one. In the new Elderhostel brochure on Page 14; September 23rd to October 2nd 2002, "The Great War: People, Places and Poetry of World War One." Here's my opportunity to travel the Western Front, actually walk on those fields just as David had done, experience and make real the cataclysm that pretty much changed the world.

My first call is to book my place and sign up for a roommate. Most tour groups plan for double occupancy. I thought it might be nice to share with a kindred soul. My second call is, of course, to David. He is excited and when he hears the dates he realizes that he and Camille, my daughter-in-law, will be finishing their vacation in the south of France as I arrive in Belgium.

"I'll stay an extra day or two and come up to Ypres. We'll go to the Somme and then..." He is off and running!

***

It is September 23 2002 and I am already in the airport, three hours ahead of boarding time as per the new regulations for overseas travel. Perched on the edge of my chair in the waiting area I am looking carefully at each man's shoes as they walk by. The awful tragic events of just a year ago, September 11, 2001, have changed many things and added a level of apprehension to flying. Just recently I read that the 9/11 hijackers all wore brand-new clothes (they were on their way to Paradise) including shiny shoes. My fears coalesced and I had a plan, a warning point. I would be relaxed, at ease as long as no man was wearing new shoes. Amazing what the mind will conjure up to bring relief. No matter, I am calmly maintaining my vigil.

Sneakers, roughed up casual shoes, well-worn loafers, even a few sandals later we board the plane, my panic allayed. It's a red-eye flight and will arrive in Brussels tomorrow morning at 6:15. I'm excited, a bit apprehensive about the flight itself, but mainly thrilled thinking of the adventure to come. A roommate I have never met, that's a first, traveling in an organized group, I hope we won't be herded about like cattle. Small worries. After a typical airline dinner replete with a purchased red wine I settle down. There is a small TV screen on the back of the seat in front of me and on it I watch a tiny plane, *us*, traveling up the eastern seaboard, over Cape Cod, Newfoundland. Long before it reaches Ireland I have fallen asleep. I doze on and off through the rest of the telescoped night and our six hour flight arrives in Brussels right on time at 6:15.

I am met by a greeter from Elderhostel and together we join a small group of weary looking travelers in front of a bus just outside of the airport. They have been waiting for me and a few more stragglers from later arriving planes. Boarding the bus I sit next to a woman who smiles and shares, "Hi, I'm Phyllis Carlson, and you?" A good beginning.

"I'm Marilyn Restione. I'm here because my son, David, has made a World War I buff of me!" I explain that my father was actually in that war but his service was in the navy and therefore he knew little of the land operations. Phyllis is here because of a great uncle who had been in a Nova Scotia regiment. We wonder about what has brought our companions on the tour. Conversation is easy and comfortable as we journey to Ypres and our hotel, Ariane. Checking in, we are pleased to discover that we are to be roommates for the trip.

Unpacking and settling in takes little time, and we decide to walk into town. A welcome drink and get-together at the hotel is scheduled for 5:30, so we have a couple of hours to explore. We pick up a brochure from the lobby on the way out. It gives a condensed history of this significant Belgian town. Reading aloud to each other as we walk, we learn how very important a place this is.

Ypres is truly amazing. There has been a town here since Roman times. Location on the banks of the Ieperlee River has made it pivotal to trade and a political prize for the surrounding principalities. Flourishing in medieval times as a center for linen and wool trading, it had a population of 40,000 when Oxford, England could only boast of 4,000 people. A pawn in the continental wars of the ensuing centuries, it was conquered and reconquered by France, Spain, and the Hapsburg Empire. At last, in 1831 Belgium became an independent nation and Ypres came home to stay.

It is not surprising, therefore, that Ypres was a focal point all during World War I. It fell to the German troops early in 1914. After bitter fighting in the First Battle of Ypres the town was relieved by English troops in November of that year. In the spring of 1915 at the Second Battle of Ypres the German troops used poison gas for the first time in recapturing the area. The Third Battle of Ypres, July to November 1917, also known as the Battle of Passchendaele, was the most brutal, gaining the Allies only a few ground miles and resulting in half a million casualties to all sides! At the end of the conflict Ypres lay in ruins, almost every building had been reduced to rubble. Its undaunted citizens returned to this almost demolished site and over the next few years rebuilt their town to be almost exactly as it had been.

Phyllis and I are overwhelmed as we enter the town square. The magnificent medieval Cathedral, the Town Hall and famous Cloth Hall are there, surrounded by ancient stone buildings just as they had always been. Reconstructions perhaps, but the energy, the history and the soul of these incredible structures and the people who loved and brought them back to life is truly awesome.

We see some members of our group and join them as we circle the square. Someone notices that across the pediment of one of the buildings are carved the Seven Deadly Sins, *Envy, Wrath, Sloth, Greed, Gluttony, Lust and Pride*. As we stroll back to the Ariane, we laughingly test each other on recalling all seven. Nobody does well. For the rest of the ten days of our trip this becomes an ongoing exercise. At odd moments, at equally odd places someone will call out, "Gluttony, Envy..." and we are off trying our best but rarely remembering the whole list. Meeting the rest of the group over a welcome drink followed by an orientation meeting and a very nice dinner rounds out the first day. So far, so good.

Elderhostel has partnered with Bartlett's Battlefield Journeys a British based organization that has been taking groups through the Western Front for some years. At a lecture next morning on the build-up to the hostilities David Bartlett introduces us to Michael Kelly who will be our site coordinator. They both confess they have not toured with groups from across the pond before and hope that they will be able to handle those Americans! We assure them that we are really friendly, easy to please and will be on our best behavior.

Before the lecture, our tour leader, David Bartlett, asks that we introduce ourselves and explain why we signed up for this particular tour. The group appears to be almost equally divided between couples and single individuals. Some people indicate that there is a familial connection to the war as a reason for they're being here. Several of the men have an interest in military history, battles and, in particular, WWI. Most of the married women simply say "I'm here with my husband." I wonder if their lack of personal interest will change to enthusiasm before the journey ends. I hope so.

The lecture, the fascinating ins and outs of the political machinations leading to the conflict are so absorbing that when a hotel staffer enters the room announcing, "There's a telephone call for Marilyn Restione," it takes me a baffled minute to realize, "That's me." It is rather strange getting a personal phone call within less than twenty four hours of arrival in a foreign country. King Albert II, General Pershing, President Bush? Oh, it's Camille, my daughter in law. She's calling to tell me that while she is at Orly airport in France boarding a plane to go home David is on his way to Ypres and should be there later today.

Lunch and an early afternoon guided tour of the town leads us to the "In Flanders Fields Museum." This is a living museum, as much as is possible an experience of a day in one of the four crucial battles of Ypres. Entering the darkened, smoky hallway, we begin to hear the whine of artillery shells, the thuds of their landings, the cries of wounded men, orders shouted and…

"Sure looks like a bunch of American tourists!"

It's my son David, and I am out of the line like a shot, hugging my son, happy to see him. We move out of the way, back into the shadows where he has been standing, waiting. He's actually been following the group for the last couple of blocks looking for an opportunity to surprise me. A few whispered words and we move further into the main body of the museum. It is incredible. Life size figures in dirty, ragged uniforms carrying rifles, some wearing rudimentary gas masks are crouching in a rugged landscape of dirt, potholes, barbed wire and the torn up end of a bombed out trench. Moving further into the almost murky atmosphere we stumble upon a field hospital where a nurse in a bloody apron is bending over men on stretchers offering a canteen of water. There are cries, moans. It is all so real!

Above the very realistic sounds of battle someone is reciting the tragic, powerful poems of the war. A frightened, breaking voice;

> "Gas! Gas! Quick, boys! An ecstasy of fumbling,
> fitting the clumsy helmets just in time;
> but someone still was yelling out and stumbling,
> and floundering like a man in fire or lime..."

I know this one; Wilfred Owen's "Dulce et Decorum Est." It breaks my heart.

This has been an intense experience and we are a much more subdued group as we walk back to the hotel. Over cocktails before dinner David gets the chance to meet everyone. I quickly lose him to David Bartlett who is surprised and thrilled to hear of the depth of his interest in and knowledge of the war. The two of them spend most of the evening comparing notes, sharing anecdotes, enriching each other's experiences.

"Wrath, Pride "

Next morning David sets off to visit Mons, a battlefield he had not had a chance to visit on previous trips. Knowing that we plan to spend tomorrow and the next day together I opt to spend my day with the group. After lunch we board our coach for a trip to Flanders Field American Cemetery and nearby Essex Farm where Major John MacRae wrote *In Flanders Fields*. This poem has become a standard bearer, making the poppies that grew even on muddy battlefields a symbol we still wear today to honor the millions who died.

Arriving back at the hotel I find David has returned from his exciting day and is already sharing a scotch and conversation with David Bartlett. After dinner their animated discussion now includes Michael and again I have lost him to his new World War I buddies. I enjoy watching their enthusiastic interaction. During our evening Phyllis and I continue sharing life-stories as well. We are both happy to find that we like spending time with each other. She is interesting and a bit kooky, and I like that.

Tyne Cot, Britain's largest military cemetery is our destination today. American cemeteries are austere with their crosses lined up cleanly and perfectly. This British one presents a different picture. The gravestones are solid upright rectangles of marble and their rows are fronted by rose bushes. The shadow of an English rose must pass over each stone at least once a day is a long- standing tradition at all British cemeteries. We pause at the grave of a fifteen year soldier and Michael honors him with a poem. This small ceremony will happen several times over the next days.

Poetry seems to be much more a part of ordinary life in Britain, perhaps on the continent as well. Many Americans are not comfortable with poetry and the ease with which Europeans read, recite and refer to poems so readily I find delightful and enriching. David Bartlett told us on that first evening that there will be a poetry contest with honors on a night toward the end of our tour. He encourages us all to try our hands at it. I think I will.

"Gluttony"

My David joins us and with the group we visit sites on our way back to Ypres from Sanctuary Woods where we see preserved trenches and the Cross of Sacrifice that marks the first German gas attack. This war that was nothing but a couple of boring days in my American history class is fast becoming vivid and real, engaging all our interest and emotions. Everyone seems more focused, questions are pertinent and we all crowd around Michael to hear his answers. We are a somber group at dinner. David Bartlett and Michael pass out song sheets at the evening lecture and soon, a few sophisticated sneers notwithstanding, and we are all singing, *Tiperary, Over There, Long, Long Trail Awinding, Pack Up Your*

Troubles, achieving an emotional balance to gear us up for another day along The Western Front.

My day begins as David arrives with a special itinerary for just the two of us. The group is off to visit Poperinge and the Talbot House where troops could rest and recuperate for a day or two before returning to the Front. There will be no rest for me today as we stop at site after site remembering, sometimes even with tears, the awful, tragic battles that tore apart the old ordered way of life.

We stand just above the Sunken Road where the first day of the battle of the Somme began, July 1, 1916, and ended just a few hours later with 60,000 casualties! The majority of the British troops were young untried men. Their commanders believed that the previous days of constant artillery would have decimated the German forces. The men were told "Walk steadily forward, DO NOT RUN." The shelling had not been effective and these soldiers, many of them new to the battlefield marched, line after line, into disaster, wounding and death.

There are so many battle sites, cemeteries and memorials honoring soldiers from all over the British Empire, statues, tall, sad crosses and everywhere bright red paper poppy wreaths. There are immense craters made by explosives buried deep underground in tunnels made by intrepid moles or clay-kickers. We see them all.

Emotionally exhausted I stand in front of the Monument at Thiepval Cemetery that honors 72,000 French and British soldiers who died in the Ypres Salient but whose bodies were never found. The figures are overwhelming, combined with the seemingly endless graves I have seen marked only "Here lies in honored glory a soldier known but to God."

Phyllis joins David and me the next day. David has discovered a monument listing her great uncle's regiment. With the fields of Passchendaele nearby she places a small wooden cross with a poppy attached at the site. On the way back we stop at Hellfire Corner marking a crossroads vital to the moving of troops and equipment throughout all four Ypres battles.

That evening David and I, along with the group and many others meet at the Menin Gate for a very special service performed every evening at 8:00, rain or shine since 1928. The service is to remember and honor 54,000 British troops who died defending Ypres but who are still missing. Buglers play The Last Post (equivalent to our Taps) under the gate. The only lapse in this ritual happened during World War II when the bugles were buried to keep them from the Nazis who occupied Ypres. Legend has it that as the last of the defeated German soldiers marched out of Ypres, they did so to the triumphant sounds of those hurriedly unearthed bugles! My roommate Phyllis has been asked to place a wreath on the monument and our tour coordinator, Michael, reads from the Lawrence Binyon poem, For the Fallen.

> They shall grow not old, as we that are left grow old:
> age shall not weary them, nor the years condemn.
> At the going down of the sun and in the morning
> we will remember them.

***

David leaves the next morning. It has been great to be able to share our experiences. I have learned much from him and visited significant places the rest of the group have missed. If there was any doubt in the past about my becoming a true "World War I buff" it is no longer! The last four days in Ypres have been a revelation. I had had no idea before coming here of the horror, the incredible waste of life, the insanity of four years of agony and uselessness of trench warfare which never seemed to guarantee more than a few miles of advancement to either side. The one bright spot in all of this tragedy is that one small episode on a cold winter night when a makeshift, candle-lit Christmas tree appeared in no man's land accompanied , a blending of both British and German voices, the trading of souvenirs and a robust soccer game between, for just a little while, friendly enemies. Dawn and the war came back next morning, December 26, 1914. "The Christmas Truce" was never repeated.

Today we are on our way to Chateau Thierry. A pleasant and informative young woman, Rose, is our Bus guide. As she takes care of us all we have begun to call her, "La Mere", mother, which appears to delight her. She tells us that on July 18, 1918 this was the site of the first battle fought by the American Expeditionary Force. Before we get there, however we will stop for lunch at a charming restaurant run by the family of Phillipe Corzinski, the man who by himself located and dug up a WWI tank buried beneath the fields of the battle of Cambrai. The first appearance of these large, ungainly new weapons rumbling across a field must have been frightening. Totally covered by metal, at first glance, they might have seemed impregnable but their top speed of only four miles per hour actually made them prey to artillery and bombardment. Not really successful in this first battle, improved and upgraded, they ultimately became a factor in the defeat of the German army.

"Envy, Greed, Lust"

Arriving at Chateau Thierry we learn that the American entrance into the conflict in 1917 was vitally important. It came at a time when the allied armies were much in need of active help, and this infusion of fresh new American soldiers was a godsend becoming a factor in the Allied victory.

In the darkest days of the American Revolution hope and support arrived from France in the person of the Marquis de Lafayette. He was just 19 at the time but had trained as a soldier and officer since the age of 13. He believed that the American cause was a noble one and offered his services. He fought in several battles, was wounded and earned the respect and friendship of Washington, Hamilton and Jefferson. He led troops in the battle of Yorktown when the British surrendered. His participation throughout the final years of the revolution was crucial. When he died in 1834 his son, Georges Washington, sprinkled dirt from Bunker Hill on his grave in Paris.

The gratitude and the bond between him and his beloved other country, never lessened and when the American Expeditionary Force came to the aid of France in 1917 we were paying a long-ago debt. Landing on French soil, an officer serving with General Pershing proclaimed, "Lafayette, nous sommes ici!" "Lafayette, we are here!"

The next day, continuing to move south along the Western Front we stop at battle sites, Belleau Wood, the Marne, Oise-Aisne American cemetery, Chamery, with poetry readings at each site. We drive past road signs painted black with the names of towns that were busy rural centers before the war but now are only scattered ruins. At dinner Michael reminds us to pack because tomorrow we will be on our way to Verdun. Drifting into sleep I seem to wander through gravestones and crosses sheltering the broken bodies under the ground but blank where names should be. The first lines of my poem come to me along with sleep—

> I knelt and touched the warm, wet grass
> beside your cross and in that quiet moment
> felt your hand brush mine –

***

"I am very happy to meet you all. My name is Ingrid and I will be your guide for the rest of the journey." She speaks with a **German** accent! I turn cold and when I look at my fellow travelers I see a stunned look in everyone's eyes. For the last nine days we have been immersed in the tragedies inflicted on the French people and the Allied troops by German armies. How quickly we have been conditioned to dislike and distrust anything Germanic. It takes a minute to understand and drop our reaction. The moment passes and we are able to welcome this friendly, outgoing woman who now assures us that although she was born in Germany she has lived in France for 25 years, married to a staunch French patriot.

"*Sloth*"

On the way to our next hotel, Coq Hardi, Ingrid helps us to understand about Verdun, it's emotional as well as strategic importance to France. Hundreds of years before the Common Era it was important militarily and politically. Since medieval times, battles fought here determined outcomes far bigger than just this relatively small city and area. Over the centuries Verdun became a symbol of the French soul and General Petain stated unequivocally at the beginning of the German onslaught at Verdun "Ils ne passereont pas." They shall not pass!

"To understand France you must understand Verdun" is a quote often heard to explain its importance. Knowing this, German generals came to believe that the way to win the war was to continually attack Verdun without pause, thus rendering the French army exhausted and impotent. They failed to realize that constant battles would do the same to the German troops and combined with the growing desperate conditions at home actually contributed to their eventual defeat.

We visit Fort Douaumont, Verdun, its museum and Ossuary where the bones of 130,000 unidentified soldiers are kept. Ingrid takes us into the fort itself, telling us of the appalling conditions French troops endured here during siege. They were unable to leave the protection of their underground quarters, and so lived with the dead and dying in rat infested corridors for days on end. In one dark, dank room I almost panic, feeling unable to breathe as I stumble away from the horror to a door leading to the outside and air!

We are silent for much of the trip back to the hotel. A rich red wine, a lovely dinner and a few songs go a long way to lighten the atmosphere. We are now ready for the results of the poetry contest. David had sent all the entries back to London for a committee there to make the selection. After several people have read their poems I begin to believe that mine was not considered and relax. David confesses that he tried to write poetry and has realized that he just can't do it. Then he announces, "But here's someone who can, Marilyn Restione." Wow, I am surprised and very pleased to recite:

UNKNOWN SOLDIER

I knelt and touched the warm wet grass
beside your cross and in that quiet moment
felt your hand brush mine.
Time seemed to stretch and split...
and there you were in front of me.
The years had washed away
your pain, your tears
the ugly wounds that
tore you from your life.
There you were,
clean and shining, whole
innocent again.
A miracle of sweet remembrance,
in an instant--gone
but knowing you at last
I can let you sleep,
Unknown no longer
not to me.

A field trip to the World Center for Peace next morning is particularly meaningful after all we have seen and experienced on this powerful journey back in time. We begin to relax and let go of the painful memories. At lunch I discover that Ingrid is a "Trekkie," an avid follower of the TV show, *Star Trek*, as am I. Recalling and comparing specific characters and episodes has brought me almost totally back to the present and ready for our next destinations. The Cathedral at Reims will cleanse our souls and a visit to La Champagnes Mercier will wash away the dust and sadness of the war in a champagne tasting *extraordinaire!*

We have become a real group, warm, sharing laughter, interested in each other's thoughts over the last days and as we separate at the airport next day on the way to our separate homes---

"Wrath, pride, gluttony, envy, greed, lust and sloth!"

Someone yells, "We finally got it!"

At home in France...

La Vie En Rose

My trip to France and Belgium last year along the World War I Western Front was incredible, somber, at times heart-wrenching. It was filled with the horrors of trench warfare but I would not have missed it for the world. I learned about a truly cataclysmic event that changed the face of Europe and whose outcome and resolution inevitably led to the Second World War.

I return to France this year, 2003, in a softer nostalgic mood and with very different expectations. I want to fall in love with La Belle France and Paris again as I was in 1953.

I remember sitting in a little Parisian café on one of the last days of my trip back then. I was humming along with Edith Piaf singing, *La Vie En Rose*. I know it is a love song to a man but for me it would be my love song to Paris. And here I am again!

This tour is called, "Impressionists of Normandy, The Seine  and Paris," and will take me to Rouen and Honfleur, cities in Normandy, the World War II landing beaches, and on a lovely river cruise ship along the Seine to Paris and beyond. There will be lectures about impressionist painters. I will be meeting Monet, Cezanne, Van Gogh, Seurat, Sisley, Renoir, and visiting the places where they lived and worked. I will be viewing first-hand many of the precious paintings they created that now give us so much beauty but which shook up the art world in the latter part of the 1800s. Elderhostel is giving me a chance to do all that.

My flight is an easy one and I am met at the airport by one of our group leaders, Fanny Poirier. She is wearing a colorful scarf that reminds me of India but before I get a chance to comment on it we are met by the rest of the recently arrived travelers and board our coach. On the way to Rouen we stop at Les Andelys for a traditional Normand lunch.

The Hotel Mercure is situated in the medieval center of Rouen and will be our base for day trips in the next few days. Upon arrival, I meet my roommate, Helen Delaune, and after settling in we join the group for a short orientation program. Eleanore Brisbois, our second group leader, is introduced. She seems as charming and lively as Fanny.

In the past in group situations where each person tells their name and shares brief background information I use my legal name, Marilyn, and, pretty much, give a standard, middle-aged, suburban matron story. This time, however, perhaps sparked by Fanny's beautiful scarf, I offer Bhadrena as my real name and explain that I was given it by an Indian Guru whom I visited in India in 1987 and 1988. This causes little response from the group but I am surprised to see broad grins on the faces of Fanny and Eleanore. Almost before the meeting disbands they approach me, and tell me that they have just recently returned from a long stay in Dharmsala, India where they studied with the Dalai Lama!

They continue to share their Indian adventure with me during our delicious dinner at La Pecherie. I enjoy hearing about the teachings of the laughing, peace loving Dalai Lama and what daily living was like in a Tibetan ashram in exile.

Not surprisingly Fanny's scarf did come from India, but why did she decide to wear it today? Feeling some trepidation, why did I choose to share my sannyasin name and honor my guru? Synchronicity, serendipity all in one. A wonderful way to rekindle a love affair with a country, its people, its past, and its artistic flowering.

Our lecture next morning covers the early history of Impressionism when Monet and Boudin began taking their canvases outside, *en plein aire*, to paint in the open air, to capture the moment and the actual landscapes they saw. Using quick, short brush strokes in varying colors to show light and movement, they allowed the observer to experience the scene directly. Several painters soon joined the new movement and despite outrage from established classical artists, impressionism flourished.

Following an excellent lunch at La Boucherie, the Butcher Shop, we walk through the streets of Rouen, exploring. The Market, Ste. Jeanne d'Arc church, a cross in the pavement marking the place where she was burned and medieval half-timbered houses are all on view. Wonderful. A special site is the thirteenth century Cathedral. It became an icon of Impressionism, painted at least thirty times by Monet endeavoring to capture the ever-changing light and colors. A concert of music of the time is our evening entertainment.

The Normandy countryside we pass through next morning on our way to the coastal town of Honfleur is beautiful. The landscape of little, winding streams and small farms is dotted by placid cows, munching rhythmically, posing for the tourists. A soft, warm light appears to cover everything. It is not surprising that Impressionism was born here.

We have a treat in store. Honfleur is a picturesque harbor village with lovely sixteenth to eighteenth century townhouses fronting the quay. Brightly colored sailboats dot the harbor, blue skies with large, drifting white clouds preview the paintings we will see in the local *musee*. They are by Boudin who celebrated this place, his birthplace, with these lovely pictures.

There are small, interesting shops and we are free for a while after a lunch of skate (I've never eaten that before) to wander. Before I left on this trip I read an article giving a background on French customs and suggesting how to behave in France. Here is my opportunity to put some of those ideas in practice. Entering the little souvenir shops I look immediately to see who was in charge and accordingly say, "Bonjour, Madam" or "Monsieur" or "Mademoiselle." After a brief look-around, leaving, I say, "Merci." Wonder upon wonder, I receive delighted, surprised smiles from the shop owners. The article had explained that Americans are frequently viewed as arrogant because they never acknowledge or thank French store personnel. Just a small difference in everyday customs can cause international misunderstandings. I do my bit today for good American/French relations!

Remember that skate lunch? It was good to try something new, tasty, but it is proving to be a mixed blessing. On the way back to Rouen I begin to feel slightly unwell. Oh dear, will I make it to the hotel? Gritting my teeth, calling on my American fortitude, I arrive in time. Curled up in my bed, holding my poor achy stomach I forego dinner. Eleanore comes to comfort me, telling me funny stories about mishaps in India. I fall asleep, stomach soothed and wake almost normal next morning.

I remember vividly waking early on June 6, 1944, turning on my bedside radio to hear the war news from London which is five hours ahead of us. Almost unbelievably they were talking about the invasion of Normandy by Allied troops. It had really happened. Large ships off shore firing artillery at the German outposts on the beaches, the sea almost black with smaller transport vehicles loaded to the gunwales with soldiers already leaping into shallow water to race up the sand, getting a foothold wherever possible, planes roaring, firing overhead, bodies floating in the water...chaos... INVASION at last!

Fifty-nine years later I am on my way to see that horrendous setting I could only begin to imagine that long ago morning. Our first stop is Omaha Beach where the Americans landed. Torn up concrete bunkers, scrub grassland leading to sharp cliffs down to the sea. What a forbidding place, bleak, torn, pock marked with shell craters. I ache for those brave young men who faced its almost insurmountable dangers. They must have been scared to death but they came on, into unrelenting gunfire, storming the defenses, scrambling as best they could up those escarpments, being the heroes they surely were.

We wander in small, quiet groups, reading inscriptions on the monuments scattered here and there in the empty landscape. There are poems written on some, others mark the painfully labored Allied advances, all of them trying to touch in some small part the pain, the sorrow and the ultimate victory of what happened here.

A few in tears, all silent, cold with borrowed memories we visit the American cemetery at St. Laurent, where 9,841 American soldiers are buried. We honor the dead and give heartfelt thanks for their sacrifices. In a quiet moment, remembering my tour of the World War I battlefields last year, I am struck by the terrible consequences of war itself that twice in just 31 years has ravaged France.

A subdued lunch is at a small restaurant right on the shore. A poster on the wall catches my attention. It is a painting of *Liberte*, the ship I sailed home on from that wonderful nine week European trip I took in 1953! This tour is turning out to have amazing coincidences for me. Serendipity for sure and I am delighted.

Tomorrow brings a wonderful change of pace and a lifting of spirits as we board M.S. *L'Esprit D'Europe*, the lovely river cruise ship which will be our home for the next few days. Sailing slowly along the Seine we pass quaint small villages, Mort sur Loing, Barbizon where we stop for a while to explore on our own. Each morning we have a lecture, learning about the artists who lived and painted in this area.

One afternoon we board a bus that takes us 30 miles inland to Fontainebleau Chateau, built in the sixteenth century by Francis I, and lived in by all the kings after him and Napoleon. One of the largest chateaus in France, filled with architectural and artistic treasures, it takes a couple of hours to explore only a part of it. The design, the setting, the art are all magnificent but, to be honest, it's not my cup of tea and I am happy to be back on board the lovely *D'Esprit d'Europe*.

There is a flat, open, upper deck where we sit on deck chairs, idly talking, spotting the occasional charming private homes amid the lush green of the river banks. We pass through locks, which is exciting, interesting to see how the rise and fall of the water is handled. In the mornings, somewhat embarrassed but bold, I do Tai Chi up on the deck. The graceful form feels enriched by the lovely surroundings.

The ship experience brings a touch of luxury to the tour. Meals are truly gourmet and we are offered two different wines appropriate to particular courses at each sitting. The service is deferential and excellent. Round tables make conversation easy and my tablemates make it delightful. One of the original creators of the program, *Sesame Street*, sits opposite me, and she regales us with stories about the early hectic attempts to bring it to the TV screen.

We have been passing more and more small towns, sailing under many graceful bridges. There is an excitement in the air and far ahead we see spires--Paris!

We sleep this night on the boat moored in the shadow of the Eiffel Tower.

My head is spinning, my mind sharply awake with all the amazing colors, light so real I turn to see if the sun is shining, beauty filling my eyes! Paintings almost beyond my counting hang on the walls of the two museums we visit today, the Marmottan and the D'Orsay. Seventy-one Monet canvases displayed in the first leave many more to grace the walls of the second. That is only the beginning. Manet, Renoir, Degas, Berte Morisot, Caillebotte, Sisley, are all here...I am overwhelmed.

Dinner on the boat and a lecture on the peak flowering of the Impressionist movement helps us to further appreciate not only the paintings but the effort it took to bring that gift to the world. I can't say for sure and I don't remember actual dreams but my sleep this evening is filled with color!

***

WAIT, wait! The boat is leaving Paris...oh, dear! Fanny quickly assures me, "We'll be back, we are just sailing to Auvers to visit Vincent Van Gogh's house."

She has said magic words--*Van Gogh.* Calmed for a short while and then excited all over again, this tour is encompassing so many of my small passions. I discovered the paintings of Van Gogh when I was quite young and fell in love with the colors leaping out from canvases layered thick with paint. Old enough to go to New York by myself I would detour from planned activities to run quickly uptown to the Metropolitan Museum of Art to look with delight at *Sunflowers, Cypresses, Starry Night, Wheat Field.* Now I will see his last home, those wheat fields, and his grave.

Walking slowly uphill through the small, rural town of Auvers-sur-oise, we pass the church he immortalized, the wheat fields, sites of some of his last paintings, to arrive at the graveyard where he lies next to his brother Theo, who died shortly after Vincent. My tears are for Vincent but my thanks for beauty are to both men. It is said that Van Gogh sold only one of his hundreds of paintings in his lifetime, but faithful Theo saved all the rest, allowing the world to be able to see and appreciate that wonderful body of work.

Van Gogh's style of painting moved a short step beyond, into Post-Impressionism which later was called, Expressionism. Both modes were born in the late, creative years of the 1800s.

Today L'Esprit takes us to the home of Claude Monet, to the house and gardens of Giverny where he lived and painted for the last forty years of his life. We experience everything firsthand, not his pictures, but the actual subjects of his paintings… magnificent gardens, flowers of all types and colors, the small arching bridge over the pond filled with waterlilies. They are all here. Despite difficulties with cataracts as he aged, his work continued to be lovely beyond measure. Never static, growing, he experimented until his death in 1926.

We return to Paris as Fanny promised and that evening there is a gala dinner in the lovely dining room aboard L'Esprit. Special wines, fancy desserts and a chance to thank all the gracious people who have taken such good care of us on the voyage is a great way to bid goodbye to the river Seine.

The Palais Royal Hotel, our new home, is situated right in the middle of the city. Helen and I have a room on the third floor with a great view of rooftops, broad, clunky chimneys and the lovely white church, Sacre Coeur, in the distance. I take a picture of the view out of the window as I always do in each new hotel.

We wake the next morning to our second full day in Paris and to rain! Originally scheduled for a leisurely walk through the city we opt for a Metro trip to Notre Dame. At first disappointed by the lack of sunlight, the cathedral façade almost obscured by misting rain, I begin to appreciate the magnificent interior in a different way. The glory of the Rose window, the soaring columns, the precious statue of the Virgin and Child, realistic with her loving looks and the sweet, calm face of the Baby are as beautiful as I remember. However, the darkness of the day and the crowds of people sheltering from a sudden downpour outside enable me to notice small shadowy beauties, tucked in corners that would usually be overwhelmed by objects highlighted from sun filled windows. Looking back as we are leaving, I see Quasimodo crouched, sheltering from the rain, under a gargoyle, imploring "Sanctuary," high above the square below!

The rain lets up after lunch and we are able to walk in the garden of the Rodin Museum, viewing some of this talented sculptor's most famous statues, *The Burghers of Calais*, *The Thinker* and the *Gates of Hell* in a natural setting. Stepping further outside of our Impressionist orbit, the Picasso museum delights me with hundreds of his colorful, original works. There are also paintings by Cezanne and Matisse. It is like having a banquet of every tasty, nourishing, fulfilling dish spread before us for our pleasure!

A special treat this evening is a concert in the medieval gothic Saint Chapelle. Ongoing restoration has brought a freshening of the gorgeous stained glass windows and vivid color to the interior of this royal chapel, built in the 1200s. The music is heavenly, as it should be in this ethereal place. Remember the quote, "My cup runneth over?"

And now, today, I really hear the strains of La Vie en Rose as we board a private coach that will take us on a full tour of Paris, seeing all the important sights, traveling down the Champs Elysees, stopping finally in Montmartre where we will spend the afternoon. Wandering the narrow streets to the Place du Terte we pass Renoir's apartment, The Red Mill, a small building where Picasso painted *Desmoiselles d'Avignon* and *Le Consulat*, a bistro where all the painters congregated. I recognize scene after scene I've only viewed in paintings. On up a steep incline that leads us to the highest point in Paris and the Basilique du Sacre Coeur. This church, built in the Romano-Byzantine style, so white against a bright blue sky, is almost magical. We surely have experienced the sacred and the profane at Monmartre!

Our farewell dinner this evening is at L'Aiguiere. The entire menu is in French. I do not understand anything beyond the date, *Lundi 28 Avril 2003* and *Apertif* but, no matter. It is one of the most delicious meals I have ever had. Conversation is in superlatives as we recall each marvelous sight we have seen on this excellent tour.

Bidding goodbye and many thanks to Fanny and Eleanore, with promises to keep in touch, saddens me but I have the memories of all I have witnessed and experienced. A fair exchange.

And, yes, I have fallen in love with Paris again.

La Vie en Rose.

At home in Scotland…

Land Sea and Skye

It is winter, 2004. The new Elderhostel brochure arrives. It is exciting, filled with trips all over the world, alluring, tempting, but wait, what are those little green leaves and purple blossoms falling out from the pages, and that soft, heady smell of--?

Oh, it is heather and I am going to Scotland…

Again!

It has been 51 years since Marilyn McBride and I stood at the gates of Dunvegan Castle on the Isle of Skye, proudly declaring my MacLeod lineage. Even having to pay a shilling to enter just like any old tourist couldn't dampen the excitement I felt then and now!

The tour is called "Land, Sea and Skye," which couldn't be more perfect.

I pull out my photo scrapbooks of that wonderful trip. I am amazed at how and what we did. The memories come flooding back, some almost careworn because I have relived them so many times over the years, others just surfacing now are mint, almost untouched by memory! I am full of questions. What will have changed? How will it feel? Time enough for all that, now I must call and make my reservation.

"You are one of the first to call, congratulations and I have a roommate already waiting. Her name is Kay Bailey. Ceud mile failte.

It is June 24th. A smooth, almost lullaby of a red eye flight, a night in the Glasgow Airport Hotel, meeting my roommate Kay and our fellow travelers, exploring possible connections, shared experiences, a bus ride and we are on our way to The Aigas Field Center in Beauly due west of Inverness. The bus ride is the perfect welcome back for me. As we move higher and higher into the Highlands the rough, compelling beauty of the mountains, the lochs and streams that filled my Scotland memory are actual and real. The air smells crisp and clean and I feel as though I could reach out and touch each tiny purple blossom of the heather alive on the slopes. We make a rest stop at Loch Lomond and buy silly Loch Ness monster post cards.

Of course I had seen pictures of Aigas but what a surprise it is to see from a distance as we make a highland turn in the hills an actual castle with crenelated towers, set high above a terraced lawn amidst a lush dark green landscape. I choose to forget that it was built in Victorian times and just feel the mystic rush of awe and power of the Scottish fifteenth century.

The high ceilinged ornate rooms in the castle are reserved for the members of the Lister-Kaye family whose home it is. We are housed in very comfortable heated pine lodges in the wooded gardens of the estate. Our first evening meal takes place in the flag-draped baronial hall at a long wooden table with seating for all 27 guests plus family members currently in residence. We get to meet Lord and Lady Lister-Kaye and their seven children, Warwick, Amelia, Melanie, Emma, James, Hamish and Hermione. What a delightful family it is. Sir John has a true "Lord of the Manor" persona tempered with a wry sense of humor; Lady Lucy is open, friendly and we are to discover actually cooks some of our meals. Their youngest daughter, Hermione, has come home from University to help with the planning and running of the extensive nature programs that are an integral part of the Aigas Center. Following the delicious meal, Sir John welcomes us with a brief history of how a run down, almost derelict faux *castle* became first a family home and then a well-known and respected nature center. Aigas is dedicated to not only teaching about the natural world of the Highlands but also to keeping alive a warm, enriching way of life. We learn three Gaelic words, *Gaedhealtachd*-the land of the Gaels; *Dutchas*- belonging; *urralachd*- a sense of self- belief and sufficiency.

Already feeling 'at home' my roommate Kay and I, excited and so pleased to be here, sit snug in our beds. Having filled our water glasses from the small red wine bottle I purloined from the British Airways plane we munch on the contents of the little plastic packages of trail mix I always include in my luggage We share thoughts and expectations and drift slowly off to sleep and highland dreams.

Each morning there is a short informal talk about the upcoming visits to the special places and programs on our agenda. In addition we learn more about the extensive nature programs on offer here. The staff of young Rangers provide almost daily walks through the surrounding parklands, woods, and moors, pointing out the rich plant and animal life. On our first foray into a wooded glade, we are introduced to a gorgeous lizard who barely deigns to look at us, just continuing to enjoy his blink-eyed rest underneath a gently waving fern. My head spins with all the fascinating creatures and plants we see. Aigas as a home base for our travels is truly turning out to be so much more than I had anticipated. These enthusiastic, knowledgeable young people will also travel with us and keep a written record of each day's happenings and discoveries.

On the fourth day we travel to Culloden, the historic and tragic site of the last battle fought for Bonnie Prince Charlie and Scottish independence in 1745. Standing on that bleak field dotted with simple stones bearing the names of the clans who fought here I want to cry and almost do. This battle was fought for so much more than a particular prince. Its defeat marked the beginning of the breakdown of the clan system and a systematic oppression by the English of a unique and precious Highland way of life.

Our next top is Cawdor Castle, originally constructed in 1372 on a spot where the Thane of Cawdor's donkey lay down to rest beneath a holly tree that is still there under the oldest part of the castle. The Cawdor family lives here for a good part of the year. All this is true, however, the castle lives most vividly in the fictional pages of Shakespeare's *MacBeth*. As I wander the halls I seem to hear the haunted murmurings of the distraught Lady MacBeth, "Out, out damned spot." I shiver for a moment, hurrying to catch up with my real 21st century compatriots. It is a dark, rainy, somewhat mournful day, and we look forward to the welcoming afternoon tea that awaits us back in Aigas.

The next day brings us a warm showery afternoon touched now and then with a soft summer sunlight. A wonderful lecture about the earliest people who lived here from about 8,000 BC starts off our exploration of the prehistoric sites all around the estate. I branch off from the group as we start to climb a rugged hill deep in the woods. Suddenly I am ten years old again, scrambling over rocks, through rough underbrush, scratched by tiny prickly branches that seem to spread everywhere. I am filled with that marvelous young feeling that, "I can go anywhere, everywhere, do anything and everything!" How delicious and, sad to say, how not possible. But just for a while when I reach, almost crawling now, the ruins of an old Stone Age hill fort and stand amid the ancient rubble sweaty, dirty, aching, I am the conqueror I imagined myself to be. Dropping for an instant the self-consciousness of my true 76 years I shout as loud and as long as can!

How very wonderful, wandering and traveling can be. It is never just about sites, famous spots, it can be an opening to all memories, dreams, and experiences that we carry with us all our lives. We can be and are all the beings that we have been through the years, not just in memory but in the freedom to explore them all again. My defiant, uncensored yell is actually an enormous, "Thank you!"

We have enjoyed the "Land" part of our tour and now it is time for the "Sea and Skye." We are heading west through a vigorous mountain countryside where it seems we can see forever…then onto dark roads covered with dense hanging rhododendrons that are so narrow that we almost scrape the stone walls on either sides… throat catching turns into bright air and sunlight again. It is an adventure. One of the very nice things about this tour is that the group of 27 is divided into three sections, traveling in comfortable vans instead of big, impersonal buses.

Unlike the tiny ferry, transporting three cars and many sheep which carried Marilyn McBride and me to Skye in 1953 we soar over to the Misty Isle on the new Skye Bridge. It's probably an 'old' thing but I prefer the ferry. A night in Portree with a visit to a small bakery that features Scottish Shortbread begins our new day. My purchase of eight fingers of this wonderful cookie is, of course to bring home but I am not taking bets on how long they will survive.

For the next two and half days we explore the treasure that is Skye, the Black Cuillins, sharp mountain peaks that seem in places to scrape the sky and Loch Snizort tucked away inside the softer ranges of the Red Cuillins. The loch is guarded by a colony of watchful mascara-eyed seals that dot its shores. Skye's rugged coastline, never farther than five miles from any place on the island, presents with vertical scored cliffs called, appropriately the Kilt Rocks. We see Flora MacDonald's grave and ruins of the ancient Duntulm Castle built by the Vikings who, in 1263 handed it over to the MacLeods. At this point we are only a few miles from Dunvegan Castle and I ache to see it again but, apparently it is not on our itinerary and we head off to Sleat, the southern part of Skye held by the MacDonalds, the hereditary enemies of the MacLeods! What can I do…I am outnumbered. Swearing an oath to return someday to my patrimony I graciously accept a temporary defeat.

Driving up a steep and twisty road we stop briefly at what appears to be a truly ancient camp site called a Sheiling. Our Ranger guide, Brona Doyle, explains that this was traditionally where the crofters would bring their sheep, high up the mountainside for summer grazing. The young people who would be asked to live there and care for the flock must have regarded this as a vacation to be on their own away from the arduous chores on the farm and the prying eyes of the adults. No wonder it figures often in the old poetry. Brona quotes;

> From the lone sheiling of the misty isle
> mountains divide us, and the waste of seas,
> yet still the blood is strong, the heart
> is Highland
> and in dreams we behold the Hebrides.

She confesses to not knowing where the quote is from. I call out, *The Canadian Boat Song* written about the Scottish farmers forced off their ancestral land by greedy landlords wanting to graze their ever growing flocks of sheep. Although they migrated to Nova Scotia they never lost their Skye heritage and mourned the loss of their way of life. Deep in the childish awe and love of my Scottish heritage I learned this by heart, feeling now, again, the tears I learned along with it.

Having crossed the "Sea" to the isle of "Skye" fulfilling the tour name, we are returning to the mainland. On our way back to Aigas we pass the Cloutie Well, and ask the van drivers to stop for a bit while we examine this ancient healing site. In ancient times sick people would dip a cloth in the magic well and wash their afflicted body parts. They believed that hanging the cloth on the branches of trees that surrounded the well would bring healing. Apparently some still do because there is a tree filled with cloths hanging from its limbs. Checking for broken bones, headaches and the like and finding only good health among us, we reboard our coaches and head back to Aigas, to red wine, a delicious meal and an evening recalling the Misty Isle and it magic.

The next two days are spent exploring the venerable sites of the Pictish people who left few ruins but are remembered best for their large, heavily carved Celtic crosses, some of which are still in place in the landscape. One evening we are treated to a talk by a well-known author of local books on crofting. She speaks from her own 88 year experience having grown up and subsequently owned and worked a croft herself. She is charming and a good story teller, making us really see and feel what that fast disappearing life was like. Now when traveling we spot the few authentic cottage crofts still a working part of the landscape.

When I was back in America reading about the many places I would visit, I was thrilled to discover that the archipelago of Orkney was to be a highlight. On TV I had seen programs about this group of islands off the north coast of mainland Scotland. They have been called an archaeologist's dream of ancient monuments. I was swept by such an excitement realizing I would actually, really be in Skara Brae, Maes Howe, the Ring of Brodgar! These prehistoric places are almost magical in their stark and stony mystery. This is where we are now headed.

The two hour crossing of the Pentland Firth is exciting. The day is absolutely beautiful with bright blue skies reflected in the darker blue of the water. Occasional whitecaps lifted by the wind provide sharp contrast. As we sail alongside the largest island we pass The Old Man of Hoy, a very large, slender tower of rock rising just off the beach. We wave hello as he seems to welcome us to our next adventure. We disembark at the port of Stromness and head inland.

The Polrudden Guest House just outside of the town of Kirkwall will be our home base for the next two days. We are greeted by our hostess and her large mop of a white dog who bounces all over us like the puppy he is, charming. Although late in the afternoon we head back into town to visit St. Magnus Cathedral. This Norse building begun in 1137 is constructed of local red and yellow sandstone in a polychromatic pattern called one of the best examples of medieval church building. That may be but most of us find it is also one of the ugliest examples. (Sorry, Magnus.) However it is a cathedral and I love it, pagan though I may be.

We are now so far north that the sun doesn't really set until very late and as I lie in bed at 11:00 p.m. the light is still streaming through my window. Sleep, however, comes quickly and I wake well rested in the morning light. There is a cool light breeze and again, lovely sunshine. I'm beginning to think that the talk of a rainy and gloomy British Isles is a myth, if not a downright lie.

Maes Howe is our first stop on this archaeological day of days, and we tumble eagerly from the bus to visit this chambered tomb. It is a large grass covered hill, obviously manmade, with a small entranceway that necessitates crouching almost double in order to walk down the stony passageway into the tomb itself.

As at Stonehenge, the Winter Solstice is marked here by a shaft of sunlight traveling from the entrance all the way into the heart of the grave on December 21st. The center room is high-ceilinged and holds probably as much as twenty or so people comfortably. The guide tells us that it was constructed around 2900 BC to hold the bones of their favored dead. When it was discovered in modern times there was little left to find because a group of Vikings had sheltered here for a while in the 13th century and they must have cleaned it out, making it more habitable. They also left runes scratched on the walls: "*Thornvald carved these runes--Ragnar is the most skilled of men--Ingigerth is the most beautiful of women--Thorny bedded (actually f'ked), Helgi.*" Such graffiti might be right at home on the subway walls in New York City. I guess there really is nothing new under the sun!

As we travel a short distance farther west we spot an enormous circle of standing stones, called the Ring of Brodgar. Constructed of 60 monoliths in 2800BC, it now has but 27. However at almost

350 feet in diameter surrounded by a deep trench, the henge is still very impressive. We break into small groups to wander and explore the awesome site. Standing on one of the two paths leading into the circle I look across the as yet unexcavated central sweep of rough grass, gravel and an occasional hardy, spindly wildflower. I wonder what treasures may lie beneath and around this bleak land-

scape. The salty wind is strong today and the warmth of the coaches welcomes us back from the past.

After a soup and sandwich lunch in a small local restaurant we arrive at Skara Brae, the best preserved Neolithic village in Europe. This unique community of seven houses and a workshop still littered with tools was built halfway into the ground, possibly for warmth, and connected by small passages. It is believed to have been constructed around 3100 BC. Centuries later it was abandoned and subsequently covered by sand and gravel by some monstrous storm. Lost to time and memory, it was uncovered in 1850 following another tremendous storm which swept away the sand, dirt and grass and revealed a treasure of not only the village itself but stone furnishings, jewelry, cupboards, cooking pots, built-in beds, hearths and even a rudimentary toilet in each lodging.

Supper this evening is full of talk, sentences cut off to allow another fascinating thought to come through, trying to absorb all that we've seen. We have experienced the magic, the mystery and the everyday of ancient people and places that in the scope of world history are our ancestors too. Glancing around at our fellow travelers I see a few sunburned faces. So much for gloomy Scotland!

On our way back to the mainland and Aigas on our next to last day we are in for something new, actually, literally. From the mists of antiquity we are moving to the present day. Well, close enough. We are passing the Churchill Barriers that were constructed by Italian prisoners during the Second World War to protect the port of Skapa Flow where much of the British fleet was harbored.

A group of these Italian soldiers were barracked in a small prisoner of war camp nearby and we stop to visit the site of this prison now known as the Italian Chapel. The surrounding Scottish population had also been small, and over time the two groups began to know and connect with one another, the prisoners on work details and farmers supplying food and materials. A number of the people in both groups had much in common, many were farmers or fishermen living simple lives in rural settings and a tentative social bond began to develop.

The 13 cheerless huts housing the men soon boasted cement walkways lined with flowers and shrubs built by the men themselves. In 1943 they were allowed to construct their own church. Two rounded Nissen huts were placed end to end and joined together. The camp Commandant encouraged a prisoner named Chiochetti who was a talented artist to build a sanctuary. With a creative cadre of helpers, the barren structure was transformed. Plasterboard and paneling covered the corrugated iron of the walls which were then painted. Religious pictures in bright colors all done by the men filled the body of the church. The narrow windows on each side of the molded concrete altar and railings became stain glass windows and Chiochetti's Madonna and Child, based on a holy picture he carried throughout the war graced the wall above the altar. Eventually, on the outside, a façade surmounted by a belfry was built to hide the ugly outline of the original huts.

A visiting priest conducted services for the men so far from their homes who made this lovely place out of little but scraps, paint and a great desire to bring their god to this windswept island. In 1945 when the prisoners were repatriated the Lord Lieutenant of Orkney who owned this particular island made a promise to them that the Orcadians would cherish their chapel.

A committee was formed in 1958 to look after and repair the site and in 1960 the group was able to trace the current whereabouts of the artist Chiocchetti. His traveling expenses were paid and he revisited his chapel and assisted in completing repairs. Connections between the men billeted here and the local population had never really separated and a group of the islanders subsequently visited hometowns of the men in Italy. Letters continued being sent back and forth, and in 1992--50 years after they arrived in Orkney-- eight of the then prisoners returned accompanied by their families to attend services in their very own chapel. The committee had arranged for an Italian priest to come from Italy to celebrate mass and a special luncheon followed. All those years and a sad happening in an ugly war has become a loving memory of what good people can accomplish.

Our Orkney sojourn has been remarkable in every way from prehistoric to modern day and, not least, the many sightings of incredible birds. We have seen hundreds of orange beaked puffins roosting in the cliffs, soaring seabirds who never come to land living only and always on the open ocean, Great Skua, Artic Terns, gulls of every description, even a Mute Swan.

Our last day at Aigas is a quiet one, visiting local sites, a scotch distillery for some, others, myself included, opting for a glass of red wine in a comfortable pub, packing in the afternoon and a truly grand evening feast featuring homemade haggis, laced with a dollop of brandy by Lady Lucy herself and a lone piper serenading. Evening coffee in the lounge is a warm and somewhat sad occasion with much reminiscing, reaching out for the last time to particular connections within the group. This has been an incredible tour with lovely compatible companions who, much to my delight and gratitude never once talked about their illnesses or their grandchildren.

I have enjoyed every aspect of the return to my Scottish home, and after 51 years *the blood is still strong,* and *the heart is highland!*

At home in Britain....

"Twas the schooner Hesperus"

...that sailed the wintry seas." Laughing, trying to get my quote in first, or remember another nineteenth century poem before my breakfast table companion beats me to it. *Horatius at the Bridge, In School Days, Invictus*. What a fun way to start a new adventure, meeting a fellow tour goer, John Mogan, who likes poetry and is somewhat of a renaissance man, I am to discover over the next days.

Arriving on a red-eye flight from Newark, New Jersey to London, I check in to The Thistle Hotel. Room 721 with a window overlooking the Tower of London and Tower Bridge will be my home for the next four days. This is my fifth tour with Elderhostel. "Quintessential Britain" will give me a taste of England, Wales and Scotland, a fresh, new taste actually. I visited Scotland a year ago but I last knew London and Wales in 1953! The 2005 view from my window no longer includes bombed out buildings, empty streets, homes not yet rebuilt after World War II, that was my experience during that amazing trip fifty-two years ago.

After that fun breakfast, an introductory lecture and lunch we are free for the afternoon. Now, what would you do first? Of course, a walk across Tower Bridge, stopping mid-span to look down at the Thames and eastward toward Westminster, Shakespeare's Globe Theatre, Big Ben. I join three of my fellow travelers, Gil, Charlotte and Phil. Following our walk we make a short visit to the British Museum. So much to see, we'll have to come back. A cocktail in the Thistle lounge and a great story about the Titanic from Gil rounds out the afternoon.

Yes, I will share his story.

Gil's great uncle, aunt and baby, third class passengers on the Titanic, became separated during the panic on the night of the sinking. Unable at the last minute to enter an already full lifeboat, his great aunt dropped her baby into the arms of the people in the fast lowering boat below. Dazed, bereft, she struggled through the crowds searching for her husband. An officer grabbed her and was able to thrust her into one of the last boats.

The survivors were crowded onto the deck of the Carpathian, the first ship that had steamed to Titanic's rescue. They were cold, wet, covered in blankets, weeping. Gil's great aunt heard an infant wailing. Pushing her way through the people, she saw a woman cradling a baby in her arms. Recognizing him, she rushed forward to take her son but was rebuffed by the woman who claimed that this was her child. Desperate, frantic, she suddenly realized there might be a way to resolve this and turned to the woman, "Are you Jewish?" A negative answer, and Gil's aunt grabbed the baby, tearing off his diaper to show a circumcised boy, her son!

A welcome dinner and a brief overview of the coming tour is about all we red-eye travelers can stay awake for, an early bedtime it is.

Refreshed, ready to go next morning we explore Smithfield Market, the Priory of St. Bartholomew, and after a pub lunch we tour St. Paul's Cathedral. Situated on Ludgate Hill, the highest spot in London, this church does not impress me despite its lovely setting and one of the biggest domes in the world. Inside it is too monumental, cold, and bronze statuary of important political figures, all life size, including one of Wellington on a horse, does nothing to enrich the spiritual atmosphere.

All is forgiven that evening, however, as we enjoy a tour of London at night and a visit to one of its historic pubs. Clutching my glass of red wine I maneuver through the crowds of noisy, grinning pub crawlers. Bits of conversation fly over my head to disappear into the music and general hubbub. Somehow or other we manage to stay relatively together, catching our tour bus at last, winding our way back to the hotel and bed.

A comfortable trip in our coach next morning takes us to the town of Bath for the day where water from three hot springs has been providing comfort and health since prehistoric times. Early peoples met at the natural setting of these never ending water flows, worshipping and giving thanks to the Goddess Sulis who provided them with such a miracle. The Romans, those intrepid builders, enclosed the site with buildings, rooms, dividing the pools into warm, hot and cold, creating a pleasurable environment for social interaction.

Following centuries of neglect after the Romans left, Bath became in Victorian times a mecca for high society to come and bathe and drink the *Waters* in the newly built structures encompassing the baths. We wander along the Royal Crescent, streets fronted by lovely old Victorian homes, before returning to London.

"The River Thames is liquid history" is a famous quote and today, our last full day in London, we will be time travelers figuratively touching historic sites on both sides of the river. We begin in 1070 with the Tower of London, William the Conqueror's brash statement of England's defeat and surrender to his Norman dynasty. This walled fort has maintained its importance through the centuries as royal residence, prison, menagerie, guardian of the Crown Jewels and currently, a favorite spot for tourists. There are wonderful displays of armor and medieval weaponry. The Line of Kings is an exhibit of life-size, personalized figures of all the kings since 1060 astride their special horses, amazing.

After lunch a boat trip down the Thames to Westminster is our next historic adventure. I am lucky to get a seat on the open roof of our vessel with a 360 degree view. It's a clear, bright afternoon with blue sky and drifting white clouds. Shortly after sliding under Tower Bridge, looking toward the left bank, we see a large, rounded, thatched roof building, This replica of the original 1599 Shakespeare's Globe theatre is so impressive. Light shines off its white sides as we glide by and I think I see Hamlet pacing in the courtyard.

A bit farther on and here is a different aspect of the Tower of London. It is more austere and forbidding when seen from the river. Looking right we glimpse St.Pauls, also the new ultra-modern cylindrical building topped to a point which is commonly called "The Pickle." Almost eclipsed by the large buildings around it is the monument to the Great Fire of 1666 that destroyed so much of wooden London. A tall column topped with an eagle made from shell casings honors the dead of the First World War. Ah, there's one more, for WWII.

Just coming into view, Big Ben and the Palace of Westminster, now called Parliament, which houses the government, the Commons and the House of Lords. Democracy personified, but I know a secret; the building is owned by the Queen! (Better pay the rent boys or…) Westminster Abbey is next and across the river, our destination, the London Eye.

Back on the streets again, ready to cross Westminster Bridge I stop to admire the statue of the British Queen Boadicea in her horse pulled chariot, spear raised, on her way to fight the Romans. Around 60 AD she led a successful uprising that pushed Suetonius all the way to London. Though I lack a spear and a chariot, she has always been heroine and role model for me since I discovered her in *The Journeys Through Bookland* series I devoured as a child.

Crossing the bridge we approach the Eye, this enormous, almost other-worldly structure, a gigantic bicycle wheel spinning slowly above the Thames. Everyone is excited, crowding to enter one of the 30 gondolas attached to this majestic ferris wheel that provides a spectacular view of all London in a half hour leisurely spin…but NOT me! Okay, I admit it, I am afraid of heights (well, maybe Boadicea was too) so I nonchalantly claim that I really want to sit at one of the outside cafes nearby enjoying the *passing parade*. What is in essence a cop-out is turning out to be a very pleasurable experience. Relaxing with my glass of wine, watching the crowds of people enjoying the river on this lovely day is fun. It is fascinating to see the diversity of individuals that appear to come from all parts of the world. There is every shade of complexion, bright colorful clothes, lively hair styles and gaudy carryalls.

On our trip back to the hotel the group shares their flight over London with me and I paint a picture of that happy river scene with all its life and color for them. It is an even exchange.

***

Alice in Wonderland, Harry Potter and Endeavor Morse are on the agenda today as we bid goodbye to London and head out to Oxford. Our first stop is Christ Church, the largest of Oxford's colleges. Here I am standing in the great Tudor dining hall built in 1529, amazed that I recognize the tables, chairs, the dais and the pictures on the walls, all of it. But where is Harry and Ron, Granger and Draco? Of course, this is Hogwarts! Didn't I see a white owl perched above those movable stairs that led to this place?

Actually there is a very good reason that all of this is familiar. The people responsible for the settings used in *Harry Potter* knew immediately that this site was perfect for Hogwarts, the only drawback being the too small size. Undaunted they constructed the whole scene, much enlarged, on a back lot. Harry never knew the difference.

Next is a *packed lunch*, British for picnic, on the smooth, green lawn of the Memorial Garden. Delightful. It is another clear, warm day and the magic continues. In one of the trees bordering the garden, I glimpse the Cheshire Cat grinning from ear to ear and a small blond girl running through the opening of the wall that encloses the garden. She is chasing a rabbit dressed in a waistcoat, a tiny gold watch in his paw murmuring, "I'm late, I'm late."

Why ever not, this is where Charles Dodgson, Oxford's nineteenth century mathematics professor, in his guise as Lewis Carroll wrote those wonderful *Alice* adventures for the Dean's daughter.

Finishing our pastoral lunch, we stroll leisurely through Oxford's streets. I find it very difficult to pass by the Bodleian Library without going in. Just as we are about to cross the street to return to the coach a Mark 2 bright red Jaguar flashes by with a somber looking, white haired gentlemen at the wheel. A whiff of beer lingers on the air. Could that be Thames Valley Police's very own Inspector Morse?

I have always been in awe of the centuries of learning, of the brilliant minds that fashioned Oxford. I also thought of it as a staid, extremely intellectual, perhaps even pretentious and serious place but today I carry away a different picture. There is humor here, creative whimsy, flights of fancy worthy of the Brothers Grimm, magic! I see the colleges in the round at last, and I am delighted by it all.

***

Mickleton in the Cotswolds is a quiet, almost nothing of interest place and is our next three day stopover. The Three Ways House Hotel is up to date in all respects, but quaint and welcoming in a way that the London Thistle was not. Comfortably tired from the long day I wander through the village after dinner marveling at the quiet, moonlit cottages, a respite.

Here's another place I have not been to since 1953 and I am as excited as I was all those years ago. Stratford-upon-Avon, Shakespeare's first home-place, where he grew up, married and his children were born and where, following the creative, wonder years in London he returned to die. The coach leaves us off to tour the village. We had a short lecture while driving here, and map in hand we feel quite sure we can handle ourselves. In small groups of three or four we explore Shakespeare's birthplace, his school, his wife Anne Hathaway's cottage and Holy Trinity Church where he is buried. Just below the altar, off to the left is his grave. I am vividly aware that his bones, dust by now, are beneath my feet and, overwhelmed, I shed a few tears. It is difficult to say how much I honor and love this man whose words give so much color and vibrancy to my world. Maybe if I tell you that I always, instinctively, want to capitalize all His pronouns you will understand.

A special treat is in store the next evening. When we arrived, Gil realized that The Royal Shakespeare Theatre was here and offered to arrange tickets for anyone interested. There were six of us lucky to obtain tickets and here we are anxiously awaiting the opening of *Twelth Night*.

This is an up-to-date version of the play performed in modern clothes. Seated in the first row of the balcony I am a bit unsettled to see the props, tables, chairs, writing desks complete with inkstand and heaps of free floating paper suspended on long wires from the ceiling, moving down to the stage as needed for the action and levitating back up when the scene changes. All of this as back drop to those marvelous, unchanging sixteenth century words.

Isn't traveling wonderful? There are always out of the box surprises, moments that shift perception and turn old established ideas upside down, like unexpected Christmas presents. Sometimes the world shifts, or the mind stretches with new understanding...this one was just fun!

The Cotswolds cover a fairly large area that in the past was mostly given over to sheep-farming. Villages, scarcely altered since that time, have kept their very original names, many derived from some obscure, now unknown event or person. As we travel in our coach from town to town, there is much conjecture as to the meaning of Stowe on-the–Wold, Chipping Camden, Upper and Lower Slaughter, and Great Rollright. Actually, some of our ideas are quite amusing and, laughing, we entertain ourselves all the way to Chester where we will spend two days on our way to Wales.

Hoole Hall Hotel, located a few miles outside of Chester is quite luxurious, situated in a park-like setting of green lawns and lush gardens. I take advantage of this lovely privacy and rise early both mornings to do Tai Chi in the garden.

On the face of a brochure, a quote, "Chester is still an antique town, and medieval England sits bravely under her gables" is very apt. There are half-timbered houses everywhere, old sandstone churches, monuments from the past and the city walls that enclose them all were constructed in Roman and Medieval times. A couple of hours exploring uncovers only one jarring note, *Woolworths*, a sign above a store in the middle of town is definitely not in keeping with the era evoked by its surroundings.

Leaving Chester, but not medieval times, we travel through the beautiful, mountainous views of Snowdonia along the northern coast of Wales to Conwy and its awesome castle built by Edward I in 1289 to keep the rebellious Welsh in line. The area here is in sharp contrast to the landscapes I saw in 1953 along the southern coast of Wales whose mountains were heaps of slag and coal dust dug up from the ubiquitous coal mines. I liked Swansea, experiencing a bit of the real *How Green was my Valley* remains vivid in my memory but that was a whole different country.

Conwy castle is incredible. Enclosed by eight enormous towers connected by walls 30 feet high these ruins awaken my childhood desire. If I couldn't be Queen Boadicea, to be a chivalrous, shining knight in armor runs a close second. Our guide is full of clever, interesting information about castle living. He also touches on the enmity of the Welsh for the conquering English, which in a moderated form still exists in many places today. The Welsh language is, at last, being taught in the schools, and its strong Celtic sounds are heard just about everywhere. (Eat your heart out, Edward.)

***

On our way to York we make a brief stop in Haworth to visit the Brontes, Charlotte who wrote, *Jane Eyre*, Anne, who wrote *Agnes Grey*, and Emily, my favorite, author of that wonderful gothic novel, *Wuthering Heights*. We can't stay long but I sign the Visitor's Book so Emily will know that I was there to say, thank you.

Time to back up a bit. Remember my new friend John, he of the nineteenth century poetry, one-upmanship breakfast? He is a delightful person with a good sense of the ridiculous. Whenever we find ourselves seated on the coach together or at another breakfast table, conversation doesn't flow, it jumps, it sparks from one poetic absurdity to another. Oh, we talk of other things as well, and somewhere along the line we become hooked on the Scottish, "Och, aye" which is now a watchword. This is the first time that my assigned roommate and I are not really interested in each other, so having this connection with John is pleasant and rewarding.

On our approach to the extensive and really beautiful ruins of Rievaulx Abbey we are distracted by people dressed in medieval clothing, moving about in a settlement of tents, apparently cooking over open fires, shaking out bedclothes, washing utensils in wooden buckets. In other words, living here. When the coach parks most of the tour group go ahead to visit the Abbey, but I turn back to the encampment and, I soon learn, back to the thirteen century.

Although busy with chores, the people are friendly. Some of them speak to me in Olde English, others take pity on me and revert to present day. They are reenactors who meet for a couple of weeks each summer to live as close as they can to their period, in this case 13ᵗʰ century. One of the women, shivering slightly, shows me the blankets and shawls she used last night to try and keep warm (no sleeping bags allowed). She takes me to the doctor's stall where he offers me amulets in the shapes of body parts so that I might buy the one that will banish the troubles I have in that area. The meals they cook are as close as possible to true rustic fare although she says there are occasional runs to the nearest fast food place. I love this visit and upon learning that there are comparable groups all over the British Isles celebrating many different eras, I wonder if there might be one which reverts to Roman Britain where I could be... Queen Boadicea. This request brings only blank stares and a few giggles. Thanking everyone and wishing them warmer weather, I run to catch up with the tour.

Rievaulx Abbey was founded in 1132. The Cistercians were a strict order and obviously talented in business because, over the centuries, they became quite wealthy due to a flourishing wool trade. By 1538 when the Abbey was closed by Henry VIII, the buildings covered much of the lovely green valley. Through the years people have confiscated many of the stones and other building materials to make their homes but the ruins that are left are extensive and really awesome. The village has encroached somewhat onto the Abbey grounds with small, red roofed cottages scattered between the white stone gothic remains. The partnership this engenders is actually comfortable and pleasing. A lovely lunch in the village hall has been prepared for us by local women and they entertain us with good conversation and impromptu stories. Although this visit might be viewed as just a side trip among all the grand, important places we see, I think it will figure happily and large in my memory.

And now there is York!

What an intriguing place, beautiful abbey ruins, tight, twisting narrow streets with interesting names, Newbiggin, Middlecave and

Maiden Greve and a wonderful wall surrounding the city. Gates in that wall are called Bars and the streets are called Gates and then there are combinations with names, Micklegate Bar and Walmgate Bar. Asking for directions must get confusing. Fortunately, we have a guide to steer us through.

We enter the city through the massive Monk Bar and soon find ourselves traipsing down a gate so narrow that the protruding second stories on the fourteenth century buildings almost touch. There are runnels in the center of the street and wicked looking hooks hang over wooden shelves outside some of the store fronts. This is "The Shambles," called Fleshammels in medieval times, meaning flesh-shelves. Of course, it was the street of the butchers who slaughtered their produce in the back yards, exhibited the choice cuts on those hooks and wooden shelves, letting the offal and blood run down the middle of the gate. This lasted for five hundred years but cleaned up, scoured I hope, these small stores are now filled with quaint gifts and souvenirs for the tourists!

We wander a bit, discovering in a parklike setting, medieval walls that were just built on top of ancient Roman ones. *Waste not, want not* works very well for us modern seekers. A few old royal buildings and we are ready for our fish and chips lunch. I notice we are not offered meat, perhaps in deference to those among us who don't seem to be able to forget the graphic experience of the Shambles.

Above all the sites we have seen this morning are the lovely, soaring bell towers of York Minster, one of the largest Gothic cathedrals in northern Europe. It has been difficult, at times, to tear my eyes away from its splendor and pay attention to what was happening here on earth. Built mainly in the Perpendicular style of Gothic the creamy white limestone walls soar upward, reaching for God and the sky. It is simply beautiful.

As we approach the entrance, looking up, I see that scattered among the lovely tracery of the façade are carved gargoyles, funny, ugly, wickedly leering, dark little creatures with wings. Poking their sinful, human faces into the serenity and beauty of this ethereal space brings a balance and I love it!

Shortly before we board the coach to begin our next adventure I run to a little souvenir shop and buy a two inch gargoyle replete with wings and a wicked expression to bring home. The loveliness of the Minster needs no material reminder and is already alive in my mind.

Traveling on from York, being quintessential, we arrive in Edinburgh, Scotland. Our hotel, The Thistle, sister to our London digs will be home base for our last three days. Instead of a scheduled walking tour this morning, John and I opt for a double decker Tourist Bus go-round that travels in a circle and, replete with guide, encompasses the city, old and new. These bus tours are in many large cities. They are popular because a ticket allows getting off, exploring, and getting back on the bus as many times as one wishes.

Scheduled in the afternoon is a visit to the Castle, but there is little time for a proper tour. I was here in 1953 and toured extensively so I choose to wander down the Royal Mile, that total, touristy street whose stores on both sides flaunt everything Scottish endlessly, over and over, and all the same. Sounds dreadful doesn't it. But actually, it is so over the top that it becomes fun, a joy in itself. The street wanders all the way down the hill to Holyrood House, the palace where the Royals stay when they are in town. They are not in residence, however, so we return to the hotel to prepare for tomorrow's visit to the Trossachs, Loch Lomond and Loch Katrine.

Preparation is important because the weather has turned and we have left early summer behind. Day dawns with heavy, dark clouds racing across the sky. No rain despite their threatening appearance and I can see a bit of pale blue every great once in a while, but it is COLD! Like the woman reenactor at Rievaulx Abbey, I'm layering. Our first stop, Trossach National Park is on the shores of Loch Lomond. There is an interesting lecture by a young Park Ranger about the work they are doing in reintroducing endangered species to the area. He is proud to report that they are celebrating 50 years of abundant Ospreys who were once almost unknown locally.

Soup and a sandwich lunch gets us warmed up for a trek along the edge of the lake. We have a choice of taking the low road, staying right along the shore or taking the high road, a more ambitious climb to a lookout spot. Mindful that I am not Queen Boadicea, I decide to play it safe and do a leisurely walk. I don't know who I'm fooling, trying to be a practical adult, I have hardly walked 20 minutes before I want to climb. Looking around, I see the group is no longer in sight so I just take what might be a path and grabbing trees and stumbling over rocks I begin to haul my intrepid, young self up the hill. I never find the group but I do suddenly happen upon a wonderful lookout clearing and, like Balboa at Panama sighting the Pacific Ocean for the first time, I am silent with admiration for the magnificent view. Stretching for miles, dotted with heavily wooded islands, this beautiful loch is the border between the Lowlands and the Highlands of Scotland. I yearn a bit toward the north for a moment before beginning my descent. Slipping, sliding over stones and under branches, barely upright, I make my precipitous return. Scratched a little, out of breath, but elated at my brief return to childhood I am, once more, a part of the group.

Moving on, we board a small boat for a trip around nearby Loch Katrine, one of Scotland's loveliest lochs. This was a well-planned activity because the scenery is particularly beautiful as viewed from the water. However, we must take that statement on faith because it is so cold that we spend the entire time crowded into the small cabin below deck drinking Scottish Whiskey!

The weather lightens somewhat next day and removing one layer of warmth I am excited about our day trip to Glasgow. Although we will not be visiting the Glasgow School of Art or any of the tea rooms designed by Charles Rennie Mackintosh, architect, designer and artist, I am happy to be in the city he enriched with his lovely

Scottish Arts and Crafts buildings, furniture and designs. It goes right on top of my growing list, Next time…

Much of our time today will be spent in the People's Palace and Winter Gardens. Lunch is served at small tables scattered among exotic plants in the Winter Gardens conservatory, an enormous greenhouse called the glasshouse. Each table has an umbrella which can be opened to protect from the sun's rays on bright days. Our sky is overcast so we can look directly up through the delicately curved glass ceiling at a flock of small birds circling overhead.

I wish there was someone besides the few unassuming guides whom I might properly thank for this very special museum. The People's Palace is a perfect name because it chronicles the ordinary lives of Glaswegians from 1750 to the present day. Yes, there are some old museum-type displays from the past but since the 1940's, when it began to record a true social history of Glasgow, it has been a celebration of people in their everyday work and leisure…not a lord or lady in the bunch!

The Palace was built in 1889 in one of the most overcrowded, unhealthy sections of the city with a stated mission of bringing light, culture and learning to the people. "A palace of pleasure and imagination around which the people may place their affections and which may give them a home on which their memory may rest."

Wandering among the exhibits, enjoying the photos of workers, of solemn looking children in high button shoes sitting in small, dark classrooms, their mothers on wash day, smiling self-consciously for the old Brownie camera, mills and factories belching smoke, a picnic, a special day at the seaside almost totally covered from head to foot in bulky clothes, I'm beginning to know a little about ordinary people and their ordinary lives in a real way. There is a greater surprise waiting for me around the corner.

A few years ago a friend gave me a book on tape called *The Holy City*. It is a fictionalized account of the actual Nazi bombing of Clydebank, neighbor to Glasgow, on two horrendous, consecutive nights in March 1941. Those tragic events are told through the story of a particular family, the MacLeods. They lived in a tenement in a group of flat-roofed sandy colored buildings that from a distance faintly resembled Jerusalem as seen by a sailor returning from a voyage to the Middle East. The nickname, the Holy City, stuck and soon became the way the residents referred to their homes. The story was so well told and descriptions of the bombings, agonizingly real.

I first listened to the tapes while driving in my car on a trip to north Jersey. As I approached the twelve toll booths at the entrance of the bridge over the Raritan River, a point of no return, tragic events were occurring on the tape and I was sobbing uncontrollably. Barely able to maneuver in the traffic and almost blind to the directional signs I count it as a miracle I did not end up in the river!

Now, an entire section of the Museum, around that corner is devoted to pictures and actual quotes from victims of the Holy City bombings. Much of what is recounted on the tapes is absolutely, heart-breakingly real. Feats of heroism by ordinary people, all on their own, without government aid is totally in keeping with the meaning of the Palace. Again, I look for someone to thank for this impressive place. Making do with a bow and a whisper of appreciation to the air I rejoin the group.

Our farewell dinner in the hotel that evening is, whether you believe it or not, truly gourmet. I realize that Britain is not particularly celebrated for its food; however, a menu that includes, chicken liver pate, roast pork coated in an apple and cider sauce, and Black Forest Gateau describes a gastronomical feat worthy of being called gourmet.

Our guides throughout the trip, Belle and Peter, have been fond of sharing the occasional limerick. Rounding out the evening in honor of the conclusion of such a great tour, several participants have composed offerings. Amid much laughter we take turns reciting our original efforts.

Filled with memories, already a bit sad for this journey to end
I offer my contribution:

> We have a fine group…let me tell you,
> congenial, sweet-tempered, true-blue.
> We've become good friends,
> but everything ends…
> So, thanks everyone…..toodle-oo!

At home in St. Kilda...

This voyage originally appeared in *A Treasure Hunt*. If you have read it already please just take a cat nap and move on.

Celtic Quest

"It is an expedition. That's what an expedition means. A long line of everybody. On a sort of boat, I think. And we are going to discover something."

A.A. Milne, *Winnie the Pooh*

Almost desperate, I want to go on this trip soooo much, "Has anyone called who could room with me?" They only book double occupancy on the ship and I have been checking every couple of days--no luck so far! I explain that I had just spoken with my son in Seattle and he would also like to be put on the waiting list. There is a somewhat confused pause, "Would you and your son room together?" Of course! Why didn't we think of that?? We get the last stateroom!

So begins our journey on "The Little Red Ship." That's not her legal name, of course, but she's been carrying people to exciting places for a good number of years and all those grateful passengers have lovingly given her that nickname. She has recently returned from a trip to Antarctica, been refitted, and now will carry 90 people on a Celtic quest around the periphery of Scotland, visiting the islands of the inner and outer Hebrides, Orkney, touching the Shetlands and down the east coast to Edinburgh Because it will be almost impossible for a ship this size to actually dock at these ports, we will travel from the ship to the shore in big rubber Zodiacs. There is planned, as well, a very special stop at an island 40 miles outside the very edge of Scotland in the North Atlantic Ocean, St. Kilda. This comes with a stipulation that the ocean must be calm enough for the ship to approach and the Zodiacs to land. A trip of a lifetime in so many ways!

I have traveled quite a bit since my husband died in 1980 and with the exception of two trips to India in the 80's and a couple of visits to the Restione families in Italy, the trips have all been with group tours, usually, Elderhostel. This voyage has been arranged by the Archeological Institute of America, but it is also the beginning of a wonderful collaboration with my son, Daniel. We will travel together, making our own plans for the next several years. I'm quite sure that Dan has some small misgivings this first time, about "traveling with his mother," but I also know that it won't be long before any doubts are stilled. We get along so well, many of our interests the same, no mother/son role playing, and equal voice decisions, probably the fact that his incredible snoring bothers me not at all is a clincher! I grew up with a father whose snores shook the house and lived with a husband who came a close second in night-time noise production. I am impervious!

The trip begins for Dan with a long, interrupted red eye flight from Seattle to Philly airport where I pick him up and drive us home to Cape May Court House, south Jersey. Washing clothes, buying flip flops in Acme, and eating at Lucky Bones finishes that day for both of us. In order to fly non-stop to Glasgow we must leave from Newark International Airport. This necessitates a long, long ride on a local bus which seems to stop at every street corner ("oh, you're late today," "can you drop me off at the Chinese restaurant?") but we do arrive and take off on schedule! Lights dim, the hum of the engines is like white noise and dozing on and off brings us an early touch down in Glasgow. We book into the Thistle Hotel. After a breakfast of eggs and haggis we take a sight-seeing stroll through the city. A few hours into the walk I crump out but Dan continues to travel all over Glasgow. He returns with a sharp new pair of reflecting sunglasses he purchased at the Pound Store. Crisps (that's British for potato chips) and sandwiches in the bar, staggering to our room and sleep, at last, at 8:00. Sleep straight through to 7:00, wake feeling great. Another fine eggs, haggis and croissant breakfast and we are off to explore Glasgow on a public tour bus that allows one to get on and off whenever there is an interesting site. I am thrilled to visit the Charles Rennie Macintosh House at the Hunterion Gallery. This artist is a favorite of mine and I soak up all the art and displays! We actually ride the bus two times round, enjoying this warm, sunny day. Later that evening we get a snack, haggis spring rolls, and drinks in the pub room along with a very noisy, very drunk Irish soccer team that's been playing locally. They are so funny and for some reason decide to become friends with 'these peculiar Americans'-- us. They soon have us laughing and joking and feeling very welcome.

Following a meeting of all the participants the next morning, we board buses that take us for a final look at the city on our way to Greenock and a first sight of our little red ship. Boarding is easy, finding our stateroom not quite so but after we figure out that there are two staircases leading down, one for each separate side of the ship and finally find ours, we are set and climb all the way up to the top deck to survey our new kingdom! We keep grinning at each other, so excited and happy to actually be here, on deck, watching a group of young people on the dock below, dressed in kilts, playing the pipes for us as the ship begins to sail out to sea.

Dinner, a rather disorganized practice boat drill, introduction of staff, plans for tomorrow and we are off to bed.

"Wake up," softly, a clink of china on the nightstand, the smell of coffee. Each morning now Dan will wake me with coffee and a croissant. (I knew I had this child for a reason.) We are just ahead of a booming voice over the speaker system lilting and tinged with a Scandinavian accent, "GOOD MORNING, GOOD MORNING, GOOD MORNING!" and the first day of this fabulous voyage begins!

Wow, the ship is doing an IrXXish, Scottish jig, pitching, rolling up, down, sideways. I'm in bed tight in the covers actually enjoying the pandemonium. I've never been seasick so this is almost a treat for me. Earlier in the evening when the Captain warned that it would be rough passage tonight I gave my seasick pills (I'm always prepared) to a table mate, Violet, who already looked green and queasy although we were still docked. It had been an exciting day; our first two slippery, scary zodiac landings, first at Jura and then at Islay, an island where there are twice as many deer as people. It was also headquarters for the medieval "Lord of the Isles" who ruled the Scottish Hebrides for a couple of hundred years. Dan is a good sailor as well and is already asleep. The ship rocks my cradle and Daniel's snoring provides a lullaby and I, too, am off in dreamland.

"GOOD MORNING, GOOD MORNING, GOOD MORNING"

I almost shout aloud into the whispery silence of the Skye Genealogical Library on the Isle of Skye, "It's my mother's name, and mine AND even my children--we are all listed here!" I'm standing and waving the book, entitled, *THE MAC LEODS*, *The Genealogy of a Clan.*" Everyone is excited now, people are looking up from their intense, silent searching for themselves in the old records to smile and laugh at my exuberance. Ted Gowan, the Ship's

Historian hears the hullabaloo and asks if I will share my discovery with everyone after dinner tonight.

"William Clearich, Fifth Chief of the Clan MacLeod of Harris and Dunvegan, a great warrior chief, born in the late 1300's on the Isle of Skye is my, and Dan's great, great, great, great…grandpa."

I revel in the ancient stories I've heard, and my captive audience appears to be enjoying them as well! I knew it! I knew it! Watered down, off on the end of a wispy branch on the family tree, yet I AM A MACLEOD! From then on Dan and I are greeted, "Hi, MacLeods".

This wonderful day is crowned with an adventurous scramble around beautiful Loch Coruisk ending with a leisurely zodiac trip, flirting with curious seals who bat their gorgeous eyelashes at us, on the way back to the ship.

"GOOD MORNING, GOOD MORNING, GOOD MORNING"

Dougie MacLean, a famous Scottish musician, is traveling with us and this morning serenades us from a shiny, wet ledge deep inside Fingal's Cave. The tide is rising so we can't stay long and leaving Dougie on his slippery site we return to the ship. I am happy to say that I hear his guitar rippling out on deck later and assume he made it back without incident! We are heading now for Iona, the blessed isle, home of St. Columba who brought Christanity to Scotland in AD 563. The Abbey, ruins and ancient graveyard where many Scottish Chiefs, including MacLeods, are buried are all spectacular. What I love, though, are the sheep that wander in and out of the holy places, unperturbed, nibbling the grass, totally at home on this lovely, quiet, unassuming isle. Dan wears a small, silver pentacle around his neck and on the little beach he stops to wash it in the clear, gentle waves idly slapping on the shore.

"GOOD MORNING, GOOD MORNING, GOOD MORNING"

In the morning a birding trip takes our Zodiac quite far from the ship and we are seeing Razorbills, Puffins and even a Whooper Swan! The island of Barra with its Kisimul Castle sitting just a few hundred yards offshore is our destination this afternoon. Barra is not a tourist mecca, fortunately, and the guides in the castle leave much to be desired in the way of information although they try their best. It isn't long before Dan, who know so much about the history of Scotland, is entertaining the group with medieval facts, funny anecdotes, explanations and demonstrations of how the staircases mounted always on the left wall, allowed soldiers a free right hand for swordplay.

That evening there is the Ceidleh! A sometimes wild, always noisy, musical and happy Scottish party. This one is no exception, local women 'tweed waulking' the wool, singing in Gaelic, two young Barra girls doing a dance, pints of lager being passed hand over hand from bar to thirsty watchers. A traveler from our ship recites a story and over all playing against the walls a 1950's movie, "Whiskey Galore". It is filled with sites actually filmed on Barra and watched by me 50 years ago in the US! Amazing, like so many other happenings on this 'trip of a lifetime."

"GOOD MORNING, GOOD MORNING, GOOD MORNING"

Dan misses this 'morning greeting' because he has been up on deck since 3:30 a.m. watching for the first dawn sight of St. Kilda. This incredible island chain lies 40 miles off the west coast of Scotland far out in the Atlantic Ocean. It arose from an erupting volcano millions of years ago and has been inhabited since prehistoric peoples arrived in the Stone Age. Where they and their small brown Soay sheep drifted in from is not known. Actually, the existence of St. Kilda was not known either until the 1700's when it was discovered and subsequently claimed by the MacLeods (we get around don't we?). The tenants paid their rents in bird feathers and oil taken from the enormous populations of seabirds that still nest on the cliffs. Being in touch with the mainland eventually proved to be the undoing of the island way of life. As years passed the chance of an easier, more exciting and rewarding living drew the young people away to the mainland and by the 1930's there were so few inhabitants left that the government insisted they be brought to live on the mainland coast of Scotland. The name St. KIlda is actually the corruption of a Viking name Skilda and not the domain of a saint. The austere, craggy, wind-swept views, the wheeling, screeching seabirds, the seemingly endless blue ocean exerts a strong pull on the emotions, an enchantment felt by the many visitors who continue to risk the rough surf and dangerous currents to experience this amazing isle!

And here WE ARE, caught by the magic. When we arrived in our zodiacs, Dan was second in line to go ashore but, Dougie MacLean, knowing how much this day meant to him, said, "Let the MacLeod go first", and moved out of his way. Wandering alone or in small groups we fan out from this tiny harbor, exploring the ruins of the "village street" and the the rock strewn cemetery, Dan is off to the cliffs to be dive bombed by the nesting birds! Squelching through a swampy patch covered in little blue flowers I move onto firmer ground and find a seat on the low wall of what was once a two foot thick foundation. Just then, a smattering of raindrops, gone before I can stick out my tongue to taste their cool. Suddenly I see a tiny bird tripping along an opposite wall darting in and out among some loose stones. It is the St.Kilda wren found nowhere else in the world! A bird to add to my 'life list.' What a treat for a birder like me!

Dan and I meet up with the Ranger who is in charge of the staff of The National Trust of Scotland that takes care of the island.

Dan boldly extends his hand and says, "We are here to collect the back rents due to the MacLeod!" which first calls forth a bewildered expression that then turns into a smile.

I am overwhelmed by all that we have seen and felt today; tantalizing strips of old stories, of childhood adventures of Scottish heroes that I made up and played, songs I sang to put my children to sleep, *My Heart's in the Highlands*, poems scanning to the beat of my heart, "from the lone shieling on the misty isle, mountains divide

us and the waste of seas, but the blood is strong, the heart is Highland, and in dreams we behold the Hebrides." What a capacity for joy I seem to have. How very lucky I am to be able to visit and make real dreams that were planted long, long ago in childhood!

As we sail away from St. Kilda, Dan takes a wonderful sunset picture that is one of the treasures we bring back.

"GOOD MORNING, GOOD MORNING, GOOD MORNING"

The isle of Lewis, a big island, is, in the words of Ted Gowan, our bus guide today, "Nothing but miles and miles of bugger all!" Although we have stopped at a couple of interesting sites and wandered through Stornaway, actually there isn't much to see except peaty, low scrub scenery until, all of a sudden out the window high up on a hill I see magic. Callanish. Standing stones, natural, tall, graceful, primordial, stretched against the beautiful blue sky are even more impressive up close. Unlike Stonehenge they are loosely gathered into a short avenue leading to this almost happenstance grouping around the very tall Magician's stone. There is no mystery here for me. I know what they are! Long, long ago a group of young women, on their way to market were excited, happy and dancing in the bright morning when the Magician saw them in their joy and, capturing this sweet moment, turned them into stone so they might dance forever.

"GOOD MORNING, GOOD MORNING, GOOD MORNING"

Standing on deck I wave to the 'old Man of Hoy', a tall, red sandstone rock jutting out from the main island in the Orkney archipelago. I think he recognizes me from when I was here in 2004 with an Elderhostel group tour. I remember the intense excitement I felt then, I was going to actually visit prehistoric sites, Skara Brae, Maes Howe, Brodgar, places I had only ever dreamed about. Now here I am, three years later, mellowed a bit but still somewhat in awe about visiting them all again. Skara Brae, a Neolithic village of eight homes built around 3180 BC, abandoned approximately 2500 BC, subsequently buried under centuries of drifting sand and unearthed in the 1850's by an enormous, fierce storm. Incredible. It almost feels as though I am revisiting old friends. Maes Howe, a chambered cairn, used by those same Stone Age people for burials evokes wonder all over again, as does the immense stone circle of Brodgar.

Dan is feeling miserable. A toothache which is beginning to swell his left jaw makes any real pleasure in the day almost impossible for him and by suppertime I go looking for Dr. Vlad (!), ship's physician, to get him some relief. Antibiotics and ordinary pain killers don't do much good and by the next morning I am in the doctor's office again, this time yelling that he MUST do something!! Codeine, at last, is helping.

"GOOD MORNING, GOOD MORNING, GOOD MORNING"

Zodiac trips to the Shetland islands of Foula and Papa Stour are planned today but I decide to make this a time of relaxation, catching up on my journal, and poking my head into our stateroom periodically to see how 'the patient' is faring. By 5:30 in the afternoon Dan is lying quietly tucked up in his bed, smiling beatifically, high as a kite on the codeine and, at last, "Feeeeling fiiiiine."

"GOOD MORNING, GOOD MORNING, GOOD MORNING"

And a good morning it is, with Dan, up, dressed and "3 trillion times better!" A calm, easy Zodiac ride takes us to Fair Isle, midway between Orkney and Shetland, where we are greeted by several of the 70 inhabitants. Oh, wait, it's actually 71 we are told, a new baby last night! Dan and I wander all over this lovely place, stopping at a little museum to see the beautiful Fair Isle sweaters that they weave by hand and ship all around the world. The patterns are unique, the wool and the colors, gorgeous. Prices are equivalent, however, and I must forego. Dan stops to pet a friendly, black dog and we see, for the very first time on this trip an actual iconic, red telephone booth. That evening, on the ship, a group of singers from the Isle come to serenade us.

"GOOD MORNING, GOOD MORNING, GOOD MORNING"

"Okay, Dan, look medieval." I'm taking his picture as he leans out from a tower of Dunottar Castle. This unique forbidding fortification situated high on the Scottish North Sea cliffs has been almost impregnable throughout the centuries; however, in the 900s it was stormed and captured by a group of Vikings. Ted Gowan, our historian, assures me that almost undoubtedly some of my ancestors, the MacLeods (we do get around) were part of that conquering body!

The Zodiac landing this morning and the return to the ship later in the day were our last trips in those big rubber boats. The last, ever so scary climbs down and eventually up the rickety, metal stairs that hang on the side of the ship swaying back and forth with the waves with only a strong right arm clasp from the zodiac crewman to bridge that gap between ship and boat. Today, for the first time I actually wasn't afraid. I certainly pick a strange time to become used to that panicky transfer! Tomorrow we will leave 'the little red ship' for the last time so it is mad packing before bed.

"GOOD MORNING, GOOD MORNING, GOOD MORNING"

Dan decides to go with a group who are taking a taxi directly to Edinburgh rather than exploring St. Andrews and Falkland Palace. Years ago he had lived in Edinburgh and wanted to revisit some of his old haunts. Despite a cold, cloudy morning I opted to wander the austere but beautiful ruins of the St. Andrews Cathedral and see Falkland where Mary Queen of Scots had her own apartments. There was traffic on our bus trip to Edinburgh and we did not arrive until 6:00. There was Dan, sitting outside the hotel, room key in hand, waiting to greet me. We stashed our luggage and proceeded to walk to Grey Friars Bobby pub. Of course we petted the statue of "Bobby" that wonderful, faithful dog who stayed, watching over his deceased owner's grave for fourteen years, leaving only to eat, until he, too, died and is still honored for his devotion today.

Don't you just love the Scots?

We are in the hotel so no "GOOD MORNINGS" today.

Flight home is long but uneventful. Daughter, Pamela, meets us and drives us to her home. Michael, Stephen and Kelly have been eagerly awaiting special time with their much admired and loved uncle Dan and the stories, laughter and excitement last until way into the night. At 8:00 (2:00 am Scottish time) I fold and creep away to bed. Pam drives us home the next morning and two days later, May 20th I hug Dan tightly, avoiding his quiesant but still swollen jaw, before letting him go back to Seattle, both of us calling out, "NEXT YEAR, NEXT YEAR!!!"

Aftermath: I am so full of memories of the trip, quicksilver pictures float in and out of my mind. Words, snatches of Dougie's guitar playing, all the lectures, the history, the magnificent landscapes that take my breath away, the unbelievable bright sunny weather, so unlike Scotland, day after day. I am so full I feel three feet wide and nine feet tall!! I can't stop talking about it all and go looking for people to hear my stories. When they hear me say, "It was absolutely the trip of a lifetime!" they are eager to listen. However, as the monologue stretches out I notice that the light in their eyes is dimming. They are beginning to glaze over and I feel their attention slipping. Actually, I know that their idea of a trip of a lifetime is of Paris nightlife, London theatres, Italian 'dolce vita,' not the wind swept islands, the bleak ancient ruins and the mystic pull of the wild grey sea of the Scottish Hebrides but I CAN'T HELP MYSELF! Like the Ancient Mariner who "stoppeth one of three..." I keep on speaking until the audience has shamefacedly drifted away. I really don't care and just go on talking and talking to myself.

Afteraftermath: Thanksgiving morning, early. I am at Pam's and she is shaking me awake, "Dan's on the phone! He needs to talk to you right away!"

"Mom, turn on the TV, the news, 'the little red ship' struck submerged ice in Antarctica and people are hanging on ropes, sliding down the tilted side of the ship into lifeboats! She's sinking!"

Later we see that everyone has been saved, a Norwegian ship was nearby and rescued the survivors. But, our jaunty little ship, our snug stateroom, all the 'Blethers', the daily schedules posted on the wall, the wooden "In and Out Board" we had to sign whenever we traveled ashore, the bottles of red wine that toasted each occasion, will soon lie, forever still, uncorrupted, frozen on the bottom of the Antarctic sea.

Like Grey Friars Bobby I want to build a statue to honor that sweet, adventurous home that was for me, and, I'm sure many others, "the trip of a lifetime!"

At home in Salisbury...

A Cascade Yankee in King Arthur's Kitchen

A small, 3" by 3" box wrapped in green tissue paper sticks out of the top of my Christmas stocking. It is 2008 and I am sitting wrapped in my bathrobe in the midst of a paper and package strewn family room with my son, David, and daughter in law, Camille. We are in their home in Maryland and it is just the latest in a long line of wonderful, traditional, old-fashioned Christmases. There are seemingly endless gifts, many of them bear tags with riddles that must be solved before they can be opened. I am having trouble with finding the answer to this one so Camille makes a reference to my having seen famous ruins that stand on the Wilshire Plain outside of Salisbury, England.

"What? I've never been to Stonehenge!"

She snatches the tag from my present and picking up a pen, scratches a new riddle and hands it back to me.

If you build it...you will go.

Of course, it is a little 3D jigsaw puzzle of Stonehenge. Of course, I build it, and, of course, I will go!

June 6th 2009. Another red-eye from Philly airport to Toronto to Heathrow, this time on Canadian Air Lines, good food and

FREE wine. Dan also flew Canadian from Seattle to London two days ago and he will be meeting me when I arrive.

There he is….thinner, handsome, big smile, long hair to his shoulders. I love it.

This is a new kind of adventure in some ways. Dan and I first traveled together on that trip of a lifetime Celtic Quest in 2007 but we were part of a group tour led by the Archaeological Society. There was a lot of freedom of choice but always within the pre-planned structure. This time, we are really on our own. It was great being in charge of our itinerary, perusing many brochures, endless cross-country conversations with Dan, choosing where to stay, what to do, calling the local Tourist Information Centre and making the final choices. Being totally involved in all this planning for the first time made this yearly trip begin four months ahead of the actual date of departure, stretching the excitement and anticipation of the entire adventure.

An interesting addition to our enjoyment as well as to the title of this sojourn, is Dan's assignment to share our eating experiences with the audience of Seattle's KIRO Radio station through his blog, entitled, "A Cascade Yankee in King Arthur's Kitchen." Dan is somewhat of a foodie and has reviewed many Seattle restaurants for his "Stick a Fork in It" program on this CBS affiliate station where he is News Manager.

A short distance away from those amazing stone circles, Stonehenge and Avebury, home to one of England's most beautiful cathedrals, and many ancient and interesting restaurants, Salisbury is an easy choice. People have been living here since prehistoric times; the Romans called it Sorviodunum and when they left the Saxons and then the Normans made it a royal site with a castle and a cathedral. Eleanor of Aquitaine, mother of Richard the Lionheart and the infamous King John of Magna Carta fame was imprisoned here by her husband Henry II. In the 1200's following a disastrous fire in the cathedral the Bishop moved the site a few miles down the road to New Sarum, now called Salisbury. Everyone else soon followed and the abandoned town became Old Sarum, now a destination for historically minded tourists.

After an enthusiastic reunion (I don't seem to be able to repress a loud, "DANNY" whenever I first see him, as I do only once a year.) Dan drags his two bags and my "rolley" through the streets to the Mercure White Hart Hotel. He has an uncanny way of always knowing how to find our lodgings. Which, in this case, is pretty remarkable because the street keeps changing names each couple of blocks, Exeter, John, Catherine and Endless Street.

This 17th century hotel is actually made up of individual buildings attached together over the centuries to make one interesting establishment. The long halls are interrupted every so often with steps going up or down, to accommodate the original levels, I assume. We love the old English atmosphere and after settling in we decide to visit the lovely gothic cathedral and the surrounding group of attractive old homes built for the clergy called The Close. It is delightful.

Following a dinner in the hotel we trek down those halls, *Mind the steps, please* to our room. I'm for bed and fall asleep watching Dan busily recording his first *Cascade Yankee* blog, giving the hotel restaurant only a *so-so* review (bland, adequate but boring.) Breakfast is a different story, scrambled eggs, tomato slices, sausages, blood pudding, croissants, all done to perfection. A cup of tea with saucer and spoon is on the table and when a coffee cup also with saucer and spoon is brought, at my request, I am temporarily fascinated by the two spoons. Oh, dear! I slip one into my pocket. How tacky!

Rested and well-fed (feeling a bit guilty) we are ready for a Salisbury adventure. First stop is the Tourist Information Centre. It is nice to meet some of the people I had spoken with over the last few weeks of preparation. Stepping backwards into Salisbury's past seems the best way to begin and we ask for help in visiting Old

Sarum. We are given a map and told that an ambling walk will get us there in about a half an hour. I have a notoriously poor sense of direction so Dan becomes the navigator. It is a lovely amble, there are gardens everywhere, sweet smelling pink and coral and yellow flowers poke through white fences in front of almost every cottage. There are small parks and a river we stroll along. We are a bit carried away by all this English perfection. A casual glance at the map makes us realize however, that somewhere along the way we must have deviated from the path. Dan is great at finding lodgings but not destinations, apparently. A friendly woman responds to our request for guidance by not only giving us verbal directions but even walks with us a short way. She explains that soon we should go through a park that has a Five Rivers Swimming and Leisure Centre. She wishes us well and we continue on our way. The landscape has become somewhat more rural now, there are patches of tall grass, small meadows, more trees, even the path is rougher. A bit of doubt creeps in, more than an hour has passed since we started and "Oh, there it is…the Leisure Centre!"

Confidence restored, in true English fashion we keep calm and carry on. Conversation never lags and Dan has time now to regale me with his two day adventure in London before I arrived. He visited 221b Baker Street to say hello to Sherlock Holmes, ate a lot of street food, fish and chips, Cornish pasties, and arranged to take a "Jack the Ripper Tour". This was the highlight of course because he had immersed himself in that whole awful story with all its ramifications. After numerous questions, interruptions, comments, etc. the Guide took him aside and suggested that they go for a pint in a local pub after the tour to really get into the nitty gritty that most of the current audience were not really interested in. Several pints later they had not yet solved the mystery of WHO but, all in all, British/American interests had been firmly cemented!

These tales of his London visit quite take my attention until I suddenly notice we are passing another Leisure Centre…what a surprise! We hadn't realized that the population of Salisbury and environs was big enough to warrant two such centres. It actually takes us both at least 15 minutes before the awful truth sinks in. There is only one centre and for the last 45 minutes we have been walking in a big circle. Somewhat desperate now, we are already two and half hours into our half hour amble, we again ask directions from the nearest passerby. As we begin to follow the instructions we have been given we are stopped by a loud hail, "Not THAT way, turn LEFT!" Unbelievable!

When the entrance through the large berm that surrounds Old Sarum comes into view, exhausted, demoralized, we actually turn aside and head for the Harvester Pub to recoup. As I gratefully sink into a soft, plump chair I hear Dan regretfully say to the bar tender, "I've been dragging my poor 80-year-old mother all over England!" Red wine for me, a cider for Dan, a couple of silent moments and suddenly, spontaneously we have dissolved into loud whooping gusts of laughter! *Frick and Frack on Tour!*

Old Sarum's extensive hilltop within the surrounding henge, ditch, is dotted with the ruins of church, castle and several buildings once used to service the active life that happened here so long ago. Broad history as well as anecdotes and stories of human interest are all well recorded on the placards at each site. Our struggle to reach this interesting goal was well worth it and immersion in the Medieval is our reward! That said, however, I opt to take a bus back to our hotel. Stalwart Dan sets out on foot, but on a straight-shot road well marked on the map.

Surprisingly, we arrive within fifteen minutes of each other. It is already mid- afternoon but, unwilling to give in to a strong desire to nap, we visit the lovely gothic cathedral again. There are no guided tours but helpful docents are ever ready to give information and answer questions. There is a special moment looking at one of the only four copies of the Magna Carta still in existence. A luscious blueberry muffin and coffee in the shop suffices for lunch. One of the most enjoyable things to do in any cathedral or church is attendance at late afternoon Evensong and we gratefully sit for a while listening to the choir fill the awesome space with soft, sweet music.

A well-deserved quiet evening at home is a perfect choice and after a fish and chips snack in the lounge it is exactly what we opt for. Dan is manfully resisting sleep to do his blog. A wonderful hot bath, snuggled into the covers I drift for a while remembering the day and so much more. I am incredibly lucky to be here, in this moment, in this place, in this world, in this life! An epiphany of sorts recalling with thankfulness everything and everyone that has brought me here!

I wake the next morning to a feeling of excitement and anticipation. A month ago at home I had booked a *bespoke* (private) tour of Stonehenge and today is the day. We will be meeting with Patrick Shelley, our guide, at 5:00 this afternoon in the town square. Ten of us will travel in two vans. This is so much nicer than a big tour bus. The late hour will enable us to experience sunset through those mystical, almost magical stones.

While waiting, we have most of the day to explore. It's Market Day and I choose to stay in town, wandering from stall to stall, talking with the vendors, snacking my lunch from goodies on offer at little stands tucked away in unexpected corners of the Square. I love times like this, feeling as though I were living in, not just visiting a place. Debenham's department store is having a sale so, of course I have to go. A brown and green enameled bracelet, reduced to ten pounds, is my first souvenir.

Dan, meanwhile decides to visit Wilton House, one of those stately English Manor Houses a couple of miles from Salisbury. It was designed by Inigo Jones and has been the country home of the Earls of Pembroke for four hundred years. Walking brings him through the parkland surrounding the magnificent building to the back rather than to the usual front entrance. Stopping for a smoke he is approached by a roughly dressed man he takes to be the gardener who thanks him for not leaving the cigarette butt on the grass. Answering Dan's questions, he shares facts about the grounds and gardens. Thanking him, Dan pays his fee and enters through the magnificent front door. There is no guided tour but a brochure offers helpful information. One room, one passageway, one gallery after another filled with treasures, amazes. Entering an area close to the Private family apartments, Dan is surprised to see the roughhewn gardener now dressed immaculately, entertaining some important looking guests. Of course, this was the 18th Earl of Pembroke himself. Catching a glimpse of Dan, he smiles briefly before turning back to his friends. Adventures also come in small happenings!

Meeting in the square, we have just a short while to share before it's time to meet Patrick Shelley and board our vans for a journey into the mystery of the very long ago past.

Stonehenge lies in the middle of the broad Wilshire plain, which is studded with Neolithic burial mounds. There's a long rectangular area resembling a race track, called the Cursus, another circle once made of gigantic wooden pillars, and a very large, newly discovered settlement, Durrington Walls. The latter is believed to be where the original builders lived. We visit them all. The day had been somewhat cloudy but it has been clearing over the last hour or two and Patrick begins to pick up the pace. Vans parked, we are walking, almost running, stumbling over rough terrain avoiding as much as possible the large cow pats scattered throughout the grass just under the crest of a low hill. He is finally satisfied with where we are and arranges us in a group facing the top of the mound. He instructs us to walk slowly, eyes wide open, to the crest. We do and there in the near distance, splendid against the reddening sky is time's mystery, the massive stones, each like a majestic exclamation point. Some are capped, some free standing and others lying quiescent on the ground, perhaps as they were when those ancient people like British giants dragged them there and got ready to lift them to the sky. I am overwhelmed. The endless post card pictures, stories about the site, all the hoopla and touristy drek drop instantly away and I see only a mystery, a miracle, a natural, stony, roughhewn cathedral from almost the beginning of time. Stonehenge!

People are no longer permitted beyond a fence several yards from the structure but because we are a special tour we have been allowed to enter this sacred place and walk freely among the stones. I catch sight of Dan just around the edge of the trilithon and we grin at each other like children at Christmas. Sunset is close now. Our individual wandering slows and we pause expectantly facing west across the Salisbury Plain toward a sunset sky, red between skinny dark clouds that no longer hide the sun. A long hushed moment, ordinary time seems to stretch, to pause breathless as the sun, framed briefly between the stones falls swiftly below the horizon.

Isn't it wonderful, despite all the past knowledge and exposure, to really experience a place fresh, entirely new, for the very first time!

This great *bespoke* tour (I love that expression) never quits until we are delivered right to the door of our hotel. We can't resist giving Patrick Shelley heartfelt hugs. *Oh, these demonstrative Americans!* He really appears to like it.

Salisbury is an important city of approximately 40,000 inhabitants but as we walk, wander, the streets the next morning it seems like a village. There are interesting looking byways, offshoots from the narrow roads that seem to change their names at each corner. Lovely old buildings hug the almost non-existent sidewalks, street crossings you can cover in just three or four long steps. It all feels comfortable, homey. My cat would have no difficulty lying down on the nearest patch of sidewalk and going to sleep.

Pubs figure high on our lists of to-dos on all our trips. Round about 3:00 each afternoon either Dan or myself casually confesses to feeling *a bit peckish* and we are off to Ye Old Alehouse, George and the Dragon, or Rose and Crown for a quick bite, a glass of wine for me and a cider, Scrumpy if possible, for Dan. Today, however, we forego this mid-day pleasure because we have reservations for dinner at The Haunch of Venison. The structure that houses the restaurant dates from 1320 when workmen who were building the Cathedral tower lived here. Later in the 14th century, it was reputed to be a brothel with an underground tunnel connecting it to the Church to save the clergy embarrassment. It is obviously haunted, there are even some who believe Churchill and Eisenhower can be seen drinking at the unique pewter bar while planning D-Day! There are crooked hallways turning this way and that, up one or two steps and a bit further on spiraling down a few. The ceilings are very low, held up by massive oak beams that are said to be from ancient sailing vessels. We are instantly thrown back to childhood, wanting to see into every nook and cranny, play hide and seek, jump out from tightly angled corners to scare people but, fortunately, better sense prevails and we meekly follow the waitress to our table snuggled up to a crooked window that looks out high above the street below. Totally in keeping with our surroundings, I order the wild boar. Dan, showing a bit more caution opts for the haunch of venison. I really overplayed it. The boar is much too strong for my taste and Dan, being the good son that he is, switches with me. He claims to really enjoy the wild pig and I find the venison melting in my mouth. Dan's blog that night is a masterpiece!

The very front seat on the second level of a big touring bus with windows all the way down to your feet is a perfect place to be if you are going to visit the magnificent stone circle of Avebury. So, of course, that is exactly where I am early on Thursday morning. Dan had walked me to the bus and then took off for his own daily explorations. The trip takes about one and a half hours. I am so thrilled with my total observational position and revel in all that I can see unimpeded. Villages, each complete with pub and church, cottages with thatched roofs, random Neolithic stones standing crooked in the middle of suburban backyards, ubiquitous sheep, and the funniest street crossing signs:

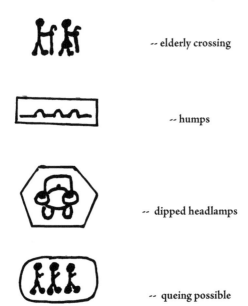

-- elderly crossing

-- humps

-- dipped headlamps

-- queing possible

Avebury is certainly an amazing place. It is the largest stone circle in Europe with a circumference of approximately 1000 feet and consists of two smaller circles, North and South, within the outer ring. Originally there were about 100 stones marking the perimeter but there are now just 60 left on guard. Unlike Stonehenge, these monoliths tend to be relatively flat, columnar or triangular in shape. Many are enormous, weighing upward of 20 tons each and all are in their natural state rather than worked smooth like the ones at Stonehenge. The setting is very different from its counterpart 17 miles to the south. A small village has grown up over the years within the circle and there is a major road running directly through the stones. Sheep graze throughout the grounds and tourists are allowed to wander right along with them. When the bus drops me off I wander as well. It is a beautiful, clear, blue-sky day with huge puffy white clouds sailing overhead.

Despite many suppositions no one really knows the meaning or purpose of these awesome Neolithic structures, but there is an aura of sanctity about them. I honor the mystery but my reaction to Avebury is very different from the way I felt at Stonehenge. The atmosphere here is warm, friendly, the stones are approachable and individual. Occasionally a sheep will rub against a rough surface, curl on the grass, and fall asleep in the giant's shadow. I might like to do the same. There is a particular monolith situated very close to the road that according to legend travels across that road every night and back again before sunrise. Obviously some of the stones have a sense of playfulness. I know it sounds silly but I have the same feeling with these giants that I have with my dog. Gazing intently at them both I know we are connected somehow and, oh, how I wish we could speak with one another. Coffee and biscuits at the Red Lion pub in the little village is a treat before I finish my wandering, board the bus and travel, bemused, back to Salisbury.

I don't know what Dan writes in his blog about our supper in the Hotel Lounge but I thoroughly enjoy a large, delicious salmon salad, crispy bread with a dipping oil and a smooth, soft red wine.

Oh, dear, Friday and it is over. Wait. That's not true. Yes, we'll be going home today but everything we've seen or experienced or felt will never leave us. We're different because of this adventure, richer, deeper, funnier perhaps, easier in ourselves, more accepting hopefully. Dan's plane leaves one hour before mine and I'm a bit teary as he walks away. Ah, he turns and calls.

Where next?

At home in Dunvegan…

Over the Sea to Skye

But first….London, Bath, York, Kyle of Localsh

Dan and I have traveled together twice in the past. In 2007 we sailed on a Celtic Quest and discovered what really great traveling companions we are. No group tour in 2009, brave souls totally on our own, we went to Salisbury, to Stonehenge and Sarum and discovered what a penchant we have for getting lost! Still brave, a bit chastened, we plan to reach for more of our dreams in 2011.

Although there is English, Irish, Scottish, Welsh and Italian in the mix, we secretly believe we are Scottish to the core! Rose Cottage is a charming little house on the grounds of Dunvegan Castle, ancestral home of the Clan Macldeod on the Isle of Skye. As members in good standing of the Clan MacLeod of MacLeod, we have rented the Rose for eight days, May 21 to May 28, fulfilling a dream of living on Skye just as though we were permanent residents.

But first…there are other dreams to be dreamed, and London is a good place to start.

Dan is flying from Seattle and I will meet him at Heathrow airport. My flight is not a good one, with two separate episodes of really rough turbulence, but I arrive safely and a short time later meet up with Dan. It is always so great to see him and I do my usual, "Daneeee," which also, as usual, embarrasses him. At home I had arranged to have a private taxi take us directly from the airport to the Ibis Hotel in Earl's Court, London. The ride is comfortable but quite expensive--the Tube next time We are very pleased at the location of the hotel Ibis on a quiet street lined with trees, apartment houses, small stores and occasional pubs. Our room 802 affords us a wonderful view of London.

Unpacking is not really a priority so we do the minimum and take off to explore this area of London new to us. At the end of our street we turn a corner into two blocks lined with lovely, white stone buildings that once might have been Edwardian private townhouses but that now are apartments. There is an aura of long ago elegance, faded now, but they are well kept and many feature small gardens or potted plants at their entrances. The streets, curving gracefully, we have named the the *Crescents*. Coming to a broad, busy main street we head for the Underground station, buy our

tickets which are called *Oysters* and are valid for several trips, "Mind the gap," and board a train to Westminster.

There she is on her chariot, brandishing a spear, defiant, rising triumphantly over the traffic across Westminster Bridge, the statue of Boadicea, the Celtic Queen who defied and, for a while, trounced the Romans in 60 AD! I love her and each time I am in London I make sure to come and say, *Slainte*. I greeted her in 2005 but I'm not sure if she remembers me.

We gaze, tourist-like, at the London Eye across the Thames, Big Ben's clock tower and the back of Westminster Abbey, saving the front for another day. The Cenotaph, Britain's primary war memorial, stands in the middle of the road, a short way beyond Westminster, in Whitehall. It is inscribed "The Glorious Dead" and although it originally honored the fallen of World War I, it is now for all soldiers killed in battles fought in the 20th and 21st centuries. Close by is an arresting monument to The Women of World War II.

True to our philosophy of staying awake for the full day following a red-eye flight we continue on to stare through the ornate metal gates in front of Number 10 Downing Street, however, the Prime Minister is not at home and this is about our waking limit. The Tube District Line takes us quickly home to Earl's Court Station. Climbing the stairs to the street, looking to the left we spot The Blackbird Pub. A warm friendly environment, a luscious dinner of smoked salmon, a spring Onion potato cake, and red wine from Montelpuciano (pub food is certainly not just fish and chips anymore) pretty much ensure that this will be our local.

We woke this morning to one of those beautiful, warm, blue-skied days that England gives us, now and then, a present between the mist and rain. I seem to be gifted this way, more than my share, and revel in the soft, clear air. For once I order, along with Dan, a full English breakfast, bacon (ham), two eggs, sausages, baked beans, tomato slice, mushrooms, blood pudding, a croissant and coffee. Almost repelled by the sight, overwhelmed, I eat about one eighth. I had to do it at least once. Dan puts his away with ease.

Instead of taking the tube all the way to the theatre, it is such a nice day, we disembark at Embankment station and walk along the north side of the Thames to cross over on Blackfriar's Bridge.

Southwark, on the south bank, is the section of London that in Shakespeare's time was home to all that north Londoners disdained: prisons, brothels, tanneries, bear-baiting halls, and, of course, theatres. Until recently it remained the ugly stepsister but the middle of the 20th century brought exciting changes to this neglected area. Modern hotels, businesses, restaurants, art galleries, and the Royal Festival Hall have replaced many of the run-down buildings. Walking leisurely along the lovely promenade that skirts the river, we pass under the Millennium Bridge. The Tate Museum is next and then--there it is!

Please do not tell me this is just a replica. I do not believe it. As I stand next to Shakespeare's Globe Theatre, the sounds of the 21st century fade away and all I hear are rough curses from the boatmen on the Thames bringing the playgoers for today's performance. The air is filled with the raw, pungent smells of everyday living in this reign of her Royal Majesty Elizabeth I. I hear the show today is a new one, *Hamlet, Prince of Denmark*, and just like the gentry we have tickets to sit in the Gallery.

This theatre, this "wooden O," built in 1599 is a delight. The two-story stage is square, jutting out from the rounded back and topped by a false ceiling supported by two pillars painted to look like marble. Color is everywhere. That ceiling, called the Heavens is covered by stylized images of the sky. There are no curtains and door-like openings in the rear allow actors to come and go. Props are scattered here and there and I see a rope tied from one pillar to the other, holding red panels pulled back, resembling curtains. Did I hear something about a "play within a play" being part of today's show?

Left of center, last row of the lower gallery, our hard, narrow, wooden bench seats give us a wall to lean against, no small advantage when the play is more than two hours long. Just below us the pit is filling up with the groundlings, the lowly standees. It's fun to watch the jostling for the area right in front where the lucky ones can lean their arms on the stage. It is really a friendly crowd and most of them sit down on the floor, relaxing, and strike up conversations with their matinee-mates. I must have returned to the 21st century because I notice many are wearing hoodies and carrying flimsy, clear, plastic rain jackets. Looking upward I see that the whole center of the thatched roof is open to the sky, providing light for the stage, and I recall a notice stating that no umbrellas are allowed. The day remains clear and sunny so I guess they are just hedging their bets.

After a while a few actors in modern dress carrying musical instruments stroll onto the stage and begin to play a jaunty melody, strange beginning to Hamlet's tragedy. If I were still in Elizabethan times I would recognize this practice, a holdover from when, not that long ago, plays were performed out of doors in inn yards and country squares. Lively music, announcing a performance, would call an audience. Actually, today, it is a good way to capture attention.

The impromptu serenade fades as the actors wander off stage. There is quiet.

Rough sentinels, armored, wrapped in warm clothes, looking over their shoulders as though fearful, walk on stage, talking of an apparition that appeared before them the night before. "Look, where it comes again!"

The Ghost of Hamlet's father...

I feel a shiver, goose bumps run down my arms. I am caught and held by this tragic tale that becomes my world for the next two and half hours. And what a world it is. Played by a young Joshua McGuire, Hamlet is fresh, vulnerable. His soliloquies are natural, spontaneous and there is none of the pretentiousness of some of the classic actors in the past. Instead of being awed, *oh, this IS Hamlet*, I believe that I am seeing the play exactly as it was for those long-ago audiences; brand-new, exciting, honest, deeply emotional but with characters as real and moving as the woman sitting in front of me or any of the enraptured crowd in the pit below. I feel gifted and I never, ever want to see any other version again!

Words tumbling over each other, Dan extolling how easy it is to understand the language once you relax and just let it flow over you, almost dancing with excitement, we head back down the promenade toward the tube station. Suddenly we are in front of The Anchor, one of London's oldest pubs. Samuel Pepys stood on its roof watching London burn in the Great Fire of 1666. Feeling peckish and thirsty we try to enter but the crowd is so dense and, promising ourselves that we will come here another day, we wander off to the Underground, The Crescents, the Ibis, and dinner in the hotel, Savoring the wonder of the day and the realization of a dream, that night I slip quietly back into the 16th century and sleep.

Waking to sun and a more normal breakfast of an egg over light, a croissant and coffee next day, we opt for a London-stroll adventure. We start by walking the Crescents to the tube station and the Direct Line to Westminster.

Morning, Boadicea.

Heading down King Charles Street to St. James Park we stop to visit The Churchill War Rooms. We tour the headquarters deep underground, from which Churchill directed the war, amazed at how immediate everything seems. There are maps on the walls and spread out on tables with flags and tiny ship models marking the Allies progress or lack thereof. Room after room contains switchboards, telephones color coded for specific emergencies, papers scattered everywhere, desks with messages on them only half written, all as though Churchill and his staff had just walked out for a minute. In a way that is exactly what happened. The moment victory was declared they did walk away leaving everything exactly as it was. For a long time the headquarters were ignored and only in recent years, restored and open to the public. I keep hearing those radio broadcasts by Edward R. Morrow and Eric Severeid from London during the Blitz with the awful sounds of bombs falling in the background.

We sit for a while at the edge of the Park, slowly coming back to 2011 and peace (of a sort). On our way to Trafalgar Square we travel the Strand until it turns into Fleet Street. Passing St. Clements Dane Church I hear long ago childish voices singing the ditty that named London's churches, *oranges and lemons say the bells of St, Clements*. We arrive at a large open square in front of Somerset House. Shooting up through the pavement there are multiple miniature fountains, which turn on and off at irregular intervals. What child, or adult for that matter, can resist running through them, trying to beat the odds and stay dry? Actually there are three children, probably five, six and three years old, the two older ones in underpants and the smallest, starkers, running through the fountains. They, of course, are trying to get wet, despite the really cool day. I shiver for them but soon the parents are there wrapping them in warm towels, with hoodies, pants and shoes ready to be donned nearby. Relieved, we move on.

Turning a corner into a narrow street we spot an interesting pub sign:

Ye Olde Cheshire Cheese
Rebuilt 1667

Samuel Pepys watched the original building burning from his vantage point on top of The Anchor, back in Southwark. As is the custom in crowded pubs, we join a man sitting in a quiet corner. The table in front of him is covered with papers that he is busily shuffling about but when he hears our American accents in greeting, he smiles and shares that although he now lives in London he is originally from Des Moines. Yanks, they're everywhere!

Still footloose, but feeling much less peckish after our snack, we continue wandering. Skirting the grounds of St. Paul's cathedral, admiring its lofty dome, we hear the sound of the bells of Mary le Beau church…*and the great Bell of Bow.* This simple, childish rhyme stops me in my tracks!

A sudden moment of awareness, of knowing and owning all that I have seen and experienced on this trip; this wonderful journey across an ocean, back in history, in the middle of Shakespeare's London, the pubs, and now surrounded by the traffic, the noise, the rushing about of the present-day city, I feel it all!

I love these spontaneous moments that set me firmly in the here and now and, renewed, I am off to the Museum of London.

Dan has done his homework well in deciding we must visit this particular museum. It is great. Entering, we step back into Londinium. Projected onto the walls are videos of everyday Romano-British life. Everything is to scale, life size, and real. I want to talk to that woman coming around a corner of what will, in 2000 years, be Fleet Street. Turning a corner, ourselves, we have moved farther back in time to "London Before London." This archaeological exhibit dates all the way back to 450,000 BC, an incredible collection of artifacts that tell a coherent history from these amazing fragments.

"Medieval London" thrills me with displays of that Great Fire of 1666 that burned most of wooden London, of the clothes and manners of Elizabethan times, and maps of Southwark's bawdy landscapes. There are paintings of the Thames teeming with ships in its busy harbor, a drawing of the year that the great river was frozen bank to bank, and a tiny mock-up of the Globe.

There is so much more to see but I am really beginning to flag. Happening upon a café in the middle of the building, I beg leave of Dan and, bidding him Godspeed, I purchase a cup of coffee, a generous slice of cake topped with lemon drizzle and sit contentedly at a small welcoming table. It is an hour later when Dan returns filled with information about all the rest of the exhibits he has seen. His stories carry us back through the Tube, down the Crescents and back to the Ibis, with one quick detour to get him a Cornish pasty that serves as an appetizer to his supper at the hotel. Replete with salmon and gravelox we spend the evening reading about and anticipating our trip to Bath tomorrow.

We have been congratulating ourselves lately about what experienced, prepared travelers we have become. Double checking our Rail Passes, purchased well in advance at home, we head off for our day in Bath.

Hubris, *pride goeth*…It seems that our passes are just fine but they must be validated by a railroad official who is asking to see our passports. I have mine but Dan cannot find his. While he is making a mad search through all his pockets, I pull what he refers to as your little old lady shit: chin wobbling pathetically, eyes tearing, imploring. It works. Reassuring the poor, old, feeble mother the official validates the rail pass of the forgetful son.

Bath is a surprise. I visited here six years ago with an Elderhostel tour but much has changed. There are now videos projected onto the walls as they were in the Museum of London, depicting the important social life of the baths. Cleanliness, the comfort of the warm pools and the exhilaration of the cooler waters were all important, but even more so was the opportunity to conduct business, meet important people, exchange the latest gossip, all in a relaxed atmosphere. The lifestyle, so different from today, becomes understandable.

Being able to explore the various sites and exhibits on our own, rather than herded in a group, really widens the experience. Dan and I particularly enjoy a display of the small bits of copper thrown into a pool by those long-ago bathers. Carved on them are curses against people that had annoyed, stolen from, or in some way angered the throwers as well as requests for the god, Sulis to do awful things to the perpetrators!

On the balustrade surrounding the largest pool there are statues of Roman heroes. Waving goodbye to Claudius, a particular favorite of ours, (having watched hours and hours of that wonderful TV show, I Claudius,) we take the return train to Earl's Court. A last supper at our local, The Blackbird and back to the Ibis. Having packed for our early departure tomorrow we settle comfortably in our beds. Reminiscing about our London, we begin to anticipate...York.

The two hour train journey through the green, orderly, English countryside is pleasant and I am remembering how much I enjoyed my visit to York in 2005 with the Elderhostel group. Plans, this time, are to see much more and it will be fun to play guide for Dan in the few places I have already been. I'm starting to develop a gruesome, explicitly bloody spiel for The Shambles as we pull into York's lovely station.

The Minster Hotel is a nice surprise. Relatively small, with a bed and breakfast ambiance of interesting nooks, corners and unexpected staircases yet it has all the amenities. I imagine it was once a very grand private residence. The feel and warmth of a home seems to linger.

Perhaps not the best prepared duo, but we have learned to be among the fastest **un**packers. Jackets in the closet, clothes in the drawers, toiletries bag hung on a hook in the bathroom, important paraphernalia laid out crisply on the table, maps, brochures, water bottles ready to hand takes only minutes and we are out the door, on the way to the new adventure.

York is an ancient, venerable city, established by the Romans, politically important through the ages since, somber…

BUT not today.

Today, York is a carnival! The massive Bootham Bar is our entrance gate to the side shows, displays in murky glass shop windows, the underground rides through Viking land, and the tiny twisting alleys called Snickleways that take us from here to who knows where. The Shambles horror street, Clifford's Tower, endless eateries, called pubs, tempting with their luscious smells, the Midway, a pedestrian mall in the center of town, filled with people calling out to one another, enjoying themselves. Wrapped around, holding it all together is the ancient carousel Wall.

Caught in a holiday mood, we slip through narrow entrances into bright lit snickleways, surfacing two streets over from where we began. Ancient second stories protrude over the narrow, twisting streets making the quirky window displays in the shops below difficult to see. Ah, the Shambles, the street of butchers where, in medieval times animals were slaughtered in the shop yards and blood and offal ran down the runnels in the middle of the road. Dan is appropriately shocked by my vivid description. Not shocked enough, apparently, to keep him from looking for the nearest pub. Which will it be, Old White Swan, Hole in the Wall, Cross Keys, the Punch Bowl? Take your pick, we will visit them all before we're through.

As we tire, the circus mood begins to fade. Dan opts to sit for a while at an outside cafe, nursing a cider, but I have one more adventure to pursue. I pay for my ticket, enter The Jorvik Museum and Viking Centre, sit in a small carriage that carries me underground and through a really wonderful exhibit of the life of the Vikings who came here in the 800s, ruling for the next 200 years. Life-sized figures in realistic settings seem so real. Blinking my eyes as I return to the present day, delighted with my excursion into the past, I endure Dan's sneering, "Tourist trap." I confess I loved it.

Winding through one snickleway after another, discovering the nooks and crannies of Old York, we find ourselves, at last, on the way back to the Minster Hotel. What a fun day. Sometimes a light-hearted, non-serious approach to sight-seeing clears the air and makes everything you see and experience new and fresh.

One more trip to the carnival next day, to the ancient wall that, like a carousel, enwraps Old York. There are still sections of the original construction by the Romans in 71AD. Restored, rebuilt, added to from medieval times up to the present it is a treasure and a Wall Walk is a must. What a delight it is to look out over the jumbled streets and snickleways and make sense of our wanderings yesterday. "Oh, look, there's the Shambles, and the Old Swan Pub, and the Jorvik Museum!" It is all laid out like a jigsaw puzzle. We stroll along the top of the wall like some Viking conquerors from the middle ages admiring our domain.

Rising tall from the city patchwork are the twin towers of the cathedral, York Minster. The next day, viewed from ground level, the lovely Gothic traceries, windows, even gargoyles on those towers are most impressive. It is a cool, gray morning with occasional spritzes of rain and we enter the cathedral's warm and welcoming light eagerly. As I have noted before, we two pagans really love cathedrals, and York is no exception.

A friendly old man with a Guide badge on his lapel welcomes us and offers to show us around. I notice as we start our tour two women placing flowers near the altar and realize that this is a working parish church. I am reminded of this again when there is an announcement that each day at 11:00 o'clock there will be a moment of silent prayer. I am somewhat chagrined at my cavalier assumption that it is here just for tourists. This new knowledge enhances my appreciation. I also feel a tiny rush of pride when our guide tells us, "You are not tourists, you are pilgrims."

This lovely, hospitable man shares the beauty of this Gothic church eagerly, wanting us to see what he sees, as though it were his home. We do. He takes us to the Chapter House, built in the late 1200s, that still figures large as a meeting place for the Canons busy with the important workings of the cathedral. He gleefully points out the amusing, small carvings in the roof. Searching, we find a tiny mouse, some cats and dogs, a jester, some figures making funny faces and, to my delight, a joyful pagan carving of a Green Man. This exuberant symbol of a man's face peering out from a profusion of green, spring-like leaves is truly ancient. It carries with it a feeling of renewal, growth and, for many, joy. No wonder that at least one of its many forms was carved in the churches built in the Middle Ages, perhaps as a promise for people whose meager lives held little hope of fulfillment.

Delighted with the lovely guide who made this magnificent cathedral as warm and intimate as a country church, with the Green Man, with the kaleidoscope of York itself, we *pub* and wander back to the Minster for a quiet evening, our last night in York.

We awake refreshed next morning, sure that we had left the carnival behind. We have no premonition of the roller-coaster day ahead. We start off easily, on time at 10:42 in the morning. British trains are comfortable, seating is usually in groups of four, two sets facing forward and two back with a table in between. The truly wide windows give great views of the passing countryside. The trip to Edinburgh takes but two and a half hours and we are able to board our connection to Inverness almost right away.

Ah, the calm before the storm, paused on the very top of the ride before the plunge.

We have no difficulty locating our seats, reserved far in advance, only to find a very unpleasant woman sitting in my window seat. She claims that the seat is hers despite my ticket which seems to show otherwise. Unable to follow her long, confusing rant delivered in a patronizing tone I decide that the better part of valor would be to sit on the aisle next to Dan and proceed to enjoy the trip. Stretching my legs forward, occupying the floor space, forbidding her spreading sideways and taking an unconscionable length of time allowing her to get out when her stop arrives gives me a childish pleasure.

The little annoyances that accompany travel sometimes seem to pile up and such was the case here. Arriving at Inverness two and half hours later I head quickly for the Restroom only to find myself confronted with a miniature but forbidding turnstile and a desperate need for twenty pee (pence) in order to enter. A kind gentleman, now next in line, seeing my frantic search through pockets and pocketbook taps my arm and hands me the magical open sesame coin. I shall keep a small, many sided twenty-pee tucked in a corner of my wallet from now on!

Comfortable in my now valid window seat I watch the last of Lowland Scotland begin to fade behind me as we pull out of the station. Looking forward, I anticipate the next three and half hours that will take us into and through the magnificent landscape of the Highlands, lush green valleys tucked between mountains covered with purple heather, glimpses of lochs studded with tiny, mysterious looking islands, small villages, toy-like from the swiftly moving train. Occasionally, individual white houses pop up amid the trees. Dan and I begin to lay claim to this or that particular one.

Excitement is beginning to pall. Conversation lapses and silent, we drift, close to dozing. It has been eight hours since we boarded in York!

It is now about 8:00. At this latitude in the beginning of summer sunset may be as late as 10:00, even 11:00 but the bright, lovely skies have begun to grey and darken. As we pull into the Kyle of Lochalsh station it starts to rain. By now, thoroughly tired of trains, weary and hungry we disembark to find ourselves the only people on the dark, wet street. Saturday night in the Kyle does not, apparently, include a great deal of nightlife. As we wander disconsolately along the cobbled street looking for the bus station which will provide our next mode of travel, if we ever find it, a lone man appears and points the way, casually mentioning the bus is about to leave! Lugging our suitcases we follow his directions, breathlessly arriving at the nearly closed doors of the bus. We have made it, paying thirteen pounds each (!) for the privilege of bouncing and rattling about on country roads for the next hour and then some, over the bridge, onto the Isle of Skye.

I have lost track of reality and this moment of arrival on the MacLeod homeland that I have looked forward to for months passes by almost unnoticed. It is not only the flesh that is weak, the spirit has also fallen into decline. But, no road so long it does not end, there is actually a taxi waiting for us at Portree! Dan had booked "Kenny the Cabbie" online two months ago and HERE HE IS patiently waiting in the rain, welcoming, talking in some weird language that claims to be English.

Rising out of my stupor which has been reintroduced by the hour long taxi trip to Dunvegan I hear Dan telling Kenny where to stop and let us off. My excellent son has, again, done his homework and saved the day.

WAIT, wait! Do you think this is the end of this endless day, think again!

We push through a rough-hewn gate and slog through mud down a path to a white stone cottage. It is so dark by now that it is difficult to see clearly and we are not convinced that this is Rose Cottage. It does strongly resemble pictures we have seen, however, instead of being situated in the open space we are expecting it appears to be in a wooded area. We had been told that there would be a key under the mat and we check and find it so. Dan is still wary and we decide to explore another nearby cottage almost hidden by trees. It is obviously empty so we check for that key but return to what we now believe is Rose Cottage, our home away from home for the next eight days.

No more questioning, we use the key and enter to find exactly what we hoped we would. A simple country cottage, somewhat worn with that lovely lived-in feel. Living room with fireplace, small dining room leading to a basic but modern kitchen. At the back of the kitchen is the bathroom. Fairly large, this appears to be part of an added on area indicating that the comfy Rose once included an outhouse. We wanted rustic but are pleased that we do not have to brave the elements to handle our basic needs. Upstairs there are two bedrooms with alcoved windows that, dark now, we hope will have lovely vistas of the nearby Loch Dunvegan come morning.

Our spirits have recovered. Dan pulls on his wellies and is tramping around outside attempting to get the lay of the land in all that Scottish mist (read rain). More practically I head for the bathroom. Newer than the rest of the house it has a small but adequate shower unit, nice soft rugs on the tile floor and the ever present heated towel rack. This delightful appliance is part of even the most obscure bathroom anywhere in all of the British Isles. A delight we in the USA have yet to import! As I pull the door to upon leaving, the inner knob comes almost out of the handle. I don't close the door fully and intend to tell Dan as soon as he comes in.

There is a soft woolen shawl draped across the back of the couch and I wrap my cold, weary self in it and begin a search for the way to turn on the heat. Dan comes back in and shedding his muddy wellies walks into the kitchen. Before I can warn him he spots the open bathroom door and pulls it closed...forever.

Plunging down the precipitous track, the roller coaster ride continues!

Exhausted, no more reserves of energy or creative thought available, philosophically, we admit defeat. Oh, well, I have already peed and Dan has the whole outdoors so "Let's go to bed" and, like Scarlet, "think about it tomorrow." Half way up the stairs, our dauntless, Scottish souls surface and, shamefaced, we confront the situation head on. Pulling on rain jackets, boots we trek back up the incline to the neighboring house, use the under the mat key, and without a qualm we use the bathroom being very careful to not leave any trace of our intrusion. Replacing the key we stumble back home and wrapped in pajamas, bathrobe and shawl I shiver to bed…at last. It is now midnight.

A short time later, "I did it, I unlocked the door, I turned on the heat, I did it!" Dan's triumphant cry. Blessing this remarkable child, warm now, I snuggle back into the covers, the roller coaster has come to rest at last and I sleep like the proverbial baby until sunrise and a new day!

Waking refreshed, back on track, eager again for what is to come, bundling up against the cool, windy day, we walk to the nearby Castle Café. Brunch is potato/leek soup, roll and coffee. Realizing that today is not only Sunday BUT the Scottish Sabbath when almost everything in rural Scotland is closed in strict conformity to Chapel rules, we buy tuna sandwiches, crispy cookies and candy to fortify us until Monday!

A bookshop is attached to the café and we stop to browse and buy before we head off home in the light rain that is beginning to fall. There is a different feel to the day, it's quite lovely. There is no urgency, no sudden panicky need to plan what comes next, no looking at the clock. Brochures and schedules are tucked away in the suitcase where they will stay for the next seven days. We live here, remember? We aren't tourists or even travelers, this is our home and, long or short the time, it will be so until we decide to move on. Our Skye dream to be *residents* is now our reality!

Waking next morning we discover that there is a lovely vista out our windows. A sloping green lawn slips down to Loch Dunvegan where the water is being whipped into whitecaps by a stiffening wind. Undaunted, Dan makes an early trip to Fosgadhs, our mini mini-mart, bringing home staples and the makings of a delicious breakfast, Scottish bacon, eggs, jam and toast. I notice him putting away ingredients for a shepherd's pie, haggis, lemon curd pudding, baps (Scottish rolls) and a bottle of red wine. We shall be eating very well this week and wonder of wonders Dan will be the chef.

He loves to cook and I don't so, again, we make a good pair. Later in the week we discover a sweet bakery in town and buy strawberry scones and a venison casserole. We actually will eat like the lords in the castle instead of the tenants.

The rain and wind that were making rough whitecaps on the loch are whipping us about as well on our walk to town. Stopping in an intriguing shop called St. Kilda, which had beautiful handmade woolens, I meet and talk with Ann, the proprietor. She explains that they are connected with the Castle and the rental office for the cottages is located in a back room. Wonderful, I can check in, window shop and have a captive audience for my reminiscences. They are actually amazed by what I remember and what is changed (very little) since my trip in 1953. I forget that Dan had decided to walk back home when I stopped at the store and, conscious of how much time has passed, I hurry back.

Dan has on his wellies, his warm yellow rain jacket with hood and he is raring to go on the eight mile walk to Coral Beaches that he has been dreaming about for months. Despite how much the weather has deteriorated, his bold MacLeod heart is ready for adventure! I'm happy to hunker down inside and busy myself with household chores, examining the well-stocked kitchen and popping some dirty clothes into the somewhat dated and very slow washing machine/dryer. Eventually I curl up on the couch to read listening with foreboding to the howling of the wind and the slashing rain against the windows.

Four hours later the brave explorer crashes through the door to stand, immobile, like a zombie, drenched and dazed in the hall. "If the wind had not been at my back coming home you would never have seen me again!"

I can't resist taking a picture before I comfort my intrepid and wasted son.

An hour later, washed and warmed and rejuvenated with a glass of wine, Dan insists upon making a truly magnificent shepherd's pie for dinner regaling me with his epic venture along cliffs and crags and wild beaches. We wander into the living room and settle in for an hour of watching TV. There are just a few stations but we are able to get the Scottish Weather channel. Even though we have endured the vicious, day long wind and deluge we are amazed to hear that this storm has wreaked havoc throughout Britain. Not only were schools and government buildings closed and planes grounded, but even many roadways were deemed too dangerous to travel on and buses were also not running in many locations. It has been the worst weather in years!

Having fallen asleep to the buffeting of our little cottage, it is a delight to waken next morning to calm, some watery sunshine and only a gentle breeze.

Dunvegan Castle, ancestral home of the MacLeods of MacLeod is an awesome place and our destination today. We are welcomed as MacLeods and are asked to sign the special book for Clan members. Joining a small group we are guided through the castle by Margaret MacLeod. I can't resist regaling everyone about my visit here in 1953. Jealous and impressed by my trip to the island of St. Kilda in 2007, they ask question after question. That ancient, fabled island had been owned by the MacLeods all through much of the 17th, 18th and 19th centuries.

In the gallery of portraits we see one of a Chief who had killed his first wife. Reading the name beneath her picture I comment, "Well, she was only a McDonald so it didn't count," touching on the ancient bloody feud between the two Clans on the island. Margaret chuckles and squeezes my arm.

We see a sword belonging to William Broadsword at the battle of 1411 and realize that he was the son of William Clearich, fifth Chief of the clan, Dan's and my great, great, great...grandpa, who died in 1408. The Faery Flag, Rory Mor's great drinking horn that each new Chief must tip up and swallow all the brandy inside in one gulp, Bonnie Prince Charlie's fancy waistcoat are all on display.

Exiting the castle to explore the extensive Gardens we find that rain and cold have returned. However, it appears that it is only a squall coming from over Loch Dunvegan and the sun returns sporadically as the day lengthens. This will be the pattern for the rest of our time here. This is my fourth visit to the Isle of Skye and always in the past the weather has been beautiful, blue skies, puffy white clouds, not warm exactly but not this cold seeping inside my jacket, making me shiver. I guess I was due for the 'usual' highland experience. No matter, it seems that really nothing can truly destroy the joy of our Skye dream!

The fitful weather; rain, sun, wind, early mists continues through the next several days. We walk to town, buy scones, books written by local authors, watch a funny fat lady on the TV Skye weather channel whose forecasts are, unfortunately, always the same, and really enjoy being 'everyday.' Dan goes on another long, adventurous trek around the southern end of Loch Dunvegan, but fares better in the improved weather. He buys a pipe and rich smelling tobacco. Making himself a fine walking stick from a fallen branch he struts about the front lawn looking lord of the manorish.

We make reservations to have dinner at Skeabost House Hotel where I had stayed with Marilyn McBride in 1953! The lobby, once the living room when this lovely building was a private home, doesn't look familiar. I don't remember much of what it looked like 53 years ago. What I do recall vividly is Angus MacLeod, then owner, in full highland regalia and three sheets to the wind weaving across the room singing, "I like MacKay and MacKay likes me," egged on by two Englishmen there for the salmon fishing. Memory is selective and this is one I definitely chose to store away.

Five days into the stay we realize that our cash has dwindled severely. I head off to Fosgadhs where I had noticed an ATM sign. The little, somewhat antiquated machine does not take my card. A visit to a similar ATM in the Post Office results in the same rejection. I am informed that all the ATM machines on the island are set up to only honor cards issued in the UK. Totally frustrated and actually frightened by now, we have plans involving cash only obligations, I head for the St. Kilda shop. Looking for some sympathy I am amazed at the response of everyone there, shop and office alike. Ann immediately goes to the cash register and takes out one hundred and fifty pounds, cash, and asking if that is enough, hands it to me. No collateral, not even a promise or a written note, just, "Pay me back when you can get into the town of Portree and the bank."

Keys left under mats available to all and sundry who might wander by, cash loaned freely to short term visitors--is it any wonder we would like to live here? Sabbath closings, just three TV channels, no supermarkets or workable ATMs--twenty years younger and I would accept them all for a chance to actually live here for a good, long time.

Our time, our Dunvegan dream is just about over. Our last day dawns sunny and warm, just letting us know it is possible! We settle our debts, bid goodbye to all the friendly people we've met and meet our driver who is taking us on a wonderful last ride southeast across the entire Isle to a ferry that will take us across the sound to the Kyle of Localsh. The road takes us past the Red Cuillins, a chain of tall, rounded hills and a bit further on we are amazed to pass through the Black Cuillins; dark, spiky, young mountains that look just like a child's drawing, MOUNTAINS On the mainland again, we bid goodbye to Skye and our intrepid driver.

Rushing through a sudden downpour (I knew it couldn't last) we board the train at the Kyle settling down for our trip to Edinburgh. Tired of sitting, Dan decides to stand in the aisle for a bit. We are both sad, quiet with memories, almost dozing, swaying with the gently rocking coach.

"Oh, my god!" Face a mask of horror, mouth wide open, Dan is gazing at a great metal key he has just pulled from his pocket, "I forgot to leave the key!" The rest of the ride passes in guilty silence, interrupted occasionally with loud protestations of how quickly he will send it back!

Our short stay in Edinburgh is filled with memories for both of us. We have each visited here a few times in the past but enjoy it all over again. A visit to the Castle is a must and this time we see the Scottish Honours, the crown jewels, along with what seems like a thousand other people enjoying the Bank Holiday. Feeling peckish, we stop at Grey Friars Bobby pub. Upon leaving we pet the statue of that wonderful faithful dog. A stroll down the Royal Mile filled with endless Scottish paraphernalia is a *deja view* experience. It appears that the window displays have never been changed since 1953. However, Dan spots a great waxed jacket in one shop and following a short shall I, shall I not, shall I, walks away looking like a true British gentleman. After all it is the last day of our marvelous trip.

A Hamlet dream fulfilled, a wave to Boadicea about to cross the Thames on her way to conquering Romans, that wonderful, quirky carnival, York, living a lifetime on the Isle of Skye with all our MacLeod ancestors in one short week, we are just about perfect traveling companions who just happen to be mother and son. What a gift!

I'm sure you have guessed by now that this is not the end of adventuring, of magic, of discovering inside and out the wonders of ourselves and the never ending, delightful world. See you next year!

Ancient ditty sung to remember the churches of old London .

Oranges and Lemons...

Oranges and lemons,
Say the bells of St. Clément's.

You owe me five farthings,
Say the bells of St. Martin's.

When will you pay me?
Say the bells of Old Bailey.

When I grow rich,
Say the bells of Shore ditch.

When will that be?
Say the bells of old Stepney.

I'm sure I don't know,
says the great bell of Bow.

At home in England and Wales....

A Canterbury Tale

> When that Aprill with his shoures soote
> the drughts of March hath perced to the roote...
> than longenfolk to goon on pilgrymamages.
> And especially from every shires ende
> of Engeland to Caunterbury they wende...
>
> Geoffrey Chaucer

And like those pilgrymms, *wende* we did!

Unlike Chaucer's Yoeman and the Widow of Bath, who began their pilgrymmage to Canterbury from the Tabard Inn in Southwark, London in 1388, a visit to St. Swithun's shrine in Winchester becomes our 2012 starting place. His tomb is in the magnificent Winchester Cathedral. Dan and I are able to waft a *Godne mergen* to him each day because the large picture window in our hotel room looks right out on the north transept of that awesome building. An auspicious beginning to a truly wonderful journey!

Dan flew to Philadelphia from his home in Seattle. An hour and a half drive brought him to Cape May Court House. After a day of catching up, cooking Taylor Ham (they just don't have it in Seattle), buying new shoes and eating at the Bellevue, a local restaurant which is the closest thing to a pub we have here, we drive to my daughter Pam's home in North Jersey. This is a special visit because Michael, Stephen and Kelly, Pam's children, adore their Uncle Dan and see him so seldom. We picnic, kayak in a nearby lake and are treated to a lovely dinner by the kids. Pam drives us to Newark airport the following afternoon for our red-eye flight to Heathrow. I doze during most of the flight but Dan isn't able to sleep at all. Subway to London, Underground to Waterloo station, train to Winchester, a long walk to the Wessex Hotel and we have arrived. We are tired but we know that the only way to beat jet-lag is to stay awake all day. An early night with eight hours sleep will get us right on track with British time. After settling in we head for the High Street to explore this ancient city, home of Alfred the

Great, See of the Winchester Bishops and Royal city of the Anglo-Saxons. Actually, after a short stroll and a cursory look around we find the Royal Oak Pub and relax gloriously into the soft leather chairs. I peer at Dan over my red wine glass and see a man, stretched out with his feet propped up on a stool, ale in hand, smiling blissfully, totally content--at home.

Later we do wander about, sightseeing, taking pictures, getting to know where we are and where we want to go over the next few days. Just a quick bite to eat and we give up and go to our room. It is only 5:00 but we've reached our limit. Dan, who has been awake for over 24 hours, falls face down on his bed, fully clothed, exhausted. I get into my pajamas. Sliding under the covers I am asleep.

I wake feeling so rested and ready for the new day. Looking out the window it appears to be a nice, clear morning. Dan is still lying fully clothed on his bed and it is not easy rousing him. He lunges upright and staggers to the door, complaining of not enough sleep, to go outside for his morning cigarette. I shower and dress. When I pull back the window drapes all the way it doesn't look quite as bright as it did earlier. Maybe some rain later. When Dan returns he has recuperated somewhat but looks a bit puzzled. "The sun's in the south," he mumbles. Shaking his head as though to clear it of left over sleep he reluctantly gets ready to go down to breakfast, still feeling that something is amiss. To further convince him that he needs to fully wake up, orient himself and 'get with it' I turn on the TV. Running along the bottom of the screen is the message… "current time is 20:00 hours."

I don't believe it--8:30 PM? I have only been asleep for three hours. I felt so good and rested. I don't believe it!

Silently, I undress and slip under the covers. Dan, forgivingly makes no comment. He has removed his shoes, is on his bed and is already asleep. When we wake the next *true* morning feeling alert and *actually* rested we laugh all through breakfast and decide we have really had one extra day of vacation. Sunrise, sunset all in three quarters of an hour! When I was young and neighborhood friends would stand at the back door calling me to come out to play, they would slur my already abbreviated name, Maril to Merle. Remembering that long ago when my most favorite thing was to make up stories, create new worlds and play all the parts we are calling my latest tilting of time the "Merle Day"!

***

This is our walkabout day. We explore the High Street, pay homage to King Alfred's mighty statue, stroll through wooded paths along the river Ichen as it wanders sedately through the city, bordering the impressive ruins of Bishop Wolvesy's castle and the medieval wall that partially surrounds it. We enter the Abbey Gardens, a public park, with some trepidation because of the sign which hangs quite prominently on the iron gate;

ANTI-SOCIAL BEHAVIOR

Rowdy and inconsiderate Behavior
will not be tolerated at any time

(so English)

Wandering sedately we exit the park. Again our rowdy and inconsiderate selves we approach Winchester Cathedral (oh, that tune in my head, I can't help but do a tiny dance step!). The first minster was built on this site in 648, its foundations are still outlined in original bricks in the grass next to the current building.

Construction of a Saxon church in 900 was followed in 1079 by the magnificent Norman sanctuary we see today. A guided tour fascinates with stories of the events that have happened here. One of my favorite adages; If it rains on St. Swithun's Day, July 15' it will rain for forty days, actually started here when the saint's bones were moved to the New Minster. Apparently he was not happy about the transfer which occurred on July 15, 971 and caused it to rain. I love the fact that the English remember almost everything with a plaque or a good tale.

Feeling a bit peckish we return to the Royal Oak, which is fast becoming our local, for fish and chips. A leisurely evening, early to bed and...

BEEP! BEEP! A loud, strident sound, flashing red light from small ceiling fixture! We are out of bed, scared, not sure of what is happening. Is the alarm just in our room? Could it be fire? Dan calls, half way out the door, "I'll find out."

I put on my coat and stand dazedly in the middle of the room. Frozen, *should I stay here and wait for Dan, should I go down to the lobby, does the window open if I have to jump?* This does not speak well for my intelligence but I am saved from further inaction by Dan's return, breathless from running up the stairs. He is fuming. In the lobby, when he realizes that it was a general fire alarm he starts for the staircase. When a man tells him that no one is allowed to go back to their room he yells, "My 83 year old mother is upstairs!" Fortunately, just then, it is determined that it was a false alarm and he is allowed go and rescue his doddering, indecisive old mum.

I must say Dan and I seem to have more than our share of misadventures on our trips. Panic, stupidity, real danger aside these are the happenings that we remember with laughter and tell over and over to whomever will listen. It's an ill wind...

We originally had thought to take a day-trip to Portsmouth, but Winchester still holds much to see so the next two days we continued our walkabout, savoring:

…the City Museum with its hands-on Roman section where Dan proceeds to make a most boring mosaic,

…the 1052 God Begot House, a sanctuary for anyone who had broken the Law (we write down that address),

…the Great Hall, displaying King Arthur's 'actual' Round Table whose painted medallion of the king suspiciously resembles Henry VIII and was really made about 700 years after Arthur's death!

…a lovely lunch at the Eclipse Pub--serving since 1540--of country pate, toast, small salad and ginger beer,

…Westgate, Kingsgate, where we give the Jane Austen House (where she died) a miss, I am not a fan,

…the Military Museum where Dan purchases a T shirt emblazoned with the arms of the Royal 95th Rifles Brigade, which would get him a free ale in any Winchester pub if he were dishonest enough to claim membership in said regiment.

…and each night falling asleep to the lovely sound of Cathedral bells.

Winchester was a great choice but St. David, the patron saint of Wales is beckoning impatiently. We leave next morning, "Diolch yn faur St. Swithun." On our rail journey to Conwy we have a two hour layover which we spend in a pub, comfortably seated at a sidewalk table overlooking the Queen's Hotel in Chester. Relaxed, happily reminiscing we sip our wine, grateful for this unexpected interim between adventures.

*****

"Iechyda da!" I am holding out my glass to Dan, who is high up on the Conwy Castle Wall. I am toasting him in Welsh from the comfort of the terrace on the Castlebank Hotel, our new home! York's city wall was an easy trek for me but the rough, uneven walk along the battlements of the castle here proved to be too much.

This is our second day in Conwy and I am in love; with our eyrie (three flights up) in the B&B, with our hosts, with this hilly, up and down town, with the amazing Conwy castle which is our next door neighbor, with Wales.

Henrique and Jo welcomed us to their B&B upon our arrival yesterday. Climbing two sets of stairs (even the houses are hilly here) we found our room, which encompasses in the space of an ordinary bedroom all the amenities of a hotel suite. There is a full sized bed in one corner and a single bed in the other, placed just under a skylight, an arched alcove with a window overlooking a lovely Conwy panorama, a sitting area with a comfortable chair, small table with reading material, a dressing table with mirror and, surprisingly, an ordinary sized closet which houses a toilet and full shower! Dan immediately claims the smaller bed, anticipating drifting off to sleep listening to rain pattering on the glass overhead or being able to open the skylight to hear the birds chirping in Welsh. Just like my cat, we are instantly *at home*.

A walk down the High Street to the quay seems the thing to do after settling in. Going down the steep slope is fun as long as I quell thoughts of the trip back up. The seaside quay is the center, the hub of the social life in Conwy, and what a good place to people-watch. There's a pub, The Liverpool Arms, old people chatting leisurely in small groups, children of all sizes and shapes running, jumping off the harbor wall onto the sand, parents calling, lovers smooching, a few buskers entertaining, and, on this occasion, two tired but happy American tourists about to join the throng and enjoy their take-out fish and chips. The harbor at low tide is lovely. Many brightly colored boats are resting on the shore while others farther out on the water swing lazily with the current. The backdrop to all this is that awesome castle looming like some medieval giant over the everyday, ordinary activities.

A delicious sausage, fried egg, mushrooms and toast breakfast cooked by Jo, herself, gets us ready for a visit to that imposing structure. Even though the distance is short, it involves--like almost everything else in Conwy--going down to the quay and up a winding street, this one to the castle entrance. A small white bench about halfway up welcomes my tired legs. Sitting below the castle walls Dan, who is a wonderful mimic, is inspired to begin a word for word rendition of several dialogs from *Monty Python and the Holy Grail*. Consumed by laughter, guffawing, embarrassed I beg him to stop but he is on a roll and it takes a few moments before he subsides! Amidst all the fantastic memories I have or will have in the future this will be an absolute favorite and set me laughing all over again whenever it surfaces.

"Okay, let's get serious!" between poorly muffled spurts of laughter.

We're off the bench and through the barbizon, the castle gate. I had briefly visited here with an early Elderhostel tour but remember little. How could I have forgotten this amazing sight? Eight huge towers linked by a massive 30 foot tall curtain wall encompass an Outer Ward with all the functional rooms and military apartments, even a large parade ground, and an Inner Ward housing the Royal chambers. Although roofless, the whole area is very well preserved and the uses and meanings of each section are easily determined. A medieval falconer in studded leather jerkin holding a beautiful falcon on his wrist wanders the grounds and thrills children when he allows them to gingerly touch the bird's feathers. I am reduced to being one with those children and I barely hold myself back from charging down the length of the parade ground on my snowy white, mailed stallion, lance in hand, ready for the battle! Yes, it's true that cowboys and Indians was my favorite childhood game but Knights in shining armor came a very close second.

We wander the grounds for the next three hours, in and out of fantasy, really awed and delighted by all we see in this very real but magic place. Back to the quay, this time dodging children in cardboard helmets brandishing plastic swords, who obviously have also been to the castle today. Shooing a couple of dogs from a likely looking place on the low harbor wall I sit down gratefully and watch Dan go off to the Liverpool Arms for our take-out fish and chips and mushy peas early supper. Fortified, we make the steep trek back up to the B&B. We rest for a while on the terrace enjoying the lovely view and an interesting conversation with Henrique. Ever since we have arrived in Britain we've seen display after display of little flags celebrating Queen Elizabeth's 60 year Diamond Jubilee and I ask him about the paucity of Union Jacks here at Castlebank. He explains seriously that after all he is Portuguese and, with a wicked sly smile, "*This IS Wales!*"

Dan wakes the next morning to the sound of those raindrops on the skylight he foretold. I follow soon after. This is our first rainy day and, surprisingly, it pleases us. Despite endless predictions of rain, cold, and being miserable in the British Isles, I have almost always enjoyed lovely weather here. Sunny, blue-skyed days with big puffy white clouds or soft, warm misty ones with the sun peeking out now and then stretch out the time and are the norm for me. Even today the rain is gentle without wind.

We are headed today for two special houses in Conwy; first the Aberconwy House built in the fourteenth century and then the Plas Mawr House, "one of the best examples in all of the British Isles of an Elizabethan residence." Walking on the at times uneven and squeaky floorboards, Jean, our guide at Aberconwy, takes us through the dark timbered passageways to the Hall. She enthusiastically points to a wooden cabinet and asks us to find the one flaw in the intricately carved designs. I am at a loss but Dan soon finds the well-hidden mistake. She explains that in medieval furnishings there had to have been at least one error because, "Only God is perfect." Moving to the tall dining table, set as though for supper, we observe that it was made for people to stand while eating. Jean tells us that this was normal practice but if there were an important person present or, perhaps, even the owner of the house, a chair might be provided. Hence the expression, the chairman of the board!

We opt to sit comfortably at our lunch at the George and Dragon. Mussels in a light cream and white wine sauce is my choice and they are wonderful. It is Sunday so Dan orders the Special Carvery, roast beef, gravy, mashed potatoes and, of course, Yorkshire Pudding. I am pleased when I hear him ask for a double portion of the Yorkshire and an extra plate. It's a wise son who knows his own mother!

The buildings all along the High Street, business and residences alike, are so tightly packed together that we go around the block twice looking for a structure we have passed by on every trip up and down to the quay. We finally recognize the white lime narrow front of Plas Mawr. Upon entering, we are surprised to see how wide and open the rooms are. This is truly a large house, the ceilings are high, light is everywhere coming through the tall mullioned windows even on this gray, rainy day. Fireplaces warm every room. An inner courtyard, open to the sky, leads to a lovely, colorful garden. There are brightly painted designs on the white plaster walls in many of the rooms and throw rugs on the floors. Matching the current inventory to the 1665 census indicates that many of the furnishings are original to the house. I am swept away by how much I like it and how at home I feel. With no problem at all I could easily and happily live here. That evening lying in bed, musing, half in dreams,

I dress myself in a many-layered, warm and colorful Elizabethan gown and proceed to do just that.

Next morning, back in the 21st century, bright blue skies and white clouds overhead, we are on our way to the local bus stop. Even before we get there a small bus pulls up next to us and asks, "Going to Llandudno? Hop in!" and we are off to what was once a premier Victorian Beach resort. It is still popular. No wonder that, the wide promenade spreading in a crescent along the lovely bay and sandy shore fronts quaint, old fashioned hotels and Guest Houses. They are lined up like frilly young Victorian maidens shyly waiting to be asked to dance. It is easy to picture tall-hatted, spatted gentlemen, arm and arm with their voluminously gowned, parasoled partners strolling here. There is a Punch and Judy Show that has delighted children since 1864. We had hoped to take the cable car up to a Neolithic copper mine high above the town, but the lines of people waiting are so long and we reluctantly return to Conwy, to the George and Dragon for mussels and two glasses of wine. Then home to Castlebank to pack and to bed.

"*Dolch yn faur, hwl nawr, St. David!* [Thank you very much…]

The train trip to London next morning is smooth, taking us to Euston Station and thence by tube to Earl's Court. We immediately recognize the Blackbird Pub which had been our local in 2011. A walk along the two curved blocks we call the Crescents brings us to the Ibis Hotel. We laugh at ourselves for being so excited to be back at these rather mediocre lodgings but there is something wonderful about returning to a familiar place so far from home in a foreign country. The ordinary, utilitarian room is actually warm and inviting and from our twelfth story window we see vintage planes soaring overhead, their red, white and blue vapor trails slowly fading over a magnificent view of London. Of course the show is for the Queen's Jubilee but we choose to think it is celebrating our return to London. Back to the Blackbird for scampi and two glasses of red wine. Home and early to bed.

I have been waiting almost a year to visit the Animals in War monument. An article in a magazine about this recently completed World War I memorial fascinated me and it became a mission to find and honor it on my next trip to London. So, here we are next day, map in hand at the entrance to Hyde Park, ready for this next *pilgrymmage*. Oh dear, *déjà vu*, Salisbury, 2007, map in hand on our way to Old Sarum, a half hour walk that took us almost three hours to complete. Fingers crossed, a mumbled prayer, "Please no getting lost, this time."

Ever optimistic and fortified by intention, we set out. It is a lovely day and this huge park in the middle of London is a treasure. There is so much to see and almost immediately a group of the Queen's Horse Guards in full uniform, mounted on enormous black horses begins to practice drill right in front of us. We watch for a while, then moving on we catch sight of the Serpentine, a lovely man-made--or should I say Queen-made--lake as it was constructed by order of Queen Caroline in 1730. Small colorful boats and regal white swans dot the surface of the rippling water. A large bird is sitting on the path nearby. An earnest looking Japanese man, camera in hand, is crouched directly in front of the motionless swan, gazing into its face silently mouthing words. Is he worried that it is in trouble or is he simply imploring the lovely bird to pose? A fleeting image, a small scene whose outcome we will never know. Perhaps, in my memory, they will still be there.

There are so many winding paths bordered by lush well-kept greenery or tall unkempt grasses, trailing this way and that through the park, and I think we wander every one. Stopping at a small café for a snack and a cappuccino, I ask the way to the Animals in War monument, double checking, recalling our penchant for getting lost. Hyde Park is so large, filled with people strolling with their dogs, with cyclists, with summer gardens tucked away behind each twist of the path, glowing with color. As truly delightful as all this is my legs are beginning to whimper, "Sit down, sit down." A bench, a chair, an upturned bucket, there is nothing and nowhere to sit! As Dan, whose legs are much younger and stronger than mine, heads off to see the Prince Albert Memorial, I am quickly learning the art of *tree leaning*. At first cautiously and soon boldly I begin to perfect my skill at finding slightly bending trees upon which I lean gratefully. It's amazing how restful this can be.

On to Speaker's Corner where I mount an empty soapbox to harangue an invisible crowd. Marble Arch is next. Oh, at last we see it, there on the edge of the park, horses, mules laden with packs, dogs dodging the hoofs caught in the moment, all in bronze, in front of and through a short curving stone wall engraved, " They Had No Choice." I had thought that it was a World War I memorial, but not so. It honors all the animals from all the 20th century wars, even the glowworms that shed their tiny light so men could read their orders in those horrible, dark trenches in World War I in France. There is a carrier pigeon depicted, as well as elephants and camels. I read that eight million horses died during the Great War alone. There is something slightly wonderful about a people who honor their animals so, and I am touched.

Crossing a wide, busy street we find ourselves back in the heart of London. Mayfair, Grosvenor Square, Berkeley Square all lined with upscale hotels, the American Embassy, Bond Street, Oxford street where windows are aglow with precious items much too expensive to have price tags. At last, Piccadilly Circus and the "Two Chairmen" pub that actually has chairs in which to sit. There is a small blackboard on the wall next to our table and I can't resist chalking a *Kilroy Was Here USA*.

No rest for the weary, St. Martin's in The Fields is next. There has been a church on this spot since 1222 and probably much before. Up until recent times it was surrounded by open fields, hence the name. Now it is an integral part of Trafalgar Square famous for music programs, but particularly for its work with and care for the homeless. A silent bow of thanks and we are on our way again.

Westminster is much too crowded so we tube to Earl's Court station, the Blackbird for scampi, trudging along our Crescents, The Ibis, and bed by 9:00. Dan tells me next morning that as we sat tucked up in our beds, recalling the long day and almost endless walk, sudden silence caused him to look over and see me, mouth open, in mid-sentence, fast asleep!

Up on a balcony, richly dressed, arrogant King Charles I is looking down on the square below, loudly arguing the divine right of kings with a shabbily garbed soldier, one of Oliver Cromwell's revolutionaries! Tourists are crowding around taking sides. I turn to the fellow beside me and whisper, the spoiler, "Charles loses the argument, the crown and his head in the Civil War of 1648."

We are in the courtyard of a huge group of stone buildings that comprise The Tower of London. Heavy, massive and forbidding it was constructed in the 1070s on the orders of the Norman, William the Conqueror (or William the Bastard, if you prefer). It was to be his statement to the defeated English that he was their true and lawful sovereign. They got the message and for the next 900 years this iconic structure housed first the royal apartments, then a prison for treasonous enemies of the monarch. Anne Boleyn lost her head here and those *poor little princes in the tower* disappeared forever in its environs. It held the royal zoo for a time and the crown jewels are still guarded here. The Beefeaters, members of a special regiment appointed by her Majesty, Queen Elizabeth II explain The Tower to the hordes of tourists who now flood the grounds. Another very important task for one of these Beefeaters is to ensure that the six ravens who wander the grounds are never allowed to fly away. The Raven Master, who zealously adheres to the ancient legend, "If the ravens leave the tower the Kingdom will fall," hedges his bets by clipping one of each of the birds wings. Despite this precaution an emergency sometimes arises. A while ago Raven George had to be replaced for eating television aerials and Raven Grog was last seen outside an East End pub.

When we arrived here I chose to go on a guided tour but Dan opts to explore on his own. Meeting up later, sheltering under a tree in a drizzly rain, sharing our experiences we decide to visit the White Tower together. This impressive stone building is the center of the Tower of London. We see its large collections of armor, medieval weaponry, the Line of Kings exhibit with its life-size figures of particular sovereigns and their particular horses. Dan discovers a display case which contains the actual sword that Henry V wielded at Agincourt! *God's body*, I can feel the rush of air as Prince Hal and his Knights gallop by followed by those amazing English long bowmen who secured the day! "For *England and St. George!*"

Pause, while I catch my breath.

If I had been here as a child, I really don't think I would ever have left. I catch a sight of Dan's eyes shining with excitement, and I know he is feeling the same!

Back on London's streets, almost wondering how we got there, we find ourselves in front of Ye Olde Cheshire Cheese, the pub that we visited in 2011. The round sign that hangs above the door reads, "Rebuilt 1667" and must have been hung the year after that incredible fire that destroyed so much of London in 1666. We enjoy a late lunch in the basement bar area, three flights down. When we leave Dan opens his jacket covertly to show me a menu he has quietly lifted/stolen. *God's eyes*, like spoon stealing mother, like son.

The day has been so full, so rich, so tiring but there is still one more special place to see. Off on the tube's Bakerloo Line, Mind the gap, to 221b Baker Street. Sherlock and Watson are not home but we leave our calling cards and wander through the little museum and shop enjoying all the Holmes memorabilia.

Along Fleet Street, through the Inns at Court, strolling the Victoria Embankment Gardens by the Thames brings us to Westminster Station and home to Ibis's George the Dragon pub. Over chicken wings, cider, wine and chips we recall our past visits to London and marvel at how differently we spend our time here than many tourists do. This is a city famous for its excellent, trend-setting theatre and most visitors put tickets to the latest plays high on their agenda. I love the stage, fondly remembering *Les Miserables* and *Phantom of the Opera*, which both began here, but Dan and I revel in history, the bold famous past but also the tiny bits and pieces we search for and find down obscure alleyways or behind tumbled down ancient Roman walls. By evening when all the lights go on and the streets are packed with excited, night-time people we are tucked down in our local pub or in our warm comfortable beds, resting those tired legs and enjoying again in memory every event and experience of the day. There is also a few moments before sleep when we let in the anticipation and excitement of tomorrow....Canterbury!

England's premier cathedral is truly awesome. Tall, imposing, almost blocking out the sky as we approach it next day and stand up close; big brother to its gentle little sister, St. Mary Ouvierie tucked away in Southwark. Because it is so large, overwhelming, we opt to explore using the audio tours. Dan is an expert and before long he disappears down some aisle, into a murky chapel, leaving me, as usual, fumbling with my electronic guide. I am so inept with these things and I disconnect before long. Relieved, free now to wander as I will and enjoy it all on my own terms! What a great surprise to find that I have actually stumbled upon the treasure. In the north transept, a small altar marks the place where Thomas a Beckett was murdered in 1170.

This somewhat obscure area, off the main body of the church, is *The Martyrdom*, the sacred ground that brings pilgrims from all over and all when to touch the stones and remember when four errant knights defied the sanctuary of the altar and slaughtered Archbishop Thomas, believing they were following King Henry II's wishes. "Who will rid me of this turbulent priest?"

Dan is at the door looking awestruck. He moves in closer and we stand together silently picturing that bloody scene and honoring stalwart Thomas who died defending the Church.

I wonder what day it was or what the weather was like when Chaucer's somewhat motley crew of pilgrymmes finally reached Caunterbury Cathedral and stood, exhausted but exalted, in front of this altar where Thomas a Beckett was foully murdered. I can feel the Yoeman, the Wife of Bath, the Miller, the Reeve, all of them jostling each other, pushing to be the first to bow and pray.

I have my own epiphany.

We have *wended*, made *our pilgrymmage,* and found our Canterbury, touched the feet of the martyr and wished him well. Now, free of those fictional, noisy, tale-telling pilgrymms we may wander as we wish. A supper at the George and Dragon of fish and chips, mushy peas, and sticky toffee pudding feels like a celebration!

***

This is Dan's day and he has a plan for us, which begins with a walk across London Bridge to Southwark, the other London, once the step-child of the fancier, more sedate city on the north banks of the Thames. Southwark was home to prisons, brothels, the poor, the outcast, and, of course, theatres. It also has been since early medieval times the southern entrance to London for people traveling to and from the continent. The broad and well-traveled Borough High Street was filled with pubs, ale-houses and coaching inns. A 1540 map of the road indicates a riot of these watering-holes lining it on both sides. The White Hart and the Tabard, from whence Chaucer's pilgrymmes began their journey are marked. Times have surely changed, Southwark is now an exciting, upcoming, modern area and those ancient, noisy, bawdy pubs have all but disappeared. One remains, the last coaching inn in London; The George is still welcoming travelers and locals alike and will figure large in our coming day, but that is not where we start.

We walk across London Bridge, and at the south end just under the place where once traitor's heads were gruesomely displayed Dan takes us down an almost hidden winding staircase to the streets below. It is so crowded with modern buildings that it takes a moment to see that we are standing in front of a small yard filled with people sitting on the grass or at well-worn picnic tables, talking, eating, relaxed. Fronting and almost enclosing this yard is the church of St. Mary Ouverie, Southwark Cathedral. For a couple of pagans we do love cathedrals, and this one is special. It has always been an integral part of Southwark life and its people. We are greeted warmly by a volunteer Guide who offers to answer any queries we might have. I mention that in all of the churches and cathedrals we have visited there is a screen that sets the high altar and priests off from the worshipers. I do not see one here at St. Mary Ouverie and wonder why. A smile, a simple reply, "There never has been one." Why am I not surprised? An excerpt from the Dean's message in the brochure explains: "It is not power, pomp and wealth that mark out Southwark's tradition, but care for the sick, poor, imprisoned and uneducated people of south London." A screen would have cut them off from immediacy with their God and Southwark would not have it so.

We are invited to wander the choir, small chapels, and the nave south aisle with its Shakespeare memorial and stained glass window depicting all those wonderful characters that he created. Oh, I had forgotten that Shakespeare's theatre, the Globe, was here in Southwark, where he lived and worked. That the winding narrow streets outside, the bankside of the Thames, the George, were all part of his everyday! This cathedral would have been his church, and while perhaps he wasn't much of a regular church-goer his feet walked where I am walking and I am filled with awe! From a family of prolific readers and talkers, I love words and this amazing writer who caught them, who invented them, turned and twisted them into a most profound and delightful mirror in which we may see ourselves has my heart. For just this once I am out of words and we leave this very special place with a five pound donation from Dan and a silent, "Next time."

On our way to the George Inn for a refresher snack, we walk through the Borough Market which has been here since 1014. The stalls and tables piled high with breads and cheeses, specialty dishes from all over the world, tempt us. The smells alone could  make us stay but we resist with a promise of a return. Dan has a surprise for me. Although he is not sure where to find it he leads us around a few corners and there it is tucked away on an almost forgotten London back street, a long rusty iron fence festooned with ribbons, flowers, jewelry, bits of poetry, full of color. It is amazing. Coming up close we see there is a medallion attached with a legend Cross Bones Graveyard. In medieval times this was an unconsecrated graveyard for prostitutes or "Winchester Geese." By the 18th century it had become a pauper burial ground, which closed in 1853. Here, local people have created a memorial shrine.

THE OUTCAST DEAD

Behind the fence there is a plot of rough unkempt and untended stony ground. It looks forlorn, but here and there are new plantings, shrubs, and flowers. Debris has been swept up into neat, small mounds ready to be carted away. A lost place surely but absolutely denied by that riotous, burgeoning display all along the fence. These gifts of love are from ordinary people, some working to save the area from a developers shovel, others perhaps just passersby, but all touched by the desperate, tragic lives of the prostitutes who once lay here. They were sponsored by the Bishop of Winchester in the 1500s. He collected their dues but refused them burial in consecrated ground because "they were sinners." They were called, even then, "the Bishop's Geese."

On a casual evening stroll in late November, 1996 a wonderful local poet, John Constable, in his alter-ego as John Crowe was visited by the soul of a medieval whore, "The Goose". She told him their story and pointed out this graveyard which had been lost to history. During recent excavations for an extension of the Jubilee tube line, thousands of skeletons had been unearthed here. The Geese were back, welcomed by John Constable and scores of people who now know the story. Who come, as we do, to tie offerings on the fence to honor the lost souls, show them they are no longer debased and forgotten. My bracelet of chunky blue stones tied with a bright red ribbon joins all the others.

Moved by the discovery of Cross Bones, still talking of the Geese, we arrive at The George. Choosing to sit outside in the coaching area now filled with tables and benches instead of the long ago horses and carriages, we drink our ginger beer and cider and begin to anticipate our next adventure. We have a date at 2:00 this afternoon with his royal Highness King Henry V at Shakespeare's Globe Theatre which I now know is just a few blocks away from where we are sitting.

A walk along the Thames brings us to the Globe, up the stairs, through slender iron gates portraying the animals, birds and plants mentioned in Shakespeare's plays, to door number 3 and to the absolutely best seats in the whole theatre. Lower Gallery, Bay H, B36 and B37, squarely center stage. The performance begins with the costumed actors singing and dancing on stage, just as all Elizabethan entertainments began. Before there were indoor theaters plays were performed outdoors, in country parks and inn-yards, and this was probably a way to get the attention of a possible audience. Indoors, tickets purchased in advance has made passing the hat no longer necessary, but here at the Globe, the tradition of actors playing rude instruments, singing and stomping around the stage persists. I must say I like it, it creates a feeling of excitement, anticipation and certainly focuses attention.

"Oh for a muse of fire," these wonderful words from Shakespeare's play, *Henry V,* first performed in the spring of 1599 at the opening of the Globe theatre, open this new production as well. Originally spoken by Chorus, one man, this afternoon we are surprised to be welcomed by a woman. She is sitting slightly off to the side of the stage, comfortable, easy in her manner. Rising she walks closer to us and in a natural, friendly voice exhorts us to "Piece out our imperfections with your thoughts," asking that we people this "wooden O" with kings, with battlefields and horses, "turning the accomplishment of many years into an hour-glass." It is hardly necessary to request this because Shakespeare's words, his phrases and the excellent actors that give them voice carry the audience wherever and whenever they require. It is magic and it works, every time.

Henry's St. Crispin's Day speech, "we happy few, we band of brothers" is usually done in a loud , heroic voice and manner, but today *our* Henry moves quietly among his men speaking in a proud but measured, almost thoughtful tone. Those famous oft quoted words become new, fresh, spoken by a real man on the eve of a crucial battle sharing his feelings and belief in a victory with his soldiers.

The entire performance, even the sometimes silly comedic scenes, is seamless, wonderful and when, at the end of the play, those great actors race back on stage to dance and stomp and sing I want so badly to jump up and join them. Celebration.

Back to The George--"Shakespeare's pub", where else?--for dinner. This time we sit inside on the second floor next to a small fireplace. Remembering the luscious, tasty mussels in a wine and cream sauce I had in Conwy I order them again here, and I am not disappointed. There is so much to talk about. This next-to-last day of our trip has been magnificent, one exciting experience after another. We speak over each other, interrupting, playing at one upmanship in who remembers what, skipping from one episode to another until we slowly fall silent and just grin like Cheshire cats at each other.

Dan still has so much expectation and energy left and is already planning for one last walkabout through his hometown of London tomorrow. I think I may need our last day to pamper my weary legs, absorb and reflect on what our lovely pilgrymmage has been all about. Early next morning I wish Dan, Godspeed as he takes off around our Crescents into his London adventure.

I bring my journal up to date, organize all the souvenir bits and pieces and do a little packing. I'm really just slowing down, sort of catching my breath, it feels good. The minutes grow longer, time is stretching and I am relaxing like the cat. After a midday snack, I read more of Bill Byson's *Shakespeare*, even take a short nap. Pulling a chair up to the window I savor that magnificent 12th story view of London, my eyes wandering from one landmark to another, recalling. I am filled with wonder at what we have done and seen and lived! This pilgrymmage was so full of special places and experiences. Just under the surface of all the laughter, excitement and awe, it really feels like a pilgrimage to the rich, exciting

British past. People we had only read or heard about became three dimensional, in color, almost alive and if I try really hard I can just about hear the soft, rough sounds of their Old English tongue.

I hear Dan using his key, now he's coming through the door, he has his camera up to his face and, mumbling softly, is taking my picture as he walks in. This, the end of hours of filming much of all that he has been seeing and experiencing. An amazing man, my son is sharing his *walkabout* with me. There is also a running commentary, naming the buildings, places he sees and, absolutely memorable, over it all, the lovely sounds of the church of St. Mary-le-Bow bells! I haven't missed a thing.

One last meal at the Blackbird, almost hiding in the back room of the pub trying to find some escape from the noisy, shouting, drinking fans of a crucial soccer game on the TV. Dan is fleshing out the adventures I've seen on the camera. The images of the tube trips showed only feet because he was afraid someone might misconstrue his taking pictures and "punch the bloke!" He went *mudlarking* just like those ragged, homeless boys who scavenged in Victorian times. Traipsing along the wet and muddy shores of the Thames, as they did, he found treasures, broken bits of long clay pipes, old coins, and handmade nails. The miles he had walked today begin to slow his speech and, I fear, the rest of the glorious stories will have to wait until another day. For the last time we *wende* down the Crescents back to the Ibis.

Next morning, with a heartfelt thanks to the Saints, Swithin, David, London's St Paul, Canterbury's Thomas a Becket, to three cathedrals, to Chaucer's haughty, naughty pilgrymmins, Conwy's quay, the Bishop's Geese, Henry and his bowmen, and everyone who smiled and welcomed us we bid "Grammarcy, God eow gehelde, fare thee well."

What a marvelous gift these yearly trips are, Scotland, Wales, England, each filled from the first to the last moment of the last day with adventures that stretch me until I feel that I am three feet wide and ten feet tall. So alive, changed from who and what I was yesterday, each day, more real, more filled with love, with gratitude for this awesome world that opens its arms to me and, like Buddha, says. "Ehi psya."

"Come and see."

"Heere taketh the makere of this book his leve"

Geoffrey Chaucer

At home in Scotland…

The Grand Tour

BLAM! The tire hits a rough, jagged piece of macadam where it had spilled over at the edge of the road, cooled and never been trimmed. Camille tries deftly to avoid it on the turn but the narrow country road leaves no space. We limp a short way further on and shudder to a stop.

Sunday afternoon, 4:00, rural outskirts of Oban, 97 miles from Glasgow, Scotland UK. A flat tire! David opens the truck, "There's no spare!"

Further examination reveals a kit with a very peculiar looking needle-like tool and instructions in French, as the car is a Renault. But, wait, turning the page he finds those same directions written in English. Small comfort, the kit is only for sealing a narrow puncture and not the tear our poor tire has experienced.

"I don't understand, we're really stuck, you have to help us!" Camille is already talking to the rental company in Glasgow."NO OFFICE closer than Glasgow open? Why?"

How could we have forgotten that the Sabbath is holy in much of Scotland, requiring closure of many services and businesses. Among them car rental companies apparently. Much conversation ensues but does not bring any better news. We must somehow get the car back to Glasgow to exchange it for another one. Next call is to Sandy MacArthur, our Bed and Breakfast host who is fast becoming the hero of the day. He arranges for a local truck and driver to pick up David, put the car onto an attached trailer bed and drive back to Glasgow. Sandy will come and pick up Camille and me and drive us back to civilization.

We feel a little guilty and really bad as we drive away, leaving David standing somewhat disconsolately next to the crippled car. No way of knowing how long he will have to keep vigil.

Bless Camille, she has brought two lovely bottles of wine in her luggage, one for our hosts and one for us. Back at Alt Na Craig, our bed and breakfast, we waste no time opening ours and relax for a bit before setting out, walking, of course, to the highly recommended restaurant close by, The Temple of the Sea. Small, perched at the top of a sloping lawn that leads down to the shore it provides a spectacular view. Despite the fact that the building once housed the toilets for the Yacht Club, the renovated, up-to-date ambiance, decorations and luscious seafood smells assure us we will have a lovely meal. Wine, the most perfect, tasty oysters I have ever eaten, halibut, a lobster for Camille, a crusty, creamy, overflowing Pavlova for dessert and we have almost forgotten poor David's travail in the wilds of Scotland!

The walk back to the B & B, allows us a good view of the lovely house. There are benches artfully placed about the lawn, and on the top of a small rise there is a wooden deck replete with comfortable chairs and a spectacular view of the harbor and beyond. We sit a while, trying to pull together this jigsaw puzzle day which really begins three days ago with our early morning arrival in Glasgow...

Calmly, surely, "Look right, remember look right." My son and daughter-law, David and Camille and I have just landed in Glasgow airport, picked up our rental car and Camille is driving in morning rush hour traffic, on the left side of the road of course!

David is the navigator "See that red car, turn as they do. Turn left, look right." They are a great traveling pair, driving, they switch off pilot and copilot functioning as one person. I settle into the back seat, sleepy but confident and secure knowing that this 180 degree swing from a logical, obvious choice to drive on the right is no match for my clever children.

Arriving at the Argyll Hotel we delight in our room with its bright red chandelier dripping with beads and tassels. Drapes, bedspreads are all in plaid and there is a plaque on the wall which states this is the Clan MacPherson room. Displayed prominently on the door is an embellished motto, "Touch not the cat without a glove." Chuckling, we assume this is a bit of Scottish humor but are soon told by our mildly offended concierge, "This is the true ancient motto of a proud clan!"

Adhering strictly to the ancient motto of the Restione clan, "you must stay awake for the whole day following a re-eye flight," we head off to our first adventure, breakfast in the original Charles Rennie Mackintosh Tea Room. Mackintosh was an architect, designer, water colorist and artist who lived and worked in the Victorian era, 1895 to approximately 1913, but who developed a new and exciting style in all those fields. Turning aside from the fancy overblown Victoriana, his work combined simple classical forms  influenced by the Arts and Crafts movement, borrowing from the then new interest in Japanese works. Austerity is relieved by flowing forms of roses and lovely silhouettes of young women.

Yes, it is hard to describe but I love his work and am so excited to be here on May 31, 2013, having breakfast in the first of a chain of tea rooms he designed and decorated.

Replete with salmon, brie cheese, toast, coffee and good conversation we are on our way to The Glasgow School of Art, Mackintosh's masterwork, still in operation teaching each new generation of artists and architects. The students are having exams today so unfortunately (for them and us), we will not be able to see the interior rooms. A visit to the gift shop and an abbreviated tour of the outside is informative and fun.

Walking and bussing it today, we have opted to leave the car behind. David is again the navigator. We are following a "walking tour of Glasgow" suggested by Rick Steves, the guru of travelers. Does he mention that it is also a climbing tour up and down seemingly endless steep streets? No matter, there is so much to see.

On the way to the Cathedral we stop to rest a moment in St. George's Square. Looking up I see an imposing statue inscribed Sir Robert Peel. Showing off my knowledge of trivia I announce that British policemen are sometimes called Bobbies because Sir Robert created the first organized Metropolitan Police. Scoffing, David is verbally doubtful until he checks his cell phone and finds out that, guess what. Mom is right. Impressed we move on.

Everyone must know by now that I truly love cathedrals and Glasgow's paean to St. Mungo, patron saint of Glasgow, is full of beauty, history, folklore and Sottish magic. We are delighted when a friendly guide, wearing a flowing robe over his full Scottish regalia, offers to share the intriguing, homey stories as well as the majestic tales of this awesome place.

St. Mungo, meaning 'good friend,' was a priest ordained in 550 AD. He was asked to find a proper burial site for a holy man, St. Fergus. The cart carrying the body was pulled by two wild bulls who were commanded to find the final resting place. They stopped near a spot called Glasgui meaning *dear green place*. St. Mungo buried Fergus and built a small church in the nearby village, renaming it Glasgow, thus becoming the future site of the Cathedral."

Saint Mungo wasn't finished yet. He figures very large in the stories that make up the city of Glasgow's ubiquitous motto displayed on buildings, in shop windows and on banners throughout the city:

> "Here is the bird that never flew.
> Here is the tree that never grew.
> Here is the bell that never rang.
> Here is the fish that never swam."

Listening to our guide's explanation of the motto's four bewildering sentences:

> Before it could really fly, St. Mungo's tame bird was accidently killed by some students. The saint breathed life back into the fledgling and it flew.

> Some students put out the fire when St. Mungo fell asleep. It being

> winter, no wood was readily available so he broke off a frozen branch,

> prayed over it, starting the fire.

> The king of Cadzow gave a ring to his queen who then gave it to her knight lover. The king, suspecting, stole it back from the sleeping knight and threw it into the river. St. Mungo caught the fish that swallowed the ring and recovered it.

> The bell was to have been rung as prayers for St. Mungo's soul but was not found.

I am totally bewildered, but the guide seems completely satisfied that these bits of whimsy actual mean, "Let Glasgow Flourish."

In a small room just off the main body of the Cathedral, there is another fascinating display: a small carved ladybug which commemorates a patrol by a torpedo boat in 1943 in the North Sea. Apparently a ladybug alighted onto the charts they were using. It was decided not to shoo it away but to change course. In so doing they avoided many dangers.

I know this is making little or no real sense to modern Americans but somewhere in the mystical, fey Celtic soul of the Scottish mystique it is clear. I am envious of that ancient spiritual world in which one sees wonders and meanings that I will never comprehend. Bewildered, I, nonetheless buy a tiny ladybug pin as my small attempt to enter that world.

Back in the 21ˢᵗ century we are suddenly aware of how tired and hungry we are and get a bus back to the Argyll. David sets out scouting pubs in the area that might have Scottish music. Camille and I decide to explore our own hotel pub. After almost being crushed in the door of the tiny, somewhat antiquated elevator, we find the dining area. It is a bit early and no patrons are here yet, but we speak to the bartender and take a look at a menu, which seems okay.

"We don't have a set musical program here," the bar tender offers, "but sometimes people come by with their instruments and we end up having a Ceilidh!"

We tell him how much we would like that.

"I'm fine with eating fish and chips here." David has returned and we order our meal. People begin to wander in greeting each other and us as well. Some of them are carrying musical instruments, and following the main meal a couple begin a simple Celtic tune. Great. A woman from a neighboring table tells a mystic story of a girl turned into a Silky, a young man begins a dramatic poem in Gaelic but falters before he gets to the end. Not professionals obviously but good effort and we applaud although we have not understood a single word. We have a feeling that the bartender has called up some of his friends to come and entertain the Americans! As the music picks up we discover a terrible, ungrateful truth; we are exhausted. My eyes keep closing and I see Camille and David fading fast. Touched by the effort of the musicians we struggle to stay awake, but before long we have lost the battle and shamefacedly creep away to our room. Being very careful to not touch the cat without a glove we are asleep in moments.

Gratefully refreshed, having slept well, we are up early the next morning. Breakfast, a 45 minute train ride and we are in Edinburgh. I have been here four times in the past, starting in 1953, and in two, possibly three of those visits I have tried to tour the Palace of Holyrood House. This is the official residence of the British monarch when in Scotland, but when they are not in residence it is open to the public and is a favorite tourist destination. On these former occasions it has always been frustratingly closed.

Holyrood is situated at the bottom of the famous Royal Mile, a long sloping avenue from Edinburgh Castle down to the palace, lined on both sides with endless, tiny shops filled to the brim with Scottish paraphernalia and souvenirs. I have faced its lures so many times it seems like my local Cape May Washington Street shopping mall. Faces averted from temptation to look or buy, we are on our way down the Royal Mile to explore the now open Palace.

A beautiful setting, impressive gateway, soaring Abbey ruins that I believe might be the remnants of the fourteenth century Holyroodhouse and lush gardens are a lovely lead in to the current palace constructed in the1670s. We buy the audio tours and for once I am able to follow the recorded directions. Room after tapestried room of gorgeous settings tell a history of extravagant rulers. The Mary Queen of Scots apartment is a particular delight and the small, narrow room just off her bed chamber where her private secretary, David Rizzo, was peremptorily and lustily stabbed fifty six times by her husband's men is a favorite with tourists.

As we finish our tour and are walking through the forecourt we hear loud, raucous voices coming from a small side street. Approaching gingerly we see a very modern sight. A protest apparently, there are barricades on either side of the roadway and angry, gesticulating groups of people are being held behind them by the police who are striding back and forth, telling everyone, "Calm down, no bad language, stop it!" Oh, how English. David and Camille pull back out of sight. They both do work for our government and are concerned about getting involved. Not so, me. I get close to a woman behind one of the obstructions. She appears to be more subdued than her compatriots. Trying to be calmly efficient like a journalist I ask, "What are the issues here?"

Face contorted, in a sudden rage she shouts, "They're Nazis!!"

"Communists, rotten communists!" from the other side. I retreat.

Searching for some calm and quiet, we stop to visit Edinburgh's St. Giles Cathedral. What a lovely church. We revel in the medieval carvings in the famous Thistle Room. Above each imposing chair we see wooden figures, a dog with a bone, a jaguar, a baying hound, a bird, each one a special signature for the knight who sits there on special visits of the queen. Tucked high up in a corner about ten inches high is a carved angel playing a full set of bagpipes!

As he has done in the past, David declares he is now off to the Castle to visit the War Rooms. Camille has discovered a hidden treasure somewhat off the Tourist Trail, the Writer's Museum, which is just around the corner. We delight in the quiet, almost reverential atmosphere honoring the works of Walter Scott, Robert Burns and Robert Lewis Stevenson. This last illuminated my childhood with his *Child's Garden of Verses*. Whispering my favorite, *The Lamplighter*, I thank this man for his lovely words.

"Oh my," it is raining as we reenter the street, well, misting really the way much rain happens in Scotland. Even so it's uncomfortable and we look for refuge. Finding it in a small attractive restaurant displaying in its window bottles of every color and design, called

The Whiskey Room. Settling into a booth we relax and Camille calls David to tell him where we are. We are welcomed by a pleasant young man who places a tiny glass of whiskey before each of us, explaining that this particular drink comes from Islay in the Hebrides inviting us to sample. I've been there. I think it may be the island where there are more deer than people, no matter, I sip despite the fact that I literally hate whiskey. I know that Camille really enjoys it and turn to watch her delight. She faces me, her face contorted, **"NASTY."**

How could I be so wrong? David loves Scotch Whiskey. He is building a fine collection. I suppose I just assumed that Camille favored it also, but now I will never forget that explicit, passionate word which so matches my own feeling.

David finds us. Making faces, laughing we gladly push our glasses in front of him, he, pleased, downs them happily. Time for a snack, I order Haggis Spring Rolls which are delicious and make up for the awful liquor.

Home to Glasgow, a late dinner in an Indian restaurant, scallops, lentils and pecoras. Lying snugly in bed recalling all that we have done today, I store the memories, slip away and fall asleep.

Bidding goodbye to that dangerous cat the next morning and being told that the weather today will be the best of the year we are on our way to Oban and to Mull and Iona the following day. It is a very scenic drive. We are inland rather than along the coast and the winding, mostly country roads are rich and green and lined with soft Scottish woods. A brief stop at Inverary Castle allows us to tour the gardens, take pictures of the gorgeous flowers and wonder at the 25 or so Ferraris neatly lined up in the parking lot, must be a convention!

The trip is 97 miles long which gives us time to reflect on the unexpected beginnings of this newest adventure. This is only the second time since 1997 that I've been on a trip with my son David and his wife Camille. Returning from our pilgrimage to Canterbury last year, 2012, Dan and I thought about how great it would be if ALL of us, David, Camille, Pamela, Dan and I could go on an adventure together in 2013. We began a no-holds-barred active operation promoting the idea, cajoling the Restione Clan to get on board and make plans.

Ah, "the best laid plans of mice and men gang aft aglay" wrote the Scottish bard, Bobby Burns and he was so right. As much as Pamela wants to go she has recently gotten a new, special job and promising to do so the next time, opts out, feeling that she really needs to stay home. David and Camille, however, decide to forgo their annual vacation plans and join in on the Scottish Grand Tour with Dan and me.

Camille is the planner supreme, and we unfairly take advantage of her skills in reserving rooms, berths on ferries and finding great out of the way places to visit. Promising to help, subconsciously knowing we won't, we rely on her, and of course she comes through beautifully. Thanks, as always, Camille.

One truly new aspect of the coming journey is the exciting fact that we will be in a car! Both Camille and David are experts on left-hand side of the road driving. There will be a big car this time, to accommodate four of us plus luggage. Dan and I are chicken when it comes to driving on the left so we have always been somewhat restricted in our choice of destination. This time we can explore every Scottish nook and cranny!

Planning becomes a noisy, exciting auction, "What will you give me for Orkney, The Isle of Skye, Ullapool, Pitlochery, a Gaelic poetry reading, The Broch of Guerness? C'mon, c'mon speak up bid on your favorites before it's too late, how about Smoo Cave, that's a good one and let's find out what happened to Neil McNab!"

We are truly on a roll when my phone rings on a Saturday morning in March. "Mom, its Dan. I'm okay, feeling good, and they don't think it was a heart attack..."

My own heart almost stops!

"... well they didn't at first but maybe it was. Please, mom don't be upset I got to the hospital in time, I have a couple of stents. I'm really doing well, have a great doctor."

"I'm coming."

"Please, don't mom. I'm home. All my friends have checked in, people at work are scheduling themselves into time slots, calling, making sure I'm well taken care of. If you come I will worry about you, fuss, plan your time, etc. Please, its better you love me from the east coast and get on with planning of the Grand Tour. I've already talked to the doctor about the trip and he said that by June I should be okay to go."

Oh, Dan, oh Dan, child of my heart, my baby! For a while I am lost, don't know where to put myself, what to do. He's 52 years old, that's all--so hard to believe it. I understand what he means by my not going out to Seattle so I will wait and see how it plays out in a day or two. I go online immediately and buy two copies of every book on heart attacks, one to be sent to him and the other for me. I call David and Camille and Pam and spend the rest of the day hugging my little dog, Phoebe. She knows there's something wrong and cuddles close in sympathy. Frozen for a while, wishing with all my will that it wasn't so I gradually come back to real time and begin to think of what I should do.

What a comfort the computer is. I pull up every place we have been thinking of visiting and check to see if there is a reputable medical facility, hospital or clinic nearby. I don't know how I really feel about him going on the trip. Many plans, reservations, tours already in the works makes cancelling difficult. As the days move on Dan has checkups, tests, rehab programs and his doctors give him the go-ahead for the journey; however I am so uneasy.

A month or so before the starting date, "Mom, everybody, I think I will not be going on the Tour. I want so much to be with you but I'm not sure how much I would hold everyone back or even to be honest how concerned I might be about my health. Everything is going so well, maybe I should just stick with the program and don't you dare think about calling it off. If you do I will have another attack, so there!"

Knowing how much we will miss him we nevertheless accept his decision and somewhat subdued planning continues. He wants to hear what we will be doing, seeing, experiencing so that in a different way he will not miss everything. No longer just my baby, Dan is truly a thoughtful, responsible man.

Gra agus chailleann tu, Dan. [Love and miss you.]

It is hard remembering that time, but talking about it now in the car on our way to Oban, sharing feelings and thoughts helps us all. A pause for a last bit of sadness and reflection and we are suddenly caught up in the Neil McNab story.

Some years ago David and Camille were staying at Skeabost House on the Isle of Skye, the same inn where I had stayed with Marilyn McBride in 1953. The bartender, one Neil McNab, became a favorite, witty, funny, charming, and an excellent teacher of true Scotch Whiskey ("don't drink the Irish stuff...bog whiskey!") Along with Neil's lessons David was plied with sample after sample of the best single malts available, barely finding his way eventually back to their room! The amount on his bill next morning was a meager five pounds.

I've heard this story many times but enjoy it nonetheless. It is a great example of the appealing Celtic characters found in all of Scotland, highly individual, somewhat fey, amusing and sharp and always beguiling. My countrymen, at least I like to think so. We are all hoping that he will still be behind that bar when we arrive in the Isle of Skye next week. Laughing all over again, our spirits raised, we approach our new guest house, Alt Na Craig Manor.

We have really outdone ourselves this time. Making the reservations, Camille chose to slip in a luxurious, over-the-top bed and breakfast stay here in Oban. What a lovely house, and our rooms are delightful. This is a suite; large room with an imposing and so comfortable looking bed, a few steps down into a cozy sitting room which has, for us, been made into my room replete with bed and all the accoutrements that go with it.

We meet our hosts, Sandy and Ina MacArthur, they are a lovely couple. Over a light but delicious brunch, we share some of our plans for the next few days. When we mention that we'll be visiting the Skeabost Inn on the Isle of Skye the MacArthurs share that they have been there several times. Having recently recalled his fun experience with Skeabost's gregarious bartender David mentions Neil McNabb.

"Oh yes we know him, too. So sad."

A small pause, "Sad? Neil McNab?" David is surprised.

A truly awful story emerges. McNab was driving his five year old son home from school when he lost control of the car and slammed into a tree, killing the child. Adding to the shock and devastation of the tragedy there were persistent rumors that he had been drunk. In a short time, unable to cope, he did drink too much and when his wife left him he moved on. Sandy and Ina thought he might be in Pitlochery. We will be staying there toward the end of our trip and decide we will try to look him up.

Subdued somewhat we finish our meal, unpack and are ready now for our first Oban excursion.

We are on our way to Kilmartin Glen where there is an extensive collection of prehistoric standing stones, Bronze Age relics, and ancient cemeteries. We are really looking forward to seeing the site and are excited about...

BLAM!

We have now come full circle since that noisy, scary wake-up call that cancelled the days outing. We are fated to never see the awesome Neolithic ruins. Meanwhile the sun has set colorfully over the sea and while sitting on a bench overlooking Oban's harbor Camille and I are reviewing all that's happened since our arrival. We try to get in touch with David but the call doesn't go through. In our room we try gamefully to stay awake waiting for the wanderer. At 11:15, despite worry and growing concerns I can no longer keep my eyes open and default to my little room and sleep.

Suddenly awake, looking at the clock, its 12 30, I'm really scared now. "Where could he be, what's happened?" I stagger out of bed and hurry to the next room to wake Camille. At the top of the step their bed comes in view. I can't believe it. David is safe in bed and fast asleep. I never heard him come in, talk with Camille, and finally crawl under the covers--home at last! All this while his selfish, uncaring mother went happily to sleep. Well, maybe that's a bit harsh but it is the way I feel.

All is forgiven next morning and David is full of his adventures, but before he starts--there is a bit of a fanatical gleam in his eye as he says, "A lot to tell, but I have to tell this first!"

"The fellow that came with his truck to get the car and me back to Glasgow was great, easy to talk with and I actually could understand his strong Scottish burr. He told me that he had been born and raised on the Isle of Skye. You know what's coming, don't you? He knew Neil McNab."

This is so incredible, we have been in Scotland three days and already we have met three people who **know Neil McNab** in addition to the two, David and Camille, from Maryland USA. What are the chances?

David hears again the sad story from his traveling friend. They arrived in Glasgow without incident and he was able to pick out a new car, smaller and with a spare tire. Hungry with no time to eat, munching on a couple of bags of crisps, he was able to grab from a kiosk in the airport, he began the long, lonely trip back to Oban. Remember those lovely Scottish woods we passed on our way here 14 hours ago? As the sun set they became for David a dark narrow passageway where only the road directly in front of him was visible. He bravely makes light of the end of a trip that was probably like a blind man's buff game searching for each turn and fork to bring him home!

Back on schedule next morning, all safe and aboard we take the ferry to the Isle of Mull. We drive on a mostly single lane road for an hour and a half to a small ferry that takes us the short distance over to Iona. Founded by St. Columba, weary from a sea trip from Ireland in 563 AD, the small monastery he built became the seat of Gaelic Christianity for the first few centuries before becoming part of the Roman church. We stop at the quaint Martyr's Bay eatery for a delicious scone. Looking out over the small bay, I remember Dan on that wonderful Celtic Quest washing his pentacle charm reverently in the cool waters of the Atlantic Ocean where they spread right here along the shore.

Gra agus chailleann tu, Dan.

On my last visit to this "sacred isle" I toured the Abbey, the ruins of the Nunnery, the small museum with its enormous Celtic Crosses and reproduction of the Book of Kells. Happy to recall them but free now to wander and look for MacLeod Chieftains in the graveyard, I join the ubiquitous sheep that graze among the awesome relics, totally at home.

Camille and David join me after their tour of the holy sites, and we make the short walk back to where the ferry awaits, and awaits, and awaits. Dense fog and we are socked in. I have faith but a touch of anxiety is niggling at my stomach. We have that long trip back and a reservation on the ferry to get us back to Oban, and we have promised ourselves a stop at Duart Castle. Along with our MacLeod ancestors are a few MacLeans and Duart is their castle.

Ahhhhh, the mist begins to clear and before long, we and the ferry are back on Mull. We are making good time and still on schedule we arrive at the castle. Aware of our time limitations, running becomes our mode of travel. We separate, Camille up to the Castle, David and I down to the small museum/gift shop. We pass a ticket booth on the way and the somewhat nondescript older man inside asks David if we want to tour the castle. "Thanks, but we don't have time!"

Twenty or so minutes later we meet up with Camille who is bubbling over with the excitement at having been guided through of the recently restored inside rooms by the Laird of the MacLean Clan himself. Of course, rebuffed by two uncaring American tourists the (nondescript) clan Chieftain spotted Camille and leaving his ticket booth hurried to share his 'home' with her, dropping the usual fee in the pleasure of her interest. Smart, lucky Camille.

We do make the ferry, actually the very last car to pull on board. I do not believe in guardian angels but every now and then…

A lovely meal in the EE-USK restaurant (Gaelic for 'fish'), more of those magnificent oysters, a last chat with our hosts, sweet dreams and we are off to the Isle of Skye next morning. It is a beautiful blue-skied day, as it should be for my fifth visit to the *Misty Isle*. Ignoring the modern Skye Bridge we trundle on to the minute ferry at Mallaig that by the look of it may actually be the same one that shipped Marilyn McBride and me over to the clan homeland in 1953.

Our check in time at Tigh Mo Chridh Bed and Breakfast isn't until 5:00. "It's still early, let's explore on our way?"

"Good idea, how about a map and some ideas?" David points to the tiny Scotland Information Centre right here on the quay. The tall young man running the center is helpful, and soon we are sharing stories. His name is Calum MacLeod and he is a sixth generation crofter on Skye. Bending down from his well over six foot height, he gives me a welcome hug when I share my MacLeod heritage. There are a few people waiting in line to pay for items while this tiny bit of family reunion is going on, but they smile and say, "No hurry." Calum suggests a side trip to Elgol, a small fishing village on Loch Scavaig with a magnificent view of the Black Cuillins. Camille has researched Elgol and is enthusiastically herding us back in the car.

A short stop at the Gabbro Bar in the Broadford hotel where, according to legend Drambuie was invented and we are on a roller coaster, single lane road through the foothills of the Cuillins. The scenery takes my breath away. The Black Cuillins are young mountains, sharply outlined against that incredibly blue, blue sky just like those simple drawings of children. Yellow gorse blankets and softens the lowest slopes of the range that surprises us by splitting into one-farm-wide valleys and tiny streams.

Rising to a high spot, a designated pull-off view area allows us to rest a bit. The single lane driving puts a strain on my intrepid children and this will allow hearts to calm and hands to loosen and relax. The almost unbelievable beauty and scope of the Scottish Highlands fills the 360 degree panorama. We stretch, stroll and try to express ourselves in mere language. An older couple are sharing the view. They smile, we approach and an interesting conversation begins. They are English but have vacationed in Scotland for more than 30 years. Hiking has been an integral part of their visits, and despite their age that is just what they have been doing today. We share some of our favorite spots and, inevitably, being on Skye, we mention Skeabost House.

"Skeabost? My dears, we stayed there for all the years that it was owned by the MacLeod family. Sorry to say it is now run by an off-shore conglomerate so we stay elsewhere."

This time we are ready. A pause, breath-holding, a quiet, "Did you know Neil McNab?"

"Oh, yes, of course. So sad, such a pleasant, funny engaging man, such a tragedy!"

Why are we not surprised? Three in Scotland, two from America, now two more from England. Magic, an alien from another world, the current reincarnation of *Everyman, WHO IS NEIL MCNAB?* We share our connection, our amazement at this ubiquitous man but with true British aplomb they smile and continue to change their hiking boots for regular shoes and offering us a homemade scenic DVD, bid us goodbye.

We travel for all sorts of reasons, historic sights, visiting places so different from our own, meeting people, enjoying interesting food, relaxing, learning, experiencing a wider view. For me, however, just below all those reasons is the possibility of an unexpected sojourn into a place where time or space or knowledge are not what they always seem. An upside down world perhaps, deliciously out of focus, empty of the usual, of rules and standard expectations that sets me on my ear free of judgement. He's only a man with an appealing manner and a sad story that has somehow, someway, very much out of the ordinary touched a number of disparate people from all over.

Not miraculous or awe-inspiring but, again for me, a glimpse, a small step into an alternate world where ordinary cause and effect play little part and rules don't always apply. I really love to be shaken up, tossed on my ear, made to question and accept quietly and without surprise unreasonable things. Thanks, Neil McNab.

As much as we would like to visit Elgol it is getting on toward 5:00 so we turn left now onto the Road of the Isles, to Dunvegan and Tigh Mo Chridh Guest House. After unpacking, we decide to go to the Isles Inn in Portree for a drink and dinner. There is local music, which we enjoy. At 8:00 a haunting sound begins to wail in from the town Square. Oh my, bagpipes of course! Rushing out the door we see a band of young pipers in full regalia marching in tight back and forth formations, playing to the skies. I am in heaven and, once again, totally at home.

Next day begins with the family, the MacLeods of course, visiting Dunvegan Castle with a short stop to take pictures of Rose Cottage where Dan and I stayed in 2011. A lovely walk through the extensive gardens brings us to Loch Dunvegan, into a small boat and a row around the loch visiting largely pregnant seals lounging lumpily on the shores. They bat their long, beautiful eyelashes at

us and we return the greeting by taking many pictures and wishing the soon-to-be mothers well.

Following a tour of the Talisker Distillery--not my idea but I guess when one is in Scotland, needs must--we stop for a more civilized cocktail at Skeabost House. We reminisce about our visits here in the past and, of course...

"Oh, sure I knew McNab." Casually, man seated at the bar.

This time there is no surprise, no wonder. Actually expected, we are right here where he worked and lived after all, but it does make seven people in six days who...

The weather has been so perfect, clear days, bright sun, puffy white clouds and that blue, blue sky. This last morning on Skye is no exception. An early ferry takes us across to Stornaway on the Isle of Lewis.

"I have some bad news," our new B and B hostess greets us. She shamefacedly explains that there has been a booking snafu. While Camille and David's double reservation is all set my single room is now occupied.

"It's such a busy time I had trouble finding another place for your mom, but," a big, forced smile appears, "my friend has a room!"

Placing my luggage back in the car, driving across town and there it is, tucked away behind the garage is what appears to be a large wooden garden shed, my home away from home! Putting my trepidation aside I am ready for a return visit to the Standing Stones of Callinish.

My heart is beating a bit faster as we glimpse their unique outline against the sky. Soon, strolling among stones I see Camille in the center, just one the girls, the lovely dancing young women, happy and singing on their way to market. Long ago they were turned into stone so that that lovely moment would be theirs forever.

Fanciful, but it is the way I see the stones and after all, we are in Scotland.

Uncaught by the long ago magic Camille is still here in the 21st and we wander, picking out individual stones, "This one's mine."

Camille and I have a brief skirmish over one choice but settle it amicably. Each lovely bending, reaching stone is near perfect. After a short stop at the Visitor's Centre we visit Doune Broch and the Black Houses of Gearannan, places I had been on the Celtic Quest with Dan in 2007.

Gra agus chaillean tu, Dan

Really hungry this evening. The remains of our varied, many course dinner at the County Hotel resemble an archealogical dig. Back in Stornaway I bid goodnight to David and Camille and settle in to my garden shed. Stuffing a towel around the bottom of the wooden door where the light (and possibly field mice) enters I forego a shower in the tiny but freezing bathroom, turn the electric heater to high and snuggle into the large, many quilted bed.

I wake early, Camille is picking me up at 5:30. We have a ferry to catch that will take us to Ullapool. I confess to her and David that I actually had one of the best night's sleep of the journey in the warm, cozy bed. Overnight my garden shed had changed into a welcoming comfortable room!

Ullapool, isn't that a wonderful name? It just rolls around your tongue like one of those round hard candies. Originally Ulla's Stead, a Viking farm, this small fishing village of 15,000 people is now well known as a center of the Arts hosting music and poetry festivals. When Camille was booking our trip she noticed that there was to be a Scottish Poetry Evening scheduled for the night we were visiting and booked us in. The hit of that evening was to be a famous Scottish poet Aonghas Dubh, Black Angus, and there would be music selections as well.

Our bed and breakfast, Ardvreck House, is lovely and our shared room has a large picture window that frames the town's curved, almost picture perfect waterfront. Our welcoming landlady recommends several interesting local sites and we are soon off to visit Corrieshalloch Gorge. There is a magnificent waterfall best viewed from a narrow suspension bridge that spans the 150 foot. deep canyon. It is modern and looks to be made of strong metal however, even from a distance I see a slight swaying in the wind that sweeps the gorge. Remember my foolish but absolutely real fear of heights. I opt for a walk along a scruffy hill away from danger. Soon I am on my own. Singing My Heart's in the Highlands at the top of my voice, I stop now and then to build tiny cairns, three or four pebbles piled on top of each making small wobbly towers, memory spots, so the rough, wild Highland earth will know that I was there. That Scottish fey may be part of me after all.

An ocean current, the North Atlantic Drift, splits off from the Gulf Stream bringing still cold but somewhat warmer water and a more temperate climate to the north coasts of Scotland. This lucky happenstance creates an excellent environment for flowers, and on the way back to Ullapool we stop to visit Inverewe Gardens. They cover most of the 2000 acres of the Estate. Hills, shore lines, small valleys are covered with trees and plants from all over the temperate world. The colors, the fragrances, the many varied and almost supernatural blossoms take my breath away. We have so little time to revel in this orgy of the senses. We must get back for our Poet's Evening but orgy we do for as long as we can.

"Let's have dinner in the Ceilidh Place restaurant, its right across from the town centre from where the readings will be." Camille is checking our itinerary.

"Great menu, I'm having smoked trout, small Scottish pancakes with crème fraiche and the tangy spring crab dish." Mouthwatering, I'm barely seated before ordering.

Camille thinks to check with the concierge about our evening plans. Approaching our table with a distressed look on her face, "They've **cancelled** the evening, not enough people bought tickets. I told them we've come all the way from America, we are so disappointed!"

Despite the luscious cuisine our meal is subdued. True, we've had a wonderful day, but we have been looking forward to this evening. Wait, there is a flurry of activity at the desk and by the end of our meal the concierge rushes over to the table, "The show is back on! Starting soon!"

David is finished and goes over to the hall, but Camille and I haven't eaten dessert yet. We are hurrying but David comes running back, "They're waiting for the Americans!" Gulping we follow him across the Centre and enter the hall with everyone staring expectantly at us. We scrunch into our seats with a quick glance around. It is a mixed audience of about 25 people, some young, white hairs here and there, and a mother with a little girl on her lap, everyone casually dressed. When the plans changed so quickly do you suppose there was a hue and cry in the town rounding up an audience for the Americans?

What an evening. There are a couple of young women with guitars, a man with a keyboard, and 70-year-old Aonghas is a delight. Long bushy white hair framing a ruddy smiling face, hands clutching small fragments of paper on which his poems seem to be written and that occasionally fall to the floor as he scrambles through them when he loses his place. Unfortunately most of them are in Gaelic or Scots but no matter, the songs, the sometimes screechy music, the high-flying poet are all so uniquely, wonderfully themselves that I am treasuring every chaotic moment. Oh, how I love this country!

This last Ullapool day is as beautiful and clear with bright blue skies as the last three or four days have been, and we are now on our way to Geodha Smoo to explore this largest coastal cave in Britain. There is a long sharply slanting, pebble scrambling climb down to the sea entrance. A sturdy fence curves all the way down and looks like it might be fun to scramble with the pebbles and a firm handhold on that fence, but mindful of the long, not so much fun climb back up I decide I will stay cliffside and let David and Camille do the adventuring.

I sit for a while at a stone table, tracing the old carved graffiti with my finger before wandering. I bend down to smell some of the tiny pink flowers that grow between the rocks, have a short, somewhat one-side conversation with a hairy Highland cow and enjoy the warm sunshine.

Yes, I'm sorry now I didn't make that trip down when I hear what a magical place the cave is. David and Camille boarded a small boat that glided through the shallow inlets leading to a spot where a natural hole in the far above ceiling let in a soft light wrapped in golden dust particles, spreading mystery into dark corners. Their guide regaled them with stories of fabled highwaymen who in the past used the cave to secrete their wealth and their prisoners, sometimes, *oh sorry be*, throwing those same unfortunates down the surface hole to the depths beneath when they would not pay!

We roll those lovely syllables round our tongues the next morning for the last time, bidding Ullapool goodbye and thanks for the wonderful exciting time we've had there.

Although there is a Cruise Ship anchored in Stromness in the archipelago of Orkney, this group of islands ten miles north of mainland Scotland well into the North Sea is probably not a place that many American tourists visit once, much less twice. I am visiting for the third time! As the ferry sails by the tall rock stack called the Old Man Hoy, I think he winks at me in welcome. We make landfall at Kirkwall and head through the town toward our next guest house. I am amazed to recognize the same inn where I stayed in 2004 with an Elderhostel tour! I had obviously looked at all the reservations that Camille had made for us but had not remembered the name. What I do recall, in addition to what Polruddan House looks like is the big shaggy dog, Sandy, and here he is wagging his tail as though he knows me. I have mentioned before that returning to a place you've stayed at in the past seems a bit special and so it is again. Room of my own this time, cozy and warm against the really cold weather outside.

We've been told that this part of Scotland was warmer in the past. A good thing for the Neolithic families that lived in this early, 3100 BCE, enclave of homes, Skara Brae. Hidden for centuries under sand and grass this group of stone dwellings built half underground, connected by covered walkways, was unearthed by a monstrous storm in the 1800s. This is a perfect start to our pre-historic trek through Orkney. Moving down the road so to speak, we stoop to walk through the narrow passageway that captures the sun on the winter solstice and brings its promise of warmth and spring into the chambered tomb of Maes Howe. A short trip to the Ring of Brodgar, a massive stone circle 340 feet in diameter is as awesome, windswept and magical as it was the last two times I stood silent in its stony shadow.

Gra agus chailleann tu, Dan.

Oh dear, we pull the car over to the side of the road at the site of truly important ancient ruins. So disappointed, we gaze at the lovely stretch of green lawn that almost covers this narrow isthmus. Covers also the latest very significant archeological finding, the Ness of Brodgar. Apparently, when the summer excavation finishes the sod and grass is placed back over the ancient treasure to protect it from the elements, and people. We are here out of the digging season so must use our imaginations to rebuild this newly discovered "Neolithic temple complex without parallel in western Europe."

Chilled, still halfway back in ancient mysteries we stop at the Kirkwall Hotel for a thawing drink. This plush, upscale Victorian hotel eases us quickly back into modern times and, spurred on by Camille who falls in love with the surroundings, we make reservations for dinner the next evening.

Each day it is easier to slip back in time and this morning is no exception. I have told Camille and David about seeing the Broch of Gurness on one of the earlier visits but don't remember quite what the site is like, "I just recall a whole lot of stones." Camille sees a pile of rocks on the roadside and says a bit disdainfully, "Is that it?"

I feel somewhat vindicated as we later approach the extensive sprawling group of rough half standing buildings that is the Broch. Oh my, how could I have forgotten these ruined houses, probably a temple, a fort surrounded by the remnants of a massive wall! Nearby there is a tiny Visitor's Centre and we stop to get information. The guide is helpful, filling us in with the Norse/Scottish background of Orkney. The extensive prehistoric sites here in Orkney indicate very early settlement by ancient peoples making this all but definitely the spiritual center of Britain prior to the building of Stonehenge. By the Middle Ages, however, civilization had passed Orkney by and the land was ready for Viking ownership and development. This island chain is now part of Scotland, but with a population a mix of Norse and Scottish, we wondered where allegiance lies. The Guide explains it this way. "Well, if Scotland and Norway were playing football NO ONE would root for the Vikings!"

Our next stop is a new one for me and I am very excited. The Isbister Chambered Cairn--known more familiarly as The Tomb of the Eagles--stands, mysterious and still, facing east over the North Sea towards the rising sun. On a summer evening in 1958 the local farmer was walking the sandstone cliffs looking for a stone to use as a corner fence post for the rock wall that marked his fields. He noticed that weather erosion had revealed a section of horizontal stones on the edge of a grassy mound. The structure appeared to be manmade rather than natural. His interest piqued, the fence post forgotten, he began to dig. A small stone chamber came into view along with what looked like fragments of bone. Darkness denied any further search, but Ron Simison was there, pick and shovel in hand, at the very crack of dawn next morning.

What he had discovered and carefully excavated over the next few weeks was a 5000 year old tomb containing about 30 human skulls and many bones of the Sea Eagle. Later years and more professional digging uncovered an area 10 feet long and five feet wide. The ceiling is seven feet high and was originally capped by stone slabs. Small side chambers held bones, skulls, pottery chards and stone jewelry items littered the floor. All these artifacts are on display in the Visitors Centre where we were introduced to Jock Tamson, Granny, and Charlie-Girl, three of the ancient skulls. These three were part of the 1958 excavation and spent the next 20 some years being lovingly protected from the elements in Ron Simison's closet under the stairs, but now greet visitors in the family owned Centre.

Crawling on hands and knees down the very narrow 10 foot long entrance tunnel is a small adventure. Part of the ceiling has been left open and light filters down into the chamber making it easy to see. The remains have been removed to safer homes, but we stoop and gaze into those eerie side openings, shivering some at the 5000 year old mystery. Moments of awe, of connection and for one magical split second I am actually, unequivocally a real person alive in that ancient time and place. I have a name and a love and a purpose but thousands

of years intervene and I have forgotten. I am left with a warm, fulfilling feeling of having touched a kindred soul.

Dinner that evening at the Kirkland Hotel is a treat. Lovely red wine, delicious seafood and a few luxurious hours recalling all of our exciting forays into the past is exactly the way to bid goodbye to Orkney.

Early morning takes us to the ferry, which sails the Pentland Firth to the mainland port of John O' Groats and the long trip southward to our next stay in Pitlochery.

Walking to town after settling in is everyone's choice after the drive. Of course we have a hidden agenda, we are on a mission to find, at last, that ubiquitous but elusive Neil McNab. We are constantly distracted by this lovely 'downtown' High Street with its interesting shops, however, David enters each bar we pass to ask for him. Sadly there is no trace, but we do discover a free whiskey tasting in McKay's pub. Camille has decided she will bite *this* bullet, and learn to like the "nasty" drink. Face contorted at each sip she keeps pace with David, I abstain. She bravely carries on with determination. Many sips later I drag my three sheets to the wind children to a table in the restaurant

area, stoking us all with food for the uphill walk back to our B & B. Surprisingly we make it without incident and, still giggling, on to bed.

Decorum returned, breakfast next morning is really special and our host makes

some great suggestions for the day. Following his recommendation, s we drive up into the hills surrounding the town. The Queen's View is a high spot giving a lovely view of the river and loch, dotted with small islands. Wisps of early mist soften everything into an impressionist painting. Through the trees that line the gently curving road we get glimpses of the loch. The mist is clearing now and we stop by an old stone bridge for a change in drivers. Camille bravely follows the narrowing to one-lane on-the edge-of blind-turns drive up into the high hills.

The car's back seat puts me lower down, giving me a clear look at the tree tops and the sky but pretty much blocking off my ability to see the road. I have the impression that we are flying around the precipitous curves and mountain edges. Heart pounding, fingers crossed I bless Camille silently, endlessly as we cross the peaks descending to a more sedate valley floor.

Several stops later we see a 5000 year old tree (or not), an old Victorian hotel where we are given a tour by the most obsequious, name-dropping man (he guided George Bush, Neil Armstrong, on and on) and pass a sign stating that a village had been decimated by plague here in 1448. Feeling a bit awed viewing a poem that Robbie Burns actually wrote on a pub wall, we eventually relax, have wine, and admire the ambiance of The Kenmore, Scotland's oldest hotel, 1572.

Refreshed we find ourselves on the shoreline of Loch Tay looking at a wooden pier leading out in the water to a cone shaped structure made of logs covered by thatch. This is a replica of an early Iron Age structure that could house several people, allowing them to farm the surrounding land but giving them a safe place to retire to at night or in times of peril. This Crannog, as it was called, would have been in ancient times just one of many dotting the shores of Scotland's lochs. I hold David's arm to walk over those rough, rounded logs of the pier, joining him and Camille inside. We hear a talk by a bearded young man dressed in the height of prehistoric clothing. It is smoky, dark but cozy beneath that tall cone shaped roof as we squat around the central fire away from the pens that sheltered goats, pigs and sheep. His talk about those long-ago lives is fascinating. Back on land, he demonstrates the clever tools that were used to strip the logs and construct this watery home, the Loch Tay Crannog.

A wonderful day, another wonderful day, and it is not over yet. Fern Cottage for a dinner of three salmon portions, poached, smoked and grilled, and we are off for a last stroll about this lovely town. There is a fish ladder across the Tummel River where salmon are encouraged to make their last trip to spawn. Although we are pretty much out of season we scan the site for salmon. David and I strike out but Camille is the lucky one, spotting a majestic silvery fish leaping high into the air to disappear beneath the roiling waters of the ladder.

We have trouble leaving next morning and extend our stay a couple of hours for shopping and making one last effort to find Neil. No one seems to know him. Do you suppose God knows where he is? I hope so and although I do not pray I whisper his name each night. Goodbye, Neil McNab, and *god bless*, wherever you are.

For all the times I have been to Scotland I have never visited Stirling Castle so I am excited to be here in the courtyard listening to a guide giving us the scoop on that famous battle of Stirling Bridge within sight of this fort. He is also very truthful about the flawed character of Robert the Bruce, a hero, yes, but also a self-serving turncoat at times. On the way here this morning we stopped at William Wallace's Tower and I am still enraptured by that true *Braveheart* hero of Scotland. We revel now in the castle's majestic rooms inside. A tiny six month old baby Queen Mary of Scots was crowned here after her father died. Later, for a while, she lived here with her mother, Marie de Guise, before a couple of disastrous marriages and being captured and imprisoned in England, never seeing her beautiful apartments at the castle again.

After dinner this evening Camille broaches her last bottle of wine. We sit around an iron table in the lovely back garden of our guest house chilling slowly but happy reminiscing about our incredible journey. Carol, our hostess slips out bringing us sweaters and snacks to make even this last short interlude memorable.

Gra agus chailleann tu, Dan.

Love and miss you, Dan, all day, every day. A whisper just before I go to sleep and again next morning as we pack and get ready for the flight back home.

A Grand Tour, certainly. Covering so many miles around the western, northern and eastern coasts of Scotland, visiting islands out of time, hobnobbing with ancient people making a unique, proud country, thumbing their noses at the Romans with their silly wall. We are feeling both the mystery and the everyday that surround each moment and place we've touched, rolling place names around our tongues, sleeping in garden sheds that turn magically into cozy warm rooms overnight. We've been following Neil McNab and all his friends until we lose him in Pitlochery, watched a ruddy faced Scottish poet who kept losing his place but with such good grace. I have tasted the most amazing oysters and enjoyed Camille's lovely, just when we needed it, wine.

Sixteen days? I don't think so--a trip to the moon, touching stars and comets along the way, a gentle singing fall back to earth, more like. What do you say?

Afters: Christmas 2013. Let's see, it's a rectangle, about 11 inches by 14 inches, not heavy but substantial, a large paperback, no lighter than that, wrapped in bright tartan paper! The paper, ripped, falls to the floor. Of course, it's a picture, but look, those wonderful standing stones of Callinish are painted here, slightly curved, bending, leaning toward each other just like people dancing! My lovely young women, laughing, on their way to market forever caught by the wizard who turned them into stone have been seen by someone else and caught again, this time on canvas. Camille tells of slipping here and there in the gift shop, trying to purchase the picture without my seeing, to gift me this Christmas.

Some trips just never end!

At home in Southwark…

Happy Birthday

"There was a star danced, and under that was I born"

Shakespeare

Where would you choose to be on your 86th birthday?

I choose to be right here, in Seat B34, second row from the stage, absolute center, Globe Theatre, London, UK, June 21 2014.

Noble Caesar lies bloodied at the feet of Marc Antony. Overwrought Roman citizens pepper the audience shouting, cursing the foul traitors who have butchered their god. I shiver as I am asked to respect Brutus because, "Brutus is an honorable man!"

I am so glad to be here with Dan in London again, chills running goose bumps down my arms, excited by Shakespeare's caustic, ironic, tantalizing words. This is truly my "Midsummer Night's Dream."

People have asked us why we keep returning to the United Kingdom. I set them straight at once and change that soubriquet to British Isles. My love and wish for a separate nation of Scotland is obvious here. So be it. Correction done, I pause and give thought to this question which, strangely enough, has not seriously occurred to me before. I love the British Isles, some parts more than others but, on balance, I feel truly connected. They are my heritage. My family tree goes back to the 15th century. Stories, childhood games of jousting knights, British history from ancient to modern times all have been a vibrant influence and interest in my life. Dan feels much the same. He is very lucky, however to also have a rich, Renaissance Italian heritage from his father. He will have to explore that as well someday but, for now, his British soul has sway.

We arrived from Durham yesterday. Checking in to the London Southwark Hotel, excited to have a room in the same building as the famed Anchor Pub. Checking in I mentioned that the next day would be my birthday. This information raised little comment from the busy efficient staff BUT this morning I find a birthday card slipped under the door, signed with personal wishes from the group who welcomed us yesterday. You ask why I keep coming back?

Walking to our hotel after the performance, slowly coming back from bloody Rome to a beautiful warm London evening we are relaxed, happy. A bit past midpoint in our latest sojourn we begin to recall the very beginning of this trip with calm and eventually much laughter.

There was little of either as we sat in the waiting room at Philadelphia International Airport on Sunday, June 15th. Everything up to this point had gone very well. Dan had been able to time his arrival from Seattle shortly before our flight time to Heathrow. I had found a pleasant driver to take me to the airport to meet him at our Gate. Hugs, my usual but, by now, subdued *Daneeee* greeting and we settled down for the short wait until boarding time.

I pause here for a moment to collect the fitful, scattered memories of the next 24 plus hours…

Sitting at Gate 23 Dan and I talking over each other at times, catching up on the all the news, we hardly notice that the scheduled boarding time has passed. However, when the next announcement comes of a delay we **do** notice. It isn't until the third call that an explanation is given, "Technical difficulties."

The crowd is restive but most of us are glad the airline is being extra careful of our safety. Two hours later we finally are allowed to board and settle into our seats. Another hour is passed sitting on the runway. Workmen are hurrying up and down the aisles looking important and serious. Someone, at last, responds to our questions as to the exact situation. We are told that there is a technical problem with the on board TVs! A ripple of anger and amazement travels through this captive audience—holding us back from flying to our destinations because it doesn't work on a red eye flight when most people sleep -- incredible!

As one of the workmen passes us Dan, frustrated, worn out, tired from his flight from Seattle, surreptitiously raises his middle finger and whispers a "F – you." Not very nice, but. A short time later a stewardess comes up to us, leans over to confront Dan and testily asks him if he had threatened the workman. Thinking quickly, realizing we can be put off the plane if guilty, Dan raises his thumb in the time honored up position and says, glibly, "I said, good job." Not totally convinced but maybe frustrated as well, she nods and accepts his heartfelt explanation.

We finally take off. Three hours and a half late! But this is just the beginning...

At home, before leaving, I had arranged and paid for tickets for a train ride from Heathrow to Durham, the first stop on our journey. By now, being an experienced traveler I had taken into consideration a possible delayed arrival from the States and gave us plenty of time to catch the train, BUT NOT a three and a half hour delay! Checking in at the ticket office we find that our reserved train has left a long time ago AND we must pay last minute top prices, $500.00 for the train already in the station and about to leave. Trapped, we pay and race down the platform. I am sure that I will collapse and die right there on the cement, but my robust Macleod heart is up to the challenge and I stagger into the crowded railcar. Dan has run ahead and is breathlessly pointing to an empty seat. I sit down so gratefully and he continues on to find a haven for himself.

It's a long trip to Durham and eventually we are able to secure two seats together. A snack cart comes through and bags of crisps (that's chips to Americans) become our supper, or breakfast or.... By this time we are both pretty much confused about what time it is and exhausted.

Arriving in Durham, we get a taxi to the Castleview, our bed and breakfast. At last feeling somewhat back on schedule I pay the driver and am surprised to see a stricken look on his face. He holds out the handful of Euros I had given him and says, "I can't take these!" It never ends! Of course, Britain doesn't use euros. I know that but when I changed the money at the bank I never looked to see the bills and just put them in my wallet. Dan scrounges around and finds enough British cash to pay and tip the poor man.

It is already long after our designated arrival time and we have some trouble rousing someone to let us in. We put our bags in our room and stagger gratefully up the street to Ye Old Elm Tree pub and a proper meal. There's a group of local musicians playing and for the first time in more than 24 hours we relax--at home!

Our lovely room in a gracious bed and breakfast is a welcome reward for the misadventures of travel. The en suite bathroom is pristine, glowing in white with an enormous walk-in shower. Wrapped snugly in the soft bathrobe found lying at the end of my bed I decide I want to spend the next three weeks in this haven, safe from all the vicissitudes of the outside world.

Waking the next morning from a wonderful deep night's sleep, I discover that the last two days are already becoming one of those awful memories that we will recant with gusto and humor when we get home. For now, I let them go. I am ready for adventure and all that awaits.

Finally meeting our hostess over a delicious breakfast we forego asking for directions and suggestions for sightseeing, having decided we will be real pilgrims finding our own way. Our first discovery right outside the front door is our neighbor on the right, St. Margaret of Antioch church. Small, unassuming, built of worn soft brown stones, she will become *Maggie* as we greet her each ensuing day. Beyond her modest steeple we notice the two towers of Durham's beautiful Norman Cathedral. Ah, our pole star!

We've heard so much about this magnificent building constructed almost one thousand years ago on the site of the first small, wooden White Church. That modest structure had been built to house and honor the remains of Saint Cuthbert.

There is a sculptured panel on the front of the Cathedral commemorating the legend of the Dun Cow. In the ninth century, fleeing the marauding Vikings, monks of the Holy Island of Lindisfarne off the north coast hurriedly placed St. Cuthbert's body on a rough cart and began to look for a better place to reinter his sacred bones. Many days into the mainland, frightened, lost, they saw two milkmaids searching for a wandering dun cow and followed them. Reaching a high promontory protected by a river on three sides, the cart and coffin became rooted to the ground and would not budge. Accepting that St. Cuthbert had found his special place they thanked the dun cow for leading them here and built a small wooden structure to hold the saint's remains, the first frail, humble Durham cathedral.

We have need of our own *Dun* Cow this morning. The Cathedral looks quite close, but there doesn't seem to be any direct way of getting there. Moving further into the street we see a series of sharp hills, the *ups* and *downs* as we will refer to them, between us and our desire. Needs must and off we go. At the bottom of this particular *down* is Framwell Bridge.

"Oh, look," Dan points out. "There's one of the musicians we heard last night in the pub. He's busking, playing for coins!" With a grateful smile he accepts Dan's offering of a pound or two.

We stop for a moment to look up the river then turn to face the next *up*. Somewhat winded we reach the town square. Sitting gratefully on a stone bench I am surprised how at home I feel as I look around. Of course, not only have I learned well from that cat, but the buildings that surround the Centre, some from the 16th century, all individual and unique are reminiscent of the centres I have seen on my British travels. Warm, interesting, almost with personalities they mock the cold, austere sameness of many modern buildings. No wonder I feel at home.

Refreshed, we wander down a short dark street that opens abruptly onto a large green lawn, bright in sunlight, that leads to the Cathedral. We find the Dun Cow panel and the Sanctuary Knocker on the massive front door. Anyone who uses it to knock at that door desperately seeking sanctuary is promised 37 days of protection in the church. We mark the place carefully, just in case.

What a truly beautiful whole this building is. Constructed within a relatively short time, it mirrors one awesome style, Norman, one flowing concept of beauty. Most cathedrals were in the making over 100 years or more and so reflect a myriad of styles. Awesome, magnificent, but this one has a serene continuity I have not experienced before.

Another treasure, so unexpected. The Venerable Bede is buried here! Stifle your yawns, please, he was a remarkable man and a favorite of mine. Born in 673 AD, he became a monk spending most of his life writing books on natural history, biographies of the early saints and his masterpiece, *The Church History of the English People*. This is part of the Anglo Saxon Chronicle and is the first written history of the young, coalescing nation exploding out of prehistory onto a world stage.

"So happy to meet you, Venerable, thanks," I whisper.

From the spiritual to the mundane moving several centuries ahead from our immersion in medieval splendor, we visit the Durham Museum. The humble history of the city and its people brings us back to the present. *Down* and *up* this time, we head for Ye Old Elm Tree pub. A glass of Shiraz, scampi in a basket, music and anticipation of a special tour tomorrow ends this lovely day.

I am so excited. Today is our *bespoke* tour; a private, made to order trip to Hadrian's Wall with a special guide, Tom Keating. We planned and arranged this back in the states, and both of us have been looking forward to a day with the misguided Romans who thought they could keep those Scottish barbarians walled up!

Dan built his own wall (of pebbles) some years ago when he walked The Highland Way, across Scotland alone. Sleeping in a pup tent in the rain and cold and intermittent sunshine, brave, bedraggled, but a stalwart MacLeod all the same!

Traveling in Tom's private car, we stop for our first sight of the Wall. Just off the road stretching across a green field, three stones high and four wide, walkable, and we do. It is a preview of what is to come. Seen at a distance, further on, we begin to appreciate the enormity of this ancient project. We are able to visually follow unbroken stretches over hills and through deep valleys. It is amazing how much of it remains.

Lunch under an old massive oak tree at the Roman Museum, and we are off to Vindolanda. This fort, slightly south of the Wall, actually predated it but was later incorporated into the system of forts guarding this most distant outpost of Roman rule. The ruins are extensive and we wander through them despite the heat of the day.

Catching sight of a small group of archeologists Tom calls out to ask if they have, "Found anything special today?"

"Every day! Come by later," they laugh holding up a muddy, dripping sandal.

The Museum is a treasure house of exhibits that chronicle life along the Wall. Leather shoes, jewelry, pottery, even cosmetics have been unearthed here. However, the greatest finds--now labeled officially as one of Britain's Top Treasures--are the original writing tablets. These are wooden letters written in Roman cursive to and from the ordinary soldiers. They were found preserved in deep pockets of dense, oxygen-free mires below the excavations. Painstakingly cleaned and interpreted, they make real for us these ancient people so like ourselves;

"We need more beer---"

"Will you come to my birthday party--"

"Instructions for the next day, Sir?

"I'm sending you warm socks---"

We spend the next couple of hours vicariously in the first centuries CE before the summer heat and my tired legs make Tom's car with its modern air conditioning a true refuge. The Wall, the fort, the surprisingly human ruins are all so much more than we could have anticipated.

On the trip home Tom surprises us with a stop at The White Monk Tearoom for a scrumptious fruit scone heaped with a dollop of cream! There are two further visits to Hexham and Blanchland Abbey to see their ancient churches and small quaint villages. Dan falls in love with the quiet, gentle English countryside and dreams of coming back to live as a true English gentlemen with a dog, a gun, a library filled with books, and a quintessential pub.

"Oh, Tom, this has been such a great tour and a wonderful day, thank you, thank you!"

Ye Old Elm Tree, fish and chips, wine and we are ready for bed. But, "Dan, I left my jacket in Tom's car!" However even that cannot keep me from snuggling under that welcoming duvet and sleep. Like Scarlet, "I will think about that tomorrow." But I don't have to. Leaving Castleview in the morning we find Tom waiting for us holding my jacket. He has driven into Durham with his wife and we are pleased to meet her and thank him again.

This is our quiet day, a time to collect, muse and remember. A wandering day. There is a market in the town centre and we enjoy walking in and out of the local stores and stalls heaped with "come buy me" non-essentials. I see Dan walking across the square carrying two plastic containers bulging with fish and chips to be eaten *al fresco* sitting on the stone benches. I am flooded with such a love and gratitude for my stalwart son, who two years ago had a heart attack, shattering his and my life for a while. I should not have doubted that he would take himself in hand, put all back in order and be strong and ready for another British Enterprise. Of course, but these moments when I ache with love and joy and thanks for the gift of him still sweep through me every now and then!

We wander, buy books, feel peckish around 3:00 o' clock and stop in The Shakespeare pub, have our last Durham meal and music at Ye Old Elm Tree and settle for a quiet bed, reading and reflecting.

On time, on track, comfortable, our train takes us to London the next morning. Almost like coming home, my fifth visit to this magic city. This time, however, we have opted to stay in Southwark on the south side of the Thames. This other place, for so long stepsister of greater London across the river housed prisons, brothels, theatres now is up and coming, exciting new, modern. However our hotel is part of the Anchor Pub, where Samuel Pepys stood on the roof watching the Great fire of London in 1666. Isn't this wonderful, where history is alive and living next door?

Arriving rather late in the day from our journey from Durham, we head off to two of our favorite places, Southwark Cathedral and The George for dinner. St. Mary of Ouvrie, the cathedral, is as welcoming, underplayed, everyman's as always and after a quick look-in, I pick a small, rosy flower to press in my journal and wander on to a char-grilled tuna sandwich and battered cod at The George.

Tempting smells, gorgeous cheeses, Thai food, crisp veggies, glorious spreads, Saturday madhouse, we are in the Borough Market next morning. Right in the middle of old London this has been the site of Market-Day since medieval times, and the Borough is celebrating its 1000th birthday this year. Wow, same year but I am only 86!

Still munching on a tasty snack of bread and cheese we stroll along the Bankside river walk to the Globe Theatre anticipating our attendance tonight. We are amazed to see on a low outside balcony a group of Roman-looking soldiers milling about. Oh, yes, the first performance of Shakespeare's *Julius Caesar* is the matinee today and we are witnessing actors off stage in Act I. Our turn tonight.

It's such a warm day, the buskers are out along the promenade and silver coated actors play statues for us tourists on the green side lawns of the Tate Museum. Do you think they know it's my birthday?

An early supper in the Anchor and we hurry back to the Globe. Those wonderful seats, House-center, on a level with the stage, last year it was *Henry V* who seemed to be talking directly to me. I can't wait to be eye to eye with Marc Antony, trying to stare him down. However I have a more immediate concern. Anthony Howell, who is the sergeant on TV's *Foyle's War* is playing Cassius in *Julius Caesar* and I am worried about him. I love the show and his character, Milner is a favorite so as I do with all actors that I know I feel nervous for him. I am relieved fairly quickly of this rather silly emotion as he is great, lean and hungry and perfect in the role.

Intrigue, conspiracy, assassination, betrayal, we are caught up in it all. Wearied, sobered by the tragedy. Cassius is dead, Brutus impales himself on his sword and--remember how all these magnificent plays end? Yes, the actors come to life, pick up simple instruments and DANCE across the stage. Shocked the first time I witnessed this ancient ritual, I now feel the celebration of passion and vibrant life the plays have honored and I celebrate too!

June 22nd promises to be another lovely warm summer day, fit to be the scene of my next birthday present! But that will have to wait for 2:00 this afternoon.

A short stroll along the promenade after breakfast provides us with a singular view of blue skies and puffy white clouds mirrored in the water of the Thames. Except for that brutal, cold wet week on the Isle of Skye in 2011, the weather on all my trips has been incredible. A country almost always pictured wet, misty, dark and cold has never been my Britain.

Our morning amble takes us deeper into Southwark along the Borough High Street. This busy modern avenue was the welcome-to-London access to the medieval city from Europe and beyond. Just below the traffic sounds we can hear the jostling of carts, the rough tongued myriad languages of those ancient travelers. Passing through the now silent, empty Borough Market, we visit St. George the Martyr church and loop back to the George Inn for a lunchtime snack.

What fun, we encounter a unique group of men sitting at the outdoor tables in the inn yard next to us. Pints in hand they stand up to give us a better of view of the magnificent symbols of their order. This is The British Beard Club and each one sports a remarkable hairy production sprouting from their chins; bushy, manicured or wildly free, one falling almost below a tall man's waist. The proud members of an organization that "Unites the Bearded of The British Islands" is having their yearly convention. They assure us that we are exceedingly lucky to have arrived at this auspicious time. Casting admiring glances, we concur as we leave this august group.

You ask why we keep coming back?

Its birthday present time. A two-parter, it starts with a tour of the *Outlaw Borough* given by John Constable and/or his alter-ego John Crow that takes us through Southwark's winding streets and back in time. Just for Dan and me it is less of a tour and more of a private walk. John, a wonderful poet and leader of the movement to save the medieval Crossbones Graveyard is a delight. He is so vibrant and enthusiastic. His stories of the borough's history make the past come alive and when he recites his poem, *I Am the Wind* I am thrilled.

The second part of my present happens the following evening at the Crossbones Graveyard Gate where I am asked to read my poem, *The Winchester Geese*, honoring the lost and forgotten women buried there. Happy to be back again at this special place, I think I see my blue stone chunky bracelet that I hung on the gate two years ago! This ancient cemetery and the poor souls buried here are honored every 23rd of the month by John Constable and several local people who give of their time to save the site. Progress has been made in the last few years. The plot is being cleared and a Garden of Remembrance begun. There is now a government protection in place for the next few years. The crowd this evening is a large one and they give me a nice welcome. John greets us with banjo and song, a Druid gives a short invocation and then me:

THE BISHOP'S GEESE

We know you lie, five hundred years,
cross-boned behind that iron gate.
Tight-tucked together,
so little room, so many bones.
So sweet the fresh young bodies
turned to stone.

Here on Southwark's steamy streets;
poor, bereft, you smirked and smiled
and bared yourselves as merchandise,
for gross-lipped men who pawed the virgin prize;
and paid your dues to Bishop Winchester.
He put you in his 'barnyard',
bought his golden crosses with your shame
until the syphilis destroyed what
was once fresh and clean.....
and then refused you rest in consecrated ground.
But, sisters, sinners all, your pain has made
this rough,
out-casted place...Sacred.
The stones smell sweet enwrapped by you,
We are washed and watered in your Grace.

We dress your iron fence with beads and bangles,
beribboned toys, poems, flowers to bring you joy
and set you free of guilt and shame
and show the world how wronged you were by that
infernal priest.
How cruel it took five hundred years to bring
you peace

Sweet, tattered, tawdry, bawdy, sisters all--the
Bishop's Geese.

What a glorious day!

I want to hug the whole world. I want to dance through the crooked ancient streets of Southwark, sharing the excitement and joy of being *me* ! I surely must have been born under that 'dancing star' to have the wonderful experiences that every lucky day of my life brings.

I fall asleep replete, happy...totally birthdayed!

***

"I must confess," says Dan the next morning, "I feel a bit guilty about ignoring that other London across the river. Shall we put on our best clothes and grown-up manners and cross the bridge?"

"I'm up for it, let's go."

We head for Westminster Abbey only to detour around the enormous milling crowds waiting for entrance. Maneuvering our way to the back of the Abbey we discover quiet spots of green lawn, benches, and an iconic statue of Winnie still watching over his London. We enjoy this back street trek to the British Museum.

Back in 1953, on that amazing trip with Marilyn McBride we stayed in a tiny hotel right next to this museum. The inn is gone now but here I am again visiting this awesome place. The Elgin Marbles still make me feel uncomfortable about England's ownership of these classic statues. They really belong in their home in Greece, but they are beautiful and moving and I enjoy them fully.

"Oh, look, mom, there are your people," Dan is pointing to a trio of sandaled Asian men wrapped in orange robes. A small *Namaste* in their direction and off we go to see the Rosetta Stone. We pay our respects to this original online translation site and head for a display of artifacts dug from the early medieval Suttton Hoo ship burial site.

Excavated in 1939 one of its most valuable finds is a bronze helmet almost complete. We also see the Battersea Shield. This is a bronze plaque beautifully designed to decorate a wooden shield from approximately 350 BCE. The period from 300 CE to 1100 CE is represented by numerous brooches, buckles, and metal-work objects. Almost all of them feature sculptured animals of all descriptions, tightly woven in loops of differing metals. Anglo Saxon art flourished during this period, growing finer and more subtle throughout the ensuing centuries.

The large open hall with its soaring ceiling houses the obligatory gift store. This gives us an opportunity to buy books and a key chain with a dangling Sutton Hoo helmet, a tiny replica of a Isle of Lewis chessman and a small white water bird which I choose to call a Winchester Goose, and a coke. Fortified we tube ourselves back to Southwark and the George Inn for dinner.

Our last day. This is Dan's wandering day. Brave soul, he is heading back to "the City" on this very warm, almost muggy day. Of lesser mettle, I do my wandering closer to home. Strolling leisurely along the river walk is just right for my weary legs and I truly love the 'I have no plans, nowhere to go, no time schedule' feeling. There are so many people dressed in bright summer clothes walking along with me, laughing, enjoying the tangy smells of the river the soft breeze and the endless, bendless fun of being alive.

At the Globe Theatre I admire the openwork iron gates that are peopled with Shakespeare's characters. Wandering beyond the formal entrance, about a block further on there is an entranceway and I go in. I seem to be in the back stage, almost museum-like section of the theatre with all sorts of displays of costumes and memorabilia. It's a large open area and there are small groups of people moving about. I join one of them sitting in front of a small stage where a rather uncomfortable looking but brave young man, obviously a volunteer from the audience is being dressed, layered, into a Shakespearian woman's typical costume He is being laced into a bodice, two skirts, collars, sleeves that are separate and must be tied to the arm holes, a cap with dangling ties. He curtsies awkwardly, accepting our applause.

Models of the original Globe Theatre and the reconstruction of this new replica abound. Collections of the actual outfits worn by the actors over the years give me a chance to see how many of them I can trace to known characters. All so unexpected, thoroughly enjoyable, I have apparently wandered into a part of the Globe usually only available to paying tourists. Looking around I do not see any guides or officials who could help me to legalize myself. Thus free of guilt, I continue to experience it all!

Later on, sitting at an outdoor table at the Anchor Pub drinking a glass of red wine, relaxed, recalling the day, I am somewhat overwhelmed by the synchronicity of my life. My sannyas name, Anand Bhadrena, given to me by my guru, means "blissful grace" and "grace" means the "gift unbidden." That is what has happened to me today: unlooked for, unearned, not planned, I stumbled into a rich, rewarding experience. Considering this, I realize that more and more my life plays out that way. Joseph Campbell says, "We must be willing to get rid of the life we've planned, so as to have the life that is waiting for us." Dropping preconceived ideas, opening up to new thoughts, to whatever comes, pushing limits this is what travel, wandering does. No wonder I like it so.

Dan arrives full of his adventures across the river and we share our stories over scampi and chips, a cider and a glass of shiraz. What gifts we have been given today. Words begin to slow, stories wind down, and we are left with an appreciation and awe of this latest foray into the unknown.

Later, settled into bed, almost asleep, one of us, I don't know which, suddenly begins to chuckle. Growing into a full blown laugh, the dam is broken and all the fun and excitement and happenings of the last few weeks spill out. One-upmanship is rife and exaggeration grows with each retelling. An hour passes, two, reliving, we own it all!

Exhausted finally, gloriously empty, we sleep.

At home in Seattle ...

Off to See the Wizard...

CATHCART WAY--Street sign after street sign catches our attention as we drive along a quiet road in a Seattle suburb. We begin to envision an important, upscale new development—*Washington state's most up and coming neighborhood! Theaters, a cozy little trattoria set in the middle of the bustling town square, buskers vying for one's attention, school buses tootling up and down the street, coffee shops, suburbia rampant, the Dubai of Cascadia!*

Oh dear, this is not the way to begin a new chapter. But, come to think of it, it's not your typical, by now expected chapter so, let's go with it.

Cathcart Way, we'll get there but you will have to wait a bit.

It's 2015 and different. I'm not on a red eye flight to Europe or beyond, dozing, dreaming of Shakespeare's newest play or of meeting Monet or Van Gogh in Paris, or climbing a misted peak in the Highlands. I'm sitting with Pamela on a daytime trip flying, mother and daughter, to visit Dan, not in London but in his hometown, Seattle. It is summer and the tornado strewn Midwest below us is sending up shock waves making the plane bounce and shake around like an old, creaking bus on a bumpy road thousands of feet in the air. As we approach Denver, our midway stop, the pilot apologizes for the turbulence saying that he has been unable to find a clear and relatively peaceful stretch anywhere between 30,000 and 1,000 feet! Our layover is short but we manage to compose ourselves, preparing to face another, but a good deal shorter flight to Seattle.

Here we are, we have made it safely. Flying in we passed over miles and miles of forests thick with trees of every shade and hue of green. There must be a Wizard hidden somewhere inside that verdant carpet surrounding, almost enclosing Seattle, The Emerald City.

"Danneeee!" I never can contain myself but it is so good to see him, my very own Wicca. We pick up our luggage and check into the Marriott Courtyard. The hotel, situated on the shores of Lake Union, is just the right place for wandering the parklike lakefront, talking, taking pictures and catching up on news. We stop at Daniel's Broiler for oysters, burgers and fries. Early to bed, a few moments smoothing out any residual shakes and quakes from the flight and we are asleep.

Dan doesn't own a car, so the next morning we pick up a rental and drive to Wallingford, a lovely older section of the Emerald. We drive down block after block of arts and crafts bungalows lovingly restored, surrounded by lush green shrubbery and bright blooming flowers. Fitting perfectly into this nostalgic scene is The Serpentine apartments, built in 1928. An original ad confidently stated, "combines historical elegance with modern conveniences." The entrance is set back from the flat façade, featuring a short rounded tower above a red tiled roof and rounded portico, very art deco.

Dan's first floor, corner apartment is truly his Castle. We explore, admiring his interesting and original decorations, a five foot Scottish sword, bookcases overflowing, topped by gargoyles, and brooding Celtic posters. What catches our eyes almost right away however is a round table in the middle of his living room spread with a wonderful array of silverware tastefully placed on gleaming white plates each crossed with a red rose. There is a lovely bottle of wine in a shining ice bucket and dishes of smoked salmon and crab hors d'oevres. Of course it is Mother's Day and Pam and I are being feted and celebrated. Wonderful, thoughtful host.

"This was once the Home of the Good Shepherd, run by nuns who would take in wayward girls helping them to learn to lead decent lives." Dan is taking us on a leisurely neighborhood stroll. We have walked up and down small hills, seen many quaint homes, and are now approaching a rather forbidding large stone building.

"The young women helped pay for their keep by running a laundry service, not the most pleasant way to spend one's days, but it was felt that the hard grueling work would calm many of the incorrigible girls." Oh dear, thankfully it was closed in 1973.

Pam obliges by assuming a disgruntled and lowering pose as an incorrigible. We take her picture and move on to more agreeable sights. Wallingford center, just about three or four short blocks long is fronted by original, one-of-a-kind stores. It once was and somehow remains in this big city, a village. A really nice place to live.

Before we go back to our hotel this evening I must take a break to tell about something rather wonderful and precious that is happening. Family connections, while always loving have been stretched and thinned and rubbed off in places by the 25 years of all of us living in separate cities. Danny has been most vulnerable by being 3,000 miles, a country, away. Two week vacations each year helped renew ties, but that easy everyday comfort was slowly disappearing. Here, in one and a half days a small miracle is happening. Sister, brother, mother are suddenly all on one wave length. Without effort, actually without awareness (until now) we laugh, spark one another, feel and act as though no separation had ever occurred. We are enjoying learning about our differences, forgiving past hurts, bouncing off one another recalling all the shared memories and while missing David, our fourth, basically just having a great time! Still searching for the Wizard, we start off next day in Pioneer Square that historic bottom of the hill start of old Seattle. All this is new to Pam but I have been here before so I go looking for the store window with its big sign, *Cow Chip Cookies!* There is a wonderful bookstore I also remember. The Pike Place Market captures us for a while. We laugh at the men throwing fish to one another across the open air shop, accurately, I'm happy to say. Winding our way through the myriad stalls of this tourist mecca, we come out on First Avenue.

From here on we will be climbing. Seattle started out on a small section of waterfront that was flat. It became the port for shipping the immense flow of cut timber that was 'skidded' down the muddy slopes above. This area was really too steep to successfully build anything on but shacks and became known as Skid Row. In order to capitalize on this timber-lucrative spot, it was slowly leveled by pushing the land down the slopes making a hill rather than a cliff and in time, a secure place to build a city on. A great idea as it worked and we have modern day Seattle, always hilly but just fine!

Back to climbing. Oh, here is a really important site, the first Starbucks Coffee shop, progenitor of thousands of such all over the world. Close on we see the Seattle Art Museum that boasts a 48 foot high steel statue painted black depicting a man wielding a large mallet and called, obviously, the *Hammering Man*. This impressive salute to industry, stark in two dimensions actually lowers his arm to hammer four times a minute, only resting from 1am to 5 am each night. Further on we pass the Damn the Weather bar and a quaint old-timey hotel front bearing a sign, *ROOMS, 75cents,* both making a play for Seattle's famous number of rainy days and pioneer status! A few more upward tilting blocks and we are ready for a comfortable drive into the surrounding countryside.

A soft misting rain does nothing to obscure the lush green landscape as we head for Snoqualimie Falls. Rain hoods up, we nonetheless take pictures standing above the magnificent 270 foot fall of rainbow tipped waters. From the almost spiritual beauty of the park we travel to the mundane in North Bend where the TV show *Twin Peaks* was filmed. Two of Pamela's children (grown) are ardent fans, so we stop at the Twedes Café, featured in the program, to eat a somehow significant piece of cherry pie and buy t-shirts.

The enjoyment of the day and each other continues and we stop at small unassuming antique shops, buy a trinket or two, and find ourselves on a road that begins to have rather prominently displayed signs, saying Cathcart Way. Traveling perhaps a mile further on we see a paved road  off to the left about 50 yards long leading into an empty green field stopping abruptly nowhere. Somewhat stunned we pull over, "This is Cathcart Way, THIS is Cathcart Way, THIS IS CATHCART WAY?"

We dissolve into whooping laughter, outdoing each other in descriptions of this fantastic metropolis which apparently only exists in the dreams of some demented city planner. Why this admittedly silly happening should become such an ongoing source of hilarity for the remainder of the trip and beyond I really don't know, but for pure enjoyment nothing outdoes it.

Back to Seattle, having yet to encounter the Wizard, we have a casual supper and opt for an early night. It has been a delightful day and still chuckling a bit, we fall easily to sleep.

Excited, anticipating an overnight visit to Victoria, British Columbia, clutching tickets to the famous afternoon tea at the Empress Hotel we board the ferry next morning. A pleasant two hour trip and we have arrived. The harbor is framed by wonderful old Victorian Hotels and a wide promenade. It is easy to picture fine ladies and gentlemen strolling there in their Victorian finery.

Checking into our more modern hotel equivalent--*oh dear, I can't find my credit card!* When an extensive pocket search and purse paraphernalia strewn all over the bed do not reveal the essential plastic, Pam takes over the finances and patiently helps me through the ordeal of calling, cancelling the card, getting a new one, etc.

Disturbing, but not a major glitch, and we go out to explore the city. Impressed by an awesome Native American totem pole, a quick purchase in a little bookstore, double orders of oysters in a café, a leisurely stroll along the promenade and, it is tea time!

What a lovely experience this is, surrounded by antiqued tapestries and rugs, elegant wing back chairs, seated at hand-carved tables with a soft 4 o'clock sun shining through the windows, we are each served with our own teapot and a spread worthy of a queen.

TRADITIONAL AFTERNOON TEA

$63.00

Fresh Strawberries with Empress Cream
Smoked Salmon Pinwheel with Dill Cream Cheese
Roasted Honey Ham with Tarragon Dijonnaise
Free range Egg Salad Croissant
Cucumber & Ginger Mascarpone on Butter Brioche
Moroccan Spiced Coronation Chicken on Marble Rye

***

Freshly Baked Raisin Scone with Strawberry Jam and
Empress Cream

***

Duo of Jivara & Ivoire Chocolate Delice
Raspberry Mascarpone Mousseline
Valrhona Pistachio Cremeux Tart
Rose Petal Shortbread

Subdued, bemused, replete, we wander the rest of the evening away.

Back in Seattle Danny has made plans for us to have dinner the next evening with his daughter, my granddaughter, Bonnie and her fiancé, Darin. A real treat because we have seen so little of her over the 3,000 mile away years. Bonnie has been a vegetarian since she was ten years old, so I am being introduced to Thai dishes, sans meat but delicious with everything else! Easy, interesting, catching up conversation enhances the meal. How we all wish, and not for the last time, that we could all be closer together.

North of Seattle there is a small quadrant of the Pacific Ocean bordered by British Columbia and the American mainland. It is literally strewn with islands that were discovered and charted by a Spanish explorer in 1791 who named them the San Juan Islands. Over the ensuing years they were settled and claimed by both British and American pioneers. Lying as they did between the contending nations, there were frequent small battles, and skirmishes that were finally resolved peacefully in 1872 in favor of the States. We are headed today for one of the largest in the group, San Juan Island.

Dan meets us at the ferry this morning wearing an eye patch. Actually it is more medicinal than piratical because it covers a really angry looking sty that he has been doctoring for days. Waiting in line to board the ship, reservations are being checked and when Dan's turn comes the official calls out, "Linda..." He looks up from the obviously wrong entry and, chagrined, corrects it to "Daniel." This, however, immediately becomes the justification for one of our silliest made-up stories:

"Dan was originally one of a pair of twins, he had a sister named Linda. Development of both children in the womb proceeded erratically. Composed of just a small group of cells Dan's twin stopped growing, entered his body and just now is beginning to assert herself in the form of a sty!"

Variations and contortions of this absurd conjecture keep us elaborating and laughing for the rest of the trip. Just prior to docking *Linda* gives up the ghost and drains away. Presentable and without pain Dan leaves his eye patch behind. Finding it somewhat difficult to drop our silly mood we are nonetheless captured by the beauty of Friday Harbor.

On the deck of a small quay-side restaurant we settle down, eat crab cakes and plan our brief stay at Lakedale Resorts, situated a bit inland in the wooded center of San Juan.

There are historical sites along the raveled coast line. The English Camp, the American Camp, both situated as far as possible from each other in this small territory, date from the 1800s, the years of contention, and are now actively kept alive for visitors. Roche Harbor was settled at the ancient base of the Salish people, who were and still are an essential part of the community. Beautifully scenic it still has some truly lovely old homes and the famous Hotel de Haro Hotel. These all figure in our itinerary.

"What is this in your hair?"

At Lakedale Resorts, unloading the car, settling in to our cabin, Dan startles me and I reach up to dislodge whatever flying, crawly insect has attacked me only to touch *plastic!* My lost credit card found fallen between the seats of our rental car and now used to play a joke by scaring me. A moment more of laughter and we look around our new home. A two-storied cabin, fireplace already sporting a bright fire, grouped by a couch and two overstuffed chairs, full kitchen and dining room, two bedrooms upstairs; rustic, yes, but modern comfortable and welcoming. There is also a small wraparound porch that overlooks the lake.

Pam has made an exciting discovery, "Oh, look, a hot tub in that little building behind us. Dibs on the first soak!"

We are off and running, delighted with our new three day vacation arranged so well by Seattle Dan. We spend the balance of the afternoon exploring close by, delighted to find a chess game being played on the grassy shore of the lake. Pieces are all life-sized and must be picked up and lugged around the board, which is, of course, just marked off on the grass. Forgoing the challenge, we enjoy the General Store, packed to the actual rafters with clever old-timey knickknacks. It is all color and smell and nostalgia, fun.

Evening is all about the hot tub. Pam and Dan brought bathing suits and are immersed almost as soon as we return to our cabin. Listening to their laughter I go searching for a way to join them. Okay, I have here a pair of navy blue polka dotted pajama bloomers, a frilly but substantial bra and I am off down the path to join them. A whoop of acceptance of their inventive mother and we paddle about until our fingers are all crepey and wrinkled. Dan makes a delicious dinner but bedtime presents a problem. There is just one bed in each bedroom, leaving Dan to sleep on the pull-out couch. What seems like a *bummer* however quickly becomes a *treat* when we realize his bed is in front of the toasty fire and the large puffy duvet provided looks just great. Refusing to open up the sleeper he stretches out on the couch as is, makes a cozy if somewhat rumpled nest, wriggles in up to his chin and bids us goodnight.

There is something going on at the American Camp next day. For a moment we watch what appears to be a melee of blue suited soldiers and red coats running over the grounds, but wait. They are playing games, throwing balls, tussling playfully with one another. It is okay. The American troops have invited their English counterparts to visit and help celebrate a mock fourth of July party. We salute the American flag, with its 13 stripes and 37 stars and honor the British Standard as they both wave freely above the colorful scene below.

"Sealy, sealy, sealy." Like a child Pam is calling loudly as we lean over a stone wall fronting the magnificent waters of the bay searching for a promised sighting. Laughing, feeling like 10 year olds, we are suddenly conscious of a sedate, older couple that have come up behind us. Subdued, embarrassed we slink away down the path out of earshot to double up with glee at our foolishness.

This is becoming our exploring day. Driving that afternoon toward Roche Harbor, a sign on the side of the road catches our attention and we pull over and park. An arrow directs us to a path leading up a hill into a lovely wood thick with trees and shrubs. The legend tells of a unique mausoleum built in the 1930s by and for the McMillan family. John McMillan was a wealthy industrialist, politician, a staunch Methodist and a Mason who insisted upon designing his own gravesite. Intrigued, we begin to climb. The path is well-marked and the wood is lovely but after a while, tiring. I suggest that Pam and Dan continue upward while I just wander about enjoying a level spot.

It is really nice to stop a while and just look around. It is so still and quiet that I hardly move. The scene is like an impressionist painting with sunlight glancing through rough green branches to spread in pools on the forest floor. Awed and grateful, I savor this moment as long as I can.

A rustle, a quick movement in the corner of my eye, oh, a lovely, graceful deer walks into the scene. I gasp, making an involuntary movement and she bounds away. A small cathedral built for a moment in an American wood.

I haven't really been conscious of time passing as I just wander and enjoy but soon I hear voices in the distance and realize they are calling my name, more magic? No, it is my children running breathless down the path seemingly overjoyed to see me. They explain that returning from the mausoleum they must have made a wrong turn and had been searching for me sure I had been abducted or fallen into a crevasse. Reassured of my safety they tell me of their adventure.

In a cleared space at the top of the rise is an enormous stone rotunda enclosing a large limestone table surrounded by six stone chairs. The setting is a copy of the dining room where the family would gather every evening. However here each chair is a tombstone enclosing the ashes of each McMillan with names and dates on the backs. Of course, Dan and Pam each chose a chair and proceeded to sit and make after-dinner conversation!

Together again, having shared our stories we walk back down to our car and continue on to Roche Harbor. It is such a bright blue day and the harbor alive with shiny white sailboats is another painting worthy of Monet or Renoir. We park near the famed Hotel de Haro, built in 1886 and are delighted to find an actual yellow brick road as part of the lovely Gardens. The bricks were supplied from the now closed Roche Harbor Lime and Cement Works, which was a mainstay of the old city in the early 20th century. We sit for a while on benches overlooking the harbor and the lovely old buildings from our vantage point on the yellow brick road. We talk and reminisce and plan for our departure tomorrow.

***

The dinner this evening, cooked by Dan, is a masterpiece and a fitting end to this wonderful visit, to up and down Seattle, to tea at the Empress Hotel, to this beautiful island, and most of all to the love and enjoyment of each other.

The flight next morning is a much calmer ride than our arriving one. Still teary from our goodbyes I settle back. Pam is quiet and relaxed as well. With nowhere to go and hours to fill before landing I am free to just muse, just watch the kaleidoscope of memories and begin to pick and choose which ones to relive.

Despite this routine that I have followed after all my trips there is a new element today, a deeper understanding of travel, of my travels, and a glimpse, perhaps of my future goings. Last year, leaving the British Isles Dan and I were already thinking, as we did after every trip, of where, "Next year!"

A particular city or island or historic sight, or even a coming event did not surface right away or even easily. I combed the internet, asked people, looked at atlases, etc. but a ready destination did not surface. I did not feel an urgency and was a bit bewildered by this. After a couple of months I spoke to Dan and discovered that he was feeling somewhat the same. "Maybe we take a breather, a break and wait a year." Wow, I was surprised at how sort of right that felt and relaxed.

Spring came and Pam and I began to talk about going somewhere together. Perhaps Chicago, but she'd been there, liking it but not really interested in going again. When Seattle was mentioned she became excited saying that a visit there would be great. Visiting Dan would, of course, be a big plus for both of us. She only had five or six days from work but we thought that would be really good all around. Dan was thrilled and began almost before we got off the phone to make reservations and plans.

Sitting on the plane today, remembering that being in Seattle was actually so much more and better than we hoped for I feel a tingle, a touch of something new. At 88, not as mobile as I used to be, my wanderings have become shorter, smaller, less grandiose but, judging from the recent example, just as fulfilling and rewarding as my grander efforts. A momentary sadness, regret at loss begins to fade. Flying not overseas this time but cross-country, staying only five days and not a cathedral in sight, I experience and enjoy every moment. Could it be that that old chestnut, It is quality not quantity that matters? Apparently, and looking up close is just as fulfilling as gazing far away.

If I were younger I would see it all, go everywhere, poke and pry into each corner, stand in awe in every cathedral, search out mysteries and legends and talk to everyone in the world whether I could understand them or not.

But older now, grateful for this smooth flight home, almost dozing, I begin to see that each trip, each wandering, each cat-nap--no matter how momentary or close at hand it may be--is a journey, a learning and an adventure. No restrictions, no rules, no qualifications necessary, a trip to the Acme for a loaf of bread can be an opening into a world. Ticket in hand, looking inward and outward, each moment a discovery I will wander as always.

Perhaps there really was a Wizard in the Emerald City and I have brought her home!

At home…everywhere

"Every journey…"

I put down my pen and close the page. I take a large gulp of lukewarm coffee, stand, shake myself and laugh aloud!

I am done. I've wrestled, poked and prodded memory, split it in two, molded and shaken it all the way back in time—my time, when my world began.

I have found treasure and tears, hidden moments filled with anguish or unrepentant joy. I have seen things I never knew were there, invented myself, reinvented, tossed truth in the air and watched it fall, willy-nilly, onto the page. Words drift in and out of focus, the writing stops but the joy of what I have done is with me forever!

Oh, if you need me, to ask a question or perhaps my stories have made you remember one of your own and you want to share, please come look. You will find me curled around a skinny stray cat both of us fast asleep, at home, on the steps of a cathedral…somewhere.